YEARBOOK OF SYMBOLIC ANTHROPOLOGY I

The Yearbook of Symbolic Anthropology is an independent publication supported by the staff services of the Département d'Anthropologie, Université Laval, Québec, and of the communications branch of the Faculté des Sciences Sociales at the same university. The volumes are organised by editorial committees who invite qualified authors to contribute articles. At a future date, announcements will be made requesting contributions also from uninvited authors who may have relevant material available.

Editorial Office
   Erik G. Schwimmer
   Département d'Anthropologie
   Cité Universitaire
   Québec 10, Canada G1K 7P4
   Phone (418)6563775

Editorial Board
   Conrad Arensberg, P.E. de Josselin de Jong, Luc de Heusch,
   Claude Lévi-Strauss, Pierre Maranda, Chie Nakane, E. Meletinskij,
   David M. Schneider, Victor Turner

Editorial Committee
   Edwin Ardener, Iain Prattis, Ino Rossi, Henry Selby, Yvan Simonis,
   Robert Shirley, Roy Wagner

Subscriptions as well as single copies are obtainable from the Publishers.

The Yearbook *of* Symbolic Anthropology I

Edited by Erik Schwimmer

C. HURST & COMPANY · LONDON
McGILL-QUEEN'S UNIVERSITY PRESS · MONTREAL
1978

First published in the United Kingdom by
C. Hurst & Co. (Publishers) Ltd.,
1-2 Henrietta Street, London WC2E 8PS
Published simultaneously in Canada by
McGill-Queen's University Press
1020 Pine Avenue West, Montreal H3A 1A2

ISBN 0-903983-70-2 (C. Hurst)
ISBN 0-7735-0500-8 (McGill-Queen's)
ISSN 0140-2246

Legal deposit 2nd Quarter 1978
Bibliothèque Nationale du Québec

Typeset by Red Lion Setters
Holborn, London and
printed in Great Britain by
Billing and Sons Ltd., Guildford,
London and Worcester

Contents

Introduction

ERIK SCHWIMMER

The establishment of a 'Yearbook of Symbolic Anthropology' expresses an assumption that 'symbolic anthropology' has, over the last few years, become a viable field of study in anthropology. Even twenty years ago it was certainly not a viable field of study, in spite of the galaxy of ancestors one may wish to claim for it. In the 1950s nobody went to the field to 'do symbolic anthropology'. Today, many scholars are doing just this; there is a recognised body of method and an abundance of bewildering theory to which they can refer as well as some agreement as to the kind of data they should bring back from the field.

This new sub-discipline partakes of all the headiness and confusion characteristic of fresh departures. There is hardly any agreement on what 'symbolic anthropology' is supposed to be; there is a multiplicity of schools contradicting each other without knowing too well what the others are saying; each school works somewhat like a closed circle, often coming to very much the same conclusions in different terminology, and without always recognising that a considerable body of accepted knowledge is building up in spite of apparent divergences.

The purpose of the present series is to provide those working in this ill-defined area some sense of the tradition that is being created, some idea as to who is participating and what they are doing; to provide a somewhat organised body of source material and discussion — in fact a sort of clearing house. It will take a number of issues before the series can settle down to an ideal format, and the first three have taken an approach that will not be repeated *ad infinitum*. What has been done, to get the series started, is to present a number of school-like movements in different parts of the world, just to document what each is doing. That was an easy way to start and also, we believe, a useful one, ethnographically speaking. In the first three issues, we are presenting the British 'post-structuralists', a group of Canadians trying to find their balance between United States and French culture, an American school analysing leadership among South American Indians (reminding us that symbolic anthropology has tradition-ally been much involved with political systems), and finally two rich and neglected European schools: the Danish and the Dutch, who both, again, can show us how each school finds elegant solutions to what baffles the others. We promise that after this regional display, we shall start on a few other organising principles for our Yearbooks. But only three have been prepared, at the time the first one is going to press. The introduction to the second Yearbook will announce what our future plans will be.

Yet even this first issue, in spite of its regional basis, is presenting distinctive theoretical challenges relevant to the international community of 'symbolic anthropology' practitioners. Before speaking of these distinc-tive challenges, however, some general remarks have to be made as to what 'symbolic anthropology' is, and how it is related to the more traditional fields of anthropology. On the first question, we shall have to speak most vaguely, so as to avoid making controversial statements that would seem to back one of the schools against the others. Let us therefore start with a familiar example.

There is little difficulty in saying what 'land' represents in economic anthropology: it has an actual and potential yield that can be calculated and this yield is derived either from the useholder's labour or from benefits derived by the owner when he cedes rights in land to others. Likewise, in social anthropology, a study of 'land tenure' has a clearly delineated field, including legal rules, manipulations of these rules by individuals and groups standing in a given relation to one another, transactions (customary or variant) between individuals and corporate groups and the like. In political anthropology, land is an instrument of chieftainship, a ploy in war and diplomacy. In the anthropology of religion, land is the habitat of ghosts and spirits, in particular spirits of place; it may become sacralised either permanently or temporarily. Spiritual beings and rituals may concern land in its economic, social and political aspects. I have not tried to exhaust all the possibilities, but in each case the field of reference is well established and elaborately documented in the literature.

Now what is land in symbolic anthropology? Restricting ourselves to societies where landed property and agriculture form the basis of the economic order, the answer to this question depends, as I indicated above, on the school one belongs to. For 'cognitive anthropology', the chief question would be how the society classifies different types of land, in other words, its ethnogeography. For the 'symbolic system' school, attributed to David M. Schneider, land would probably be a symbol for relationships in the social structure. For the 'semiotic' school inspired by Geertz, land transactions would be a 'text' which, if deciphered, would yield information as to a culture's basic ideology. In Turner's kind of symbolic studies the complexity of associations of 'land' would be the primary interest. In Lévi-Straussian structuralism, 'land' can be thought about only when that term is opposed to another in particular mythical or ritual contexts.

But, whatever the approach, each school would be interested in rather similar kinds of data. When a Maori says, for instance, 'This land is my backbone', there would be wide agreement that each of the following questions would be a 'good' followup in a field investigation: do you have other land that you would compare to other parts of your body? would you apply that remark to any land you inherited, or only to a certain mode of inheritance? what ethos is implied by this sentiment about land? what are the associations of the term 'backbone' which you apply to land? or: I have heard it said that a whale was stranded on that ridge you are pointing at; could you tell me more about that?

All these are, one imagines, interesting questions, but one should by no means despise the anthropologist who would ask: why do you insist so much on this land being physically attached to you? The answer might then be: because a Land Court judgment took it away from my grandfather and the judgment was based on bad information, or on bad law. We would then get to a more militant kind of symbolic anthropology, just as relevant as the others.

The above example shows both the difficulty and the possibility of defining a field of 'symbolic anthropology'. All the questions I constructed above were attempts at eliciting meaning. They were all based on different ideas as to what constitutes 'meaning'. It would not be the role of the editor of *Yearbook* to rule on the value of these different ideas. On the other hand, our example does set certain limits on relevance. It is concerned with a text taken from a particular culture, and it is not idiosyncratic within that culture; any ethnographer of the Maori would agree that it is a key metaphor within that culture. Furthermore, the questions are distinguishable from literary or linguistic or psychological or philosophical questions in as much as each of them is concerned with the specificity of the culture. Finally (and here we come to the term 'symbolic'): the text links a physical object (taken from the culture) to a multi-level concept. It links, in other words, a physical referent to a problematic signifier. It deals not only with the speaker's affective or cognitive state of mind, but just as much with an external reality, the land.

Having thus set parameters, what sub-discipline can we find within them? A brief answer would be: semiotic enquiry within an anthropological context. A minimal description of 'anthropological context' would be: the biological, physical, ecological, technological and socio-economic conditions in which sentiment and intellect combined to create the text under study. The assumptions here are that the conditions constrain and that creation is free. If we leave out the constraints we bypass anthropology; if we leave out free creation, we meet with philosophical problems beyond the present discussion. Freedom, in the sense intended here, implies that, as a general rule, constraints are such as to permit of a plurality of viable solutions to a problem.

The use of the term 'symbolic' suggested here conforms (as Benoist, Berthoud and Sabelli have recently reminded us) to the original meaning of the word: linking together an object broken in half. We apply it to the bridging of the opposition between physical constraint and creative freedom.

The papers in the first *Yearbook* illustrate well enough how such bridging is done in anthropology. Williams' paper on the dance, for instance, is concerned not only with culturally determined meanings (transformations) but also with physiological constraints (laws of motility). Strathern, again, is concerned not only with the semiotics of social behaviour (the concept of gender) but with its relation to the physiological concept of sex. Arcand, taking as his theme the Amerindian honey symbolism made famous in *Du miel aux cendres*, shows its role in the Cuiva medical system — which is freely created, as one might say, but expresses climatic constraints: extremes of wetness and drought, causing 'wet' foods to grow (in the wet season) only on treetops and 'dry' foods (in the dry season) only underground.

Elli Köngäs Maranda's 'ethnoesthetics' combines the principles of structuralist myth analysis with the notion (classically malinowskian) that a myth may systematically codify the principles of the gift exchange system. Tanner likewise develops a model of dual determination, but in a more polemical context, as he is criticising Moore's explanation of scapulimancy which was purely ecological. Whereas Moore's theory is refuted by the data, it is nonetheless clear that the ideological system reconstructed by Tanner (where scapulimancy is a rite closing a cycle of symbolic exchanges between hunters and animal spirits) is still determined 'in the last instance' by the ecological relation between man and game.

LeRoy's presentation of the relation between physical constraints and free reaction (as found in a New Guinea society) is especially elaborate and subtle. Songs are performed either by males or females. In the songs studied, the themes are pig husbandry, gardening and sex. Roy shows that in specific songs, only one theme occurs overtly, but that this theme commonly serves, at the same time, as metaphor for the others. The direct use of some of these themes is reserved to men and the direct use of others to women. Metaphoric use is not so restricted. At this point, the boundary between anthropology and literary exegesis becomes hard to draw, as the anthropologist needs semiotic skills to find the relationship between the different codes involved, while literary exegesis of the recondite cultural allusions demands considerable anthropological skills. Where these two types of skill meet, we find symbolic anthropology.

Having sketched the ideal 'structure' of the *Yearbook of Symbolic Anthropology*, we feel obliged (because of our theoretical eclecticism if for no other reason) to also trace briefly its modest history. The venture started as the *Journal of Symbolic Anthropology*, launched at the AAA conference in Toronto in 1972. The publisher was to be Mouton (it was Mouton who had originally suggested the venture), and the text was to be bilingual in English and French. The persons who still appear as members of the editorial board and committee of the *Yearbook* accepted those responsibilities for the Journal. Many of them effectively gave most valuable help. Two issues appeared and three more were fully prepared for the press. After proofreading for the third issue was completed, Mouton withdrew from the venture, claiming distribution problems.

This caused very considerable delay in publication. The market became more difficult for journals in general. The venture was taken over by the publisher C. Hurst & Co, of London, England. While this company did not in principle reject the bilingual policy of Mouton, it was more aware that good distribution in the United States was essential to success. Also, Hurst favoured the format of a *Yearbook*, as being easier to market within their organisation. This concept was in any case at least as suitable for the task we wish to perform. The change from a bilingual *Journal* to a mainly monolingual *Yearbook* was partly encouraged also by the difficulty we had in getting suitable articles in French — the Québécois authors represented in this volume submitted their work in English.

In its opening phases, the *Yearbook* thus had its share of ecological constraints, even though creative freedom was not entirely eliminated. Thus, the present volume is mainly composed of papers already accepted for the *Journal*; it is not a systematic presentation of the relevant movement in Canada and even less so as regards the English section. This is one limitation that we shall not face in future issues.

The most interesting difference between the Journal and the *Yearbook* reflects developments within anthropology as a discipline. When Victor Turner (1975) flattered us with a brief reference to the journal in his review of 'Symbolic Studies', he classified it as 'devoted mainly to neostructuralist and symbolic system analysis approaches' whereas Turner's own real preference lies in the analysis of performance and communicative events. If Turner's classification, based on the two published issues of the *Journal*, is correct, it would seem that there has been a definite shift because much attention is given in the present book to performances and communicative events, both in the ethnographic analyses (see especially Köngäs Maranda, Crépeau, Nagata, Tanner, Roy, but also Williams and Strathern) and even more so in the theoretical contributions. It would seem that Turner was, in this instance, making himself the champion of changes that were actually beginning to occur in the whole field of symbolic anthropology. Yet, these changes have not resulted necessarily in the discarding of neostructuralism and symbolic system analysis.

The second main event of the period was the rise of a new type of Marxist anthropology, represented in France by Godelier, Meillassoux, Terray, Augé, Copans and several others; and in Britain by the group brought together by Maurice Bloch in *Marxist Analysis in Social Anthropology*. In the United States, there was concurrently an interesting development of Marxist anthropology, as described by Bridget O'Laughlin, but it has not yet turned to the same extent to the analysis of symbolism. Among the chief figures of American anthropology, the closest to the Marxist symbolic approach or (as it is sometimes described) structure-marxism is Marshall Sahlins (1976a, 1976b).

The distance that existed until recently between symbolic anthropology and Marxism was due to the relative lack of attention traditionally given by Marxist scholars to 'superstructure' — a point already noted by Lévi-Strauss and taken up again by Hastrup in the present volume. Such criticism is less applicable, however, to the French anthropologists listed above than to the work alluded to by Hastrup. In so far as Marxist anthropology is concerned with the analysis of ideology, and with the thought systems by which that ideology is reproduced, it is an integral (and increasingly important) part of symbolic anthropology. Its emphasis on the history of ideological forms, and on their relation to a mode of production, hierarchy and (where applicable) class contradiction can furnish an important dimension of explanation.

While this emphasis may gradually increase in future issues of the *Yearbook* (depending on future directions in anthropology), it is already represented in two contributions to the present volume. Nagata analyses a familiar Hopi myth, but in the context of its use as justification of contemporary political action. His data are political events; his analysis is in terms of transformations made in the basic myth so as to fit the changing circumstances. He brings out that failure of one transformation leads to development of further ones. He is concerned not only with 'performances' and 'communicative events', but also very much with the kind of behaviour by dominated groups that Marxists call 'praxis'.

The second instance is Crépeau's proverb analysis, pragmatist in approach, in which it is shown that variations in the lexicon and even morphology of a traditionally structured item of oral literature can reflect and serve opposition to a dominant group. Obviously, the present volume does not exhaust the possibilities of this type of approach, either analytically or theoretically.

While the theoretical articles of this volume are by no means systematically selected to make any particular editorial point, we do find, in Hastrup's contribution, the same faith that we expressed ourselves in the convergence of the different directions in symbolic anthropology. Apart from the Marxist approach, which we discussed above, the author selects two schools for special consideration, namely the one founded by Gregory Bateson and the British school that calls itself 'post-structuralist'. The former of these is not represented here, but it is hoped that in the future we can do justice to it. Bateson's *Naven* is a seminal work whose message for anthropology has so far been only partly absorbed by the profession. As for British post-structuralism, Hastrup's paper, taken together with Ardener's, show very well its essential contribution. Without denying in the least the reality of paradigms (or what he calls p-structures) as templates for informing symbolic systems, he makes an important epistemological point in insisting that they are essentially beyond verbalisation. What is spoken can never be the paradigm but only a transformation of it, part of an event system with its own political, social and economic demands. Yet, in Ardener's estimation, if a thing is beyond language, it may still be useful to talk about it.

Williams' use of Ardener's theory is therefore especially appropriate, as neither the physical reality (and thus relevance) of the structures of dance can be doubted, nor their profound resistance to verbalisation. Nobody, least of all Williams, would minimise the role of sentiment in dance; yet performers cannot communicate without having a code, and she holds that this code is 'syntactical' rather than 'semantic'.

The two other theoretical essays in this volume (by Wagner and Crook) fit generally. into the perspective presented here. Wagner's theory of mediation expresses well the dual nature of symbolic anthropology briefly sketched in the present introduction. Crook's plea that anthropologists should make themselves into critics of contemporary social organisation has direct relevance to symbolic anthropology, in as much as Crook regards the current self-image of the social sciences as an ideological (i.e. symbolically created) barrier to change. Criticism of contemporary social organisation therefore involves of necessity an ideological criticism aimed at contemporary devices in manipulating symbols. We are pleased to publish this paper especially because, when introducing the first issue of the *Journal*, we had already indicated that social criticism ought to be one of our objectives. We may refer here to Ardener's idea that events are shaped inside a kind of black box (like a computer) of which the input is unspeakable and the output unpredictable. What, in such a universe, could be the role of criticism? It is certainly possible to look very carefully at tricks people play with the output of the black box, in our own society as well as elsewhere. But in addition, it may be that the input is not exactly what we want. Therefore, even if it is beyond language, we do not believe it is beyond change.

For the publication of this work many people have to be thanked. The publisher, Mr Christopher Hurst, has taken over under difficult circumstances and given our enterprise a new lease of life. The university at which the editorial offices are at present situated, *l'Université Laval*, Québec, has provided most generous assistance, in making staff and facilities available, notably in the communications section of the *Faculté des Sciences Sociales* whose IBM and drawing office facilities were made available to us and in the *Département d'Anthropologie*, which made available the services of Mlle Louise Thomassin as editorial and research assistant.

We should also thank the contributors who waited a long time and bore up with uncertainty. Gratitude is especially due to Mr Edwin Ardener, of St. John's College, Oxford, who organised the material concerning the post-structural movement in Britain.

Finally, as the *Yearbook* is essentially the continuation of the *Journal* in another format, the editorial board and committee remain unchanged, certainly for the present issue which contains almost entirely material brought together for the *Journal*, with the aid of the members of board and committee. The second and third issues of the *Yearbook* will be produced with the help of members of the same team.

BIBLIOGRAPHY

Bateson, Gregory 1958: *Naven*, Stanford University Press.

Berthoud, Gérald et Fabrizio Sabelli, 1976: *L'ambivalence de la production*, Paris, Presses Universitaires de France.

Bloch, Maurice 1975: *Marxist Analysis in Social Anthropology*, London, Malaby Press.

Lévi-Strauss, Claude 1966: *Du miel aux cendres*, Paris, Plon.

O'Laughlin, Bridget 1975: 'Marxist Approaches in Anthropology', *Annual Review of Anthropology*, 4:341-70.

Sahlins, Marshall 1976a: *The Use and Abuse of Biology*, Ann Arbor, University of Michigan Press.

———— 1976b: *Culture and Practical Reason*, University of Chicago Press.

Schwimmer, E.G. (ed.), 1973 and 1974: *Journal of Symbolic Anthropology/ Médiations*, The Hague, Mouton.

Turner, Victor 1975: 'Symbolic Studies', *Annual Yearbook of Anthropology*, 4:145-62.

INTRODUCTION

ERIK SCHWIMMER

Les *Annales d'Anthropologie Symbolique* fourniront des études de base à une branche de l'anthropologie qui s'est fortement développée, à l'échelle internationale, au cours des vingt dernières années. Elles suivent en général l'approche de la revue *Médiations* (*Journal of Symbolic Anthropology*) dont les premiers numéros parurent en 1973-4. Elles visent à présenter une documentation plus ou moins systématique qui servira à développer la théorie et les méthodes de l'anthropologie symbolique.

Pour les *Annales*, le terme 'symbolique', loin d'exprimer une préoccupation herméneutique, rappelle plutôt la perspective de Berthoud et de Sabelli (*L'ambivalence de la production*) c'est à dire concevoir les rapports entre l'infrastructure et les superstructures, tout en soumettant celles-ci à une analyse sémiotique approfondie.

Comme la revue *Médiations*, les Annales veulent servir les intérêts de maintes écoles qui partagent une telle préoccupation et dont les origines nationales sont très diverses. Le structuralisme français y prendra évidemment une place assez importante. L'école structuralo-marxiste (elle aussi d'origine française, mais de plus en plus répandue) s'exprimera davantage dans les numéros à venir.

On s'étonnera peut-être de ce que les *Annales* paraîssent uniquement en anglais alors que *Médiations* était bilingue, mais le bureau de redaction se trouve à présent au Département d'Anthropologie de L'Université Laval qui publie une revue en français (*Anthropologie et sociétés*) dont l'orientation se rapproche sensiblement de celle des *Annales*. Celles-ci s'adresseront donc spécifiquement à un public à l'extérieur du Québec. Elles souligneront les liens étroits entre l'anthropologie québécoise et les écoles d'ailleurs, et établiront un dialogue non pas seulement avec le monde anglophone mais aussi avec les écoles européennes, asiatiques et autres, qui utilisent l'anglais comme langue scientifique. Ainsi, dans les deuxième et troisième numéros des *Annales*, on trouvera les recueils des écoles danoises et néerlandaises, dont nous voulons faire mieux connaître les travaux en anthropologie symbolique. Il faut toutefois souligner que quatre contributions représenteront l'anthropologie québécoise dans ce premier numéro.

La diffusion des *Annales* à l'échelle internationale aurait été impossible sans l'initiative généreuse de notre éditeur, M. Christopher Hurst, de Londres. La production de cette série aurait été tout aussi impossible si l'Université Laval ne nous avait pas assurés de sa collaboration la plus totale, en mettant à notre disposition toutes les facilités techniques du service de communications de la faculté des Sciences Sociales (graphisme, composition, montage). Le département d'anthropologie nous a fourni les services de secrétariat, notamment ceux de Mlle Louise Thomassin, secrétaire de rédaction.

Résumés

BERNARD ARCAND
Faire l'amour, cést comme manger du miel ou des
fruits doux: cela provoque des caries

M. Arcand se propose de rendre intelligibles les croyances citées dans son titre, et qui font partie du système des Cuiva, petite tribu des plaines Orientales de la Colombie. Dans ce but, il analyse deux champs sémiotiques — les aliments et la physiologie. Le miel et les fruits doux occupent les positions extrêmes des deux axes d'opposition du système alimentaire: humide/sec; doux/amer. On se sert des mêmes axes d'opposition pour expliquer les maladies (qui sont causées par l'excès de l'humide ou du sec, du doux ou de l'amer), ainsi que les différences entre les sexes, l'isolation des femmes pendant leurs règales et toute la cuisine cérémonielle pratiquée pendant les rites de puberté féminins.

Les aliments interdits pendant les règles, par exemple, sont ceux qui seraient 'très mouillés' et que la cuisson ne saurait dessécher, c'est à dire le miel et les fruits doux, tandis que les femmes enceintes (supposées plus 'sèches' que les autres) préfèrent ces mêmes aliments et peuvent les consommer sans risque. Le rapport entre ces aliments et les caries s'explique parce que celles-ci gènent la mastication des aliments: si la consommation de l'humide s'ajoute à une condition déjà humide du corps, il en résulte que les dents ne peuvent désormais mastiquer que de l'humide, c'est à dire du miel et des fruits doux. Or l'amour, lui aussi, cause l'humidité.

PIERRE CRÉPEAU
L'invité envahisseur: quelques aspects de la
transmission orale des proverbes

M. Crépeau fait l'analyse sémiotique et culturelle de 70 variantes et versions du même proverbe rouandais, afin d'en construire les règles de transmission et de démontrer comment se forment les variantes et les nouvelles versions des proverbes et de la littérature orale en général. L'analyse de l'auteur nous apprend beaucoup sur sémiotique de l'architecture rouandaise, notamment sur la signification culturelle des espaces d'habitation. Il nous apprend aussi comment l'idéologie hutu interprète les rapports hiérarchiques entre eux-mêmes et les Tuutsi, leurs dominateurs traditionnels.

M. Crépeau en conclut que les matériaux de la folkloristique sont mobiles et manipulatifs et qu'ils se transforment en forme et en contenu dans le même sens que la culture totale. Il explique ces transformations par les facteurs tantôt externes, tantôt internes au processus communicatif.

RODNEY CROOK
Les observateurs comme participants: quelques remarques
sur la théorie en anthropologie et en sciences sociales

Les réflexions de M. Crook portent sur deux présuppositions qui sont, toutes les deux, assez courantes aujourd'hui: la connaissance scientifique est la seule forme valable des connaissance, et que cette connaissance est neutre par rapport aux valeurs. Ces présuppositions se contrediraient selon l'auteur, car la première, loin d'être neutre, implique déjà des valeurs qui seraient nettement nihilistes. L'idée que la connaissance scientifique soit la seule forme valable servirait de base à un mythe destructeur sousjacent à la crise idéologique de notre époque. L'auteur préfère que l'anthropologie s'occupe de la critique structurale des sociétés contemporaines et de la recherche des possibilités de création de formes nouvelles d'organisation sociale.

ELLI KÖNGÄS-MARANDA
Le don détourné: le mythe lau de la
recherche d'un échange

A partir de l'analyse ethnographique d'un texte lau ('Le don détourné'), Mme Köngäs-Maranda présente les règles poétiques de cette tribu mélanésienne. Elle démontre que cette ethno-esthétique met en relief l'importance des contenus des historiques, géographiques ainsi que sociologiques, et que l'étymologie populaire des noms des acteurs fait partie intégrante du message.

Le mythe codifie les règles qui régissent l'échange. L'auteur en rend compte au moyen d'un modèle à deux coordonnées: l'échange vertical (entre hommes et esprits, vers le haut et vers le bas), et l'échange horizontal (positif ou négatif). Les épisodes du mythe jouent sur l'un ou l'autre des secteurs de ce champ sémantique et épuisent toutes les possibilités logiques du modèle. L'ensemble reproduit l'idéologie lau de l'équilibre où les rapports sociaux, écartés de leur position stable, tendent à revenir à l'équilibre.

Le héros, homme rusé et habile, sera toujours le gagnant quand les autres oublieront les règles de la sagesse, ou bien par leur concupiscence (*Gwau*) ou bien par leur générosité démesurée (*Ilisau*). Mme Maranda croit, tout comme Malinowski, que les mythes sont des 'chartes', mais elle souligne également que 'les symboles forment un langage, parfois un métalangage'.

JOHN LE ROY
Brûler nos arbres: les métaphores dans les chants kewas

Après une discussion sommaire des fêtes des cochons des Kewas et du contexte social où se chantent les poésies appelées *rupale*, M. LeRoy présente un choix de 16 chants. Son analyse fournit les clefs des associations métaphoriques. L'auteur propose une théorie sur l'efficacité des métaphores en rapport avec le système de pensée kewa.

Le sens des métaphores ressort de la reconnaissance de certains thèmes privilégiés, notamment le brûlis de la base des arbres et la mise en terre des boutures. M. LeRoy suggère un modèle triangulaire où les hommes se servent de ces métaphores pour signifier la tuerie et la consommation des porcs, tandis que les *rupales* des femmes utilisent des métaphores du congrès sexuel pour signifier le même chose alors que les métaphores jardinières s'emploient aussi pour signifier l'acte sexuel. En appendice, l'auteur fait l'analyse thématique de son corpus total de 410 chants.

SHUICHI NAGATA
Le message de Dan Kochhongva

Les Indiens hopi croient en une prophétie selon laquelle le Frère Blanc, Pahana, reviendra de la mort pour établir le millénnium. Il ne pourra toutefois rien faire à moins que les hommes ne le reconnaîssent dès son retour. L'article de M. Nagata traite des problèmes essentiellement politiques soulevés par les tentatives d'identification du dieu revenu.

Quand M. Nagata fît son terrain chez les Hopi, un prophète nommé Dan Kochhongva, proposa deux identifications assez spectaculaires dont l'auteur décrit toutes les conséquences. Il en conclut d'abord que les mouvements millénaristes survivront, même dans des conditions précaires, tant que les difficultés qui les ont provoqués ne seront résolues; ensuite qu'il suffira d'une confirmation 'empirique' d'une identification convaincante de Pahana pour que ces mouvements n'éclatent à nouveau.

Cet article apporte à l'anthropologie symbolique un cas remarquable de l'utilisation politique des mythes. En appendice, l'auteur présente la traduction d'une lettre adressée par le prophète indien à trois chefs d'état, dont feu M. Krushchev.

ADRIAN TANNER
*Deviner et décider: explications multiples de la
scapulimancie algonquine*

La scapulimancie algonquine est une pratique de chasse que les anthropologues expliquent comme un aspect de l'idéologie religieuse

(Speck), ou une méthode objectivement efficace (parce qu'elle donnerait libre cours aux lois de la probabilité — I.K. Moore). Tout en acceptant que l'explication de Speck soit insuffisante, M. Tanner s'en prend à la théorie de Moore selon laquelle la scapulimancie ne se pratiquerait qu'après l'échec des méthodes régulières. Les recherches de M. Tanner chez les Cris de Mistassini ont démontré que la scapulimancie se pratique aussi quand la nourriture ne fait pas défaut et quand on ne manque pas d'information sur la position du gibier.

Selon l'auteur, la divination est une représentation théâtrale d'un aspect normalemant caché de la tuerie des animaux: elle rétablit le rapport avec les esprits et inaugure un cycle d'échanges entre ceux-ci et les hommes. Elle se pratique tout aussi bien en temps d'abondance; on croit alors qu'elle sert à prévenir les disettes. C'est souvent un préparatif aux activités coordonnées du groupe. Des discussions sur les signes divinatoires imposent un cadre au discours cynégétique des Cris.

Les pratiques de chasse, y compris la scapulimancie, varient beaucoup selon le type de gibier chassé par chacune des tribus algonquines. D'après la théorie de Park, la scapulimancie est contrôlée par les chefs. Or le pouvoir des chefs varie selon le type de gibier chassé et M. Tanner doute que ce pouvoir inclue, où que ce soit, le droit exclusif d'interpréter les signes divinatoires.

EDWIN ARDENER
'L'analyse des évènements — quelques problèmes à résoudre'

Tout en reprenant l'opposition notoire entre paradigme/syntagme, M. Ardener y apporte quelques précisions nouvelles. Il distingue deux oppositions souvent confondues: structures-*p* / structures-*s* et synchronie / diachronie. De plus, il introduit entre les structures-*p* et les structures-*s* une boîte noire appelée le 'mode de spécification' ou le 'mode d'enregistrement'.

L'analogie connotée ici est sans doute l'ordinateur, dont le 'programme' est représenté par les structures-*p*, tandis que les structures-*s* représentent le 'rendement'. Dans le contexte ethnographique, ce programme est le grand inconnu, surtout parce que l'ethnographe ne peut manquer d'avoir un 'programme' culturel à lui, qui ne recouvre pas normalement le programme à étudier. Celui-ci est même indicible; la langue ne peut en saisir que l'ombre. On l'entrevoit à travers les règles du système qui, elles, sont à la portée d'un bon ethnographe. Ces règles ne constituent toutefois pas le programme car, au contraire de la linguistique, l'anthropologie ne peut jamais se fier à la transmission automatique du paradigme aux syntagmes: le processus est plus lent, plus complexe — l'infrastructure y joue un rôle déterminant.

L'ensemble des rapports contenus dans la 'boîte noire' s'appelle la 'structure-monde'. L'auteur la compare aux 'mémoires' d'un ordinateur. On y trouve l'infrastructure, les règles, l'histoire et aussi des gâchettes remontant aux structures-*p*. Le projet essentiel de l'anthropologie serait donc de rendre la structure-monde consciente et de la représenter. Celle-ci comprend des 'structures' mais dans son ensemble, elle est plutôt une 'simultanéité'.

KIRSTEN HASTRUP
'La position post-structuraliste en anthropologie'

L'idée du 'post structuralisme' date du deuxième congrès décennal de l'A.S.A. à Oxford en 1973. M. Ardener en développa les principes dans un article lu pendant le congrès et inclus dans ce volume même. Mme Hastrup souligne que le 'post-structuralisme' présuppose la 'rupture épistémologique' que fut le structuralisme lévi-straussien. Elle croit toutefois que cette école s'intéressera surtout à la démarche de *La pensée sauvage*, dont elle considère l'objet 'logiquement supérieur' à celui des autres oeuvres de Lévi-Strauss. Elle présente le 'post-structuralisme' comme une synthèse des théories d'Ardener, de Bateson et de Wilden et, finalement, de l'anthropologie marxiste, dont elle discute principalement une analyse de Jonathan Friedman.

Mme Hastrup démontre que le système d'Ardener ressemble à un structuralo-marxisme en ce que l'histoire et les transformations structurales y prennent une position centrale. Friedman définit le terme 'formation sociale' comme celui de 'world-structure' (structure-monde) d'Ardener, sauf que le concept d'Ardener serait clairement sémiotique plutôt que matérialiste. Le modèle de Friedman se distingue de l'autre aussi en ce qu'il peut rendre compte de l'évolution à long terme aussi bien que de l'évolution à court terme.

Il se rapproche à cet égard du modèle cybernétique de Bateson et de Wilden qui discernent deux types d'émergence: 1. selon le programme établi du système; 2. par l'évolution d'un nouveau programme (morphogenèse). Sans négliger les différences entre Friedman et Wilden, l'auteur estime que leurs théories partagent les mêmes interprétations de la contradiction et du capitalisme. Wilden croit que les causes des morphogenèses sont toujours dues à l'intrusion de l'environnement dans le système de communications, mais il n'accepterait pas toutefois le primat des infrastructures.

Mme Hastrup conclut que les trois modèles sont de la même 'famille' car si le modèle structuralo-marxiste néglige un peu les superstructures, la pratique des 'structuralo-marxistes' en rend compte suffisamment.

MARTIN SOUTHWOLD
La définition et ses problèmes en anthropologie

Tandis que les anthropologues recherchent assidûment de bonnes
définitions qu'ils utilisent, il n'y a que peu de définitions des concepts
fondamentaux qui conviennent à l'ensemble du métier; la plupart sont
entourées de controverses. Southwold attribue cette confusion à la
classification traditionnelle des définitions: 'nominales' et 'réelles'. Il veut
introduire une distinction supplémentaire entre des définitions 'classiques'
et 'modernes', c'est à dire des définitions qu'on trouve dans les diction-
naires et dans les manuels de logique, et les définitions qui fournissent des
informations nouvelles. Les définitions qui font problème dans les sciences
sociales sont surtout du type 'moderne' et se rapportent aux faits constatés
par les recherches. Celles-ci ne sont pas 'nominales' dans le sens moderne.

Evidemment, les définitions les plus intéressantes sont réelles et
nominales à la fois. Même si une définition est nominale (c'est à dire
qu'elle énonce le sens d'un mot), elle peut énoncer indifféremment: 1. ce
qu'un mot signifie (définition descriptive); 2. ce qu'un mot signifiera
(définition stipulative); 3. ce qu'un mot devrait signifier (définition
prescriptive).

Les définitions descriptives ne posent pas de difficultés, mais elles ne
sont pas capable non plus de résoudre des problèmes. Si un terme
scientifique est mal défini en rapport avec les faits constatés, on peut
recourir à une définition 'stipulative' mais celle-ci sera particulière à un
chercheur ou même à une tribu étudiée. La normalisation du discours
scientifique exige donc les définitions prescriptives, mais celle-ci demeure-
ront insatisfaisantes à moins de ne se rattacher à une théorie (comme, par
exemple, la définition durkheimienne de la religion).

Les meilleures définitions seraient par conséquent les définitions réelles,
mais sont-elles possibles? Elles exigent une théorie globale et déductive
dans laquelle la définition serait comprise implicitement. Cependant cette
théorie pourrait être rapidement contredite par les faits, comme dans le cas
sus-cité de Durkheim.

Southwold en conclut que des défintions descriptives et stipulatives,
malgré leur valeur limitée, peuvent souvent être utiles, tandis que les
définitions prescriptives sont presque toujours ratées. Inutile donc d'en
rechercher. La définition ne progressera pas plus vite que la science
elle-même.

MARILYN STRATHERN
La performance dépend du genre plutôt que du sexe:
les paradoxes de la pensée hagenienne

Les Hageniens distinguent le sexe et le genre. Ils peuvent donc sans
contradiction attribuer le genre masculin à certaines femmes et le genre
féminin à certains hommes. Une analyse sémiotique de ces conceptions
indique que les Hageniens n'assimilent pas l'opposition masculin/féminin
à l'opposition culture/nature, mais plutôt à *nyim/korpa* (bien venu/bon
à rien). Ces termes se rapportent aux individus, au degré d'accés
aux moyens de production ainsi qu'à l'opposition entre hommes et
femmes.
    L'auteur analyse en détail le statut des femmes de genre masculin. Elle
démontre que chez les Hageniens, qui se préoccupent plutôt des rites de
pollution, les rites de passage sont absents. Au contraire des autres tribus
de cette aire culturelle, ils n'acceptent aucun lien logique entre la physiologie et les statuts sociaux. Ces statuts se lient, de préférence, à la
performance (nyim), qualité associée par définition au genre masculin.
Selon l'idéologie hagenienne, l'opposition nyim/korpa se rapporterait
réellement à la stratification sociale. Mme Strathern pense en effet qu il y a
là une hyperbole inspirée par les big-men qui dominent le système, et qui
représenteraient comme absolu et 'naturel' l'écart assez modeste séparant
les statuts sociaux.
    L'auteur retrouve l'idée des genres masculin et féminin dans le système
des couleurs utilisées dans les décorations rituelles. Ici, noir: rouge exprime
le rapport des genres masculin:féminin. Le blanc, couleur masculine,
déborde toutefois cette opposition et les hommes se servent du rouge pour
certains messages où ils s'identifient aux femmes.
    Le thème principal de cette idéologie est la peur de la pollution
supposément causée par les femmes. Cette pollution détruirait le statut des
hommes et nuirait au prestige du clan. Dans ce système, la domination des
big-men est évidente, mais ceux-ci ne peuvent pas s'emparer des moyens de
production ni établir une société de classes. L'idéologie de nyim/korpa est
donc au fond égalitaire, tout en incitant le peuple à contribuer pleinement
au prestige du clan.

ROY WAGNER
Idéologie — Théorie: le problème de la réification en anthropologie

L'idéologie contemporaine exige qu'on définisse l'anthropologie comme
une science. Or, dans la copule de toute proposition culturelle, un 'comme
si' s'interpose, parfois clairement exprimé, parfois sous-entendu. Dans une
proposition, ce 'comme si' marque le métaphorique, qu'on retrouve dans
tous les genres de discours sauf deux: la religion et la science, où la copule
exprime une identité, donc une vérité absolue.
    Quand on oublie que le métaphorique est sous-entendu dans toutes les

propositions des sciences sociales, on commet l'erreur de la réification, c'est à dire qu'on recherche un type de confirmation qui confond la méthode et l'objet. La théorie de la 'médiation', proposée par l'auteur, présuppose que dans les sciences sociales, comme dans le discours ordinaire, on ne communique que si l'imagination transforme en messages la réalité vécue. A l'intérieur des cultures on communique au moyen des mythes et des modèles spontanés, et l'anthropologue dépend essentiellement, lui aussi, de la médiation entre ces modèles et le discours scientifique.

La théorie de la 'médiation' veut surtout expliquer la créativité culturelle. L'anthropologie classique la déforme par son parti-pris, qui la réduit ou bien au cautionnement de l'idéologie indigène ou bien à l'adaptation quasi-biologique des organismes à l'environnement. C'est par leur créativité que les cultures se refusent toujours à s'enfermer dans les paradigmes des systèmes clos. Pour en rendre compte, on aura besoin des modèles extensibles.

DRID WILLIAMS
Les structures profondes de la danse

Cet ouvrage de Williams comprend deux sections. Ce recueil ne contient que la première qui porte sur les règles substantielles et séquentielles d'exécution de la danse. La deuxième (qui paraîtra dans notre prochain numéro) traite de l'espace conceptuel de la danse. Dans l'article présenté ici, il s'agit d'abord de construire une grammaire de la danse, conçue d'après un modèle chomskyen. La danse n'est pas, selon l'auteur, un phénomène purement affectif: le corps humain s'y emploie, au contraire, comme significant: chaque mouvement et chaque geste transmettent un message à tout spectateur avisé.

L'auteur dénie toutefois que ce message ait un équivalent linguistique; elle démontre que les mouvements et les gestes forment un système syntactique plutôt que sémantique. Ce système peut se construire à partir de quelques lois de motilité qui nous donnent un nombre limité de possibilités d'articuler les mouvements dans l'espace. On peut en dériver, par les règles transformationnelles, tous les mouvements des danses de toutes les cultures connues. L'auteur compare le ballet classique aux danses kathak de l'Inde du Nord afin de démontrer que les règles, bien que différentes, découlent toujours des mêmes lois de motilité, par les mêmes méthodes de transformation. Les explications éthologiques de la danse seraient incapables de rendre compte de cette rigueur syntactique, ni des recherches séculaires des maîtres-danseurs de maintes cultures qui ont réfléchi sur les manifestations les plus abstraites et les plus mathématisées du rapport entre la danse et l'intellect.

Part I
SYMBOLIC ANTHROPOLOGY IN CANADA AND QUEBEC

Making Love is Like Eating Honey or Sweet Fruit, it Causes Cavities:
an essay on Cuiva symbolism

BERNARD ARCAND

The term *Cuiva* here refers to three small groups of hunters and gatherers living in the Eastern Plains (Llanos Orientales) of Columbia near the Venezuelan frontier. In all roughly 600 persons live along the banks of the rivers Meta, Casanare, Ariporo and Agua Clara. Surely the most striking characteristic of Cuiva life today is that these people have been, at least for the last twenty years, under tremendous pressures from Colombian settlers invading their territory. While I have tried to document this situation elsewhere (Moser 1971; Arcand 1972a, 1972b, 1973), my topic here is quite unrelated.

Among other things, the Cuiva say that when a woman is menstruating, she and her husband should refrain from eating honey and sweet fruit and should also abstain from sexual intercourse. Failure to comply with any one of these restrictions will result in cavities in the teeth.

Thus the Cuiva draw an empirical connection between menstruation, sex, and the eating of honey and sweet fruit. My problem here is simply to try and make sense of this connection: why should eating honey and sweet fruit during menstruation have the same negative effects as sexual intercourse? How can an element from the conceptual domain of sex and physiology be connected in such a manner to elements from the conceptual domain of food? What congruence is there between one set of ideas relating to sex and physiology and a second set of ideas relating to food so as to allow the interchange of elements from each domain?

An interpretation of the symbolic meaning of honey and sweet fruit does seem to provide a partial explanation. From a man's point of view, a restriction on eating honey and sweet fruit is coupled with the restriction on having sexual intercourse with his wife and this is tantamount to stating that his marital relationship is suspended during the days his wife is menstruating. According to the system of food-prestations based on kinship relations, honey and sweet fruit are given to a man by his wife's parents in exchange for vegetables, drugs, and his construction of a canoe and shelter.[1] Moreover, in Cuiva culture honey is frequently associated with women: an attractive girl is literally called 'a honey' and, conversely, the beehives found in hollow trees, and especially their circular entrances, are said to be exact reproductions of a woman's sexual organs. Thus during menstruation, the denial of a woman's sexuality is accompanied by a denial of honey and sweet fruit.

This interpretation does not, however, explain why no similar restriction is placed on eating meat, which is also given to a man by his parents-in-law, or why these restrictions should apply equally to both husband and wife.

1

Nor does it explain why these restrictions should apply to this particular moment in a woman's life.

To explain such food restrictions simply on the basis that honey is often associated with women — in other words, on the basis of the symbolic value often attached to honey in Cuiva culture — would provide at best a very incomplete analysis. Instead, I suggest that the best approach is to consider each of these terms (honey, sweet fruit, menstruation, sexual intercourse) as part of a systematic ordering of ideas and to examine this system in itself in order to uncover its structure.[2] Thus, let us first consider the logical ordering of each domain — food and physiology — and then establish what congruence exists between them.

The Ordering of Food

To the best of my knowledge, the Cuiva recognize as 'edible' a total of 215 sources of food. Each one, as defined by them, forms an independent animal or vegetable species. Of these 215 sources of food, 166 are animal species which provide meat, 31 are considered 'fruit' (grow on tree-tops during the rainy season, are almost all liquid, and are often prepared as juices), and 18 are 'vegetables' (grow under ground during the dry-season, have a hard, pasty texture, and are generally cooked in leaves as a cake).

The Cuiva also discriminate between various sources of food in another way based on the simple opposition 'wet'/'dry': each type of food is placed along a continuum and judged as being relatively more or less 'wet' or 'dry' than any other. To a certain extent, this continuum from 'wet' to 'dry' is accompanied by an opposition between 'sweet' and 'bitter': very wet foods are also among the sweetest (honey and ripe fruit) and most very dry foods are said to have a bitter taste) drugs and vegetables). While all foods are placed on the 'wet'-'dry' continuum, however, the opposition between 'sweet' and 'bitter' is not applied to all.

It does not seem necessary for the purpose of this paper to detail the position of all 215 sources of food along the continua. Considering only honey, sweet fruit and the other main categories of food, the continua conceptualized by the Cuiva are as follows:

1 Opposition Wet/Dry:

Very Wet	Wet	Dry	Very Dry
Honey Sweet fruit	Meat	Vegetables	Drugs

2 Opposition Sweet/Bitter:

Very Sweet	Sweet	Bitter	Very Bitter
Honey Sweet fruit		Vegetables	Drugs

These are the normal positions of the main types of food along the two continua. According to the Cuiva, all foods left untouched will sooner or later decay and become 'rotten'. This natural process is viewed as a move away from 'dryness', with 'rottenness' as a state of extreme 'wetness'. By hunting and gathering and cooking their food, human beings interrupt, reverse, or accelerate this natural process.

The effect of cooking varies with the type of food being prepared. Cooking meat transforms it from 'wet' (raw meat) to 'dry' (cooked meat), although there is no mention of a corresponding change in taste (meat is neither 'sweet' nor 'bitter'). In this case, the effect of fire is to reverse the meat's natural progression towards 'wetness'. In contrast, cooking fruit (which is cooked only when too green to be eaten raw) accelerates its natural progression from 'bitter' to 'sweet' by making it become prematurely ripe ('edible' and 'sweet'). Cooking does not, however, alter the natural 'wetness' of fruit. Finally, the effect of cooking on vegetables creates a paradox which demonstrates that the oppositions 'wet'/'dry' and 'sweet'/'bitter' are not always strictly parallel: cooked vegetables are said to be less 'wet', but at the same time less 'bitter' than raw vegetables.

At one extreme of the continuum, honey and sweet fruits are said to be 'very wet' and are consumed without cooking (eaten raw). At the other extreme, drugs are rated as the 'dryest' of all foods and are cooked so thoroughly (in fact parched) that they stand somewhere at the limit between the categories 'cooked' and 'burnt'.

The essential point for the present argument is that honey and sweet fruit represent extremes of 'wetness'. These are two kinds of food which are eaten raw and cannot be transformed by fire.

The Ordering of Physiology and Sex

The same continuum, based on the opposition between 'wet' and 'dry', is applied to human beings. According to the Cuiva, the human body should be maintained in a state of equilibrium between wetness and dryness. This is the condition of a healthy person. To lean towards one or the other of the two extremes is considered dangerous and often causes death. When, for example, fevers produce abundant sweating, they are said 'to dry' a person. On the contrary, diarrhoea is seen as a symptom that the insides are becoming more and more 'wet'. All internal diseases, even minor ones, are seen as breaking this equilibrium one way or the other.

Although men and women are human beings, in a state of internal equilibrium, the two are nonetheless also opposed: the Cuiva say that women are 'wet' in comparison to men who are 'dry'. Women, fish, and raw meat from all animals share the characteristic of being *asuntané*. This refers to a specific smell and feel: it is a quality attached to the gluey stuff on the back of fish, to animal blood, and to menstrual blood. Women are said to be especially *asuntané* at puberty, when menstruating, and immediately after giving birth. Contact with women during these periods is considered dangerous for men, since it would result in *awapa*, an illness which makes one vomit all one's food. Fear of the same illness is also the explanation Cuiva give as to why men are always quick and careful to wash any animal blood from themselves and why hunters usually leave the preparation of raw meat to women.

Although essentially 'wet' in comparison to men, women also periodically move along the continuum: from a state of 'very wet' during menstruation, at puberty, and immediately after childbirth, through a state of 'less wet' during the days between menstruations, and finally to a state of 'dry' during childhood, pregnancy, or after menopause. Thus the continuum of 'wet' to 'dry' as applied to human beings is as follows:

Very Wet	*Wet*	*Dry*	*Very Dry*
Women when menstruating; at puberty or in childbirth	Women of childbearing age when not menstruating	Women before puberty or after menopause. Pregnant women. Men. Children	

The above ideas are expressed very clearly during the communal ritual held whenever a young girl reaches the age of puberty. Since a full description and analysis of this ritual would require more space than is available here, the following analysis is restricted to those themes which are most directly relevant to my argument.

When a girl reaches puberty the Cuiva say that she has become 'very wet'. She has left the state of 'dryness' common to all children and becoming 'wet' is an indication that she has become a woman. The central problem with which the ritual deals is that the young girl, like all women, must periodically be able to become 'less wet' in order for men to approach her. Through the ritual she must be 'dried' and brought into the second phase of her periodicity.

During the ritual, Cuiva men make a special effort to obtain as much meat as they can, while women make a similar concerted effort to gather vegetables. All this food is brought to the shelter of the girl's parents where it is cooked on a stand. This is a slow process during which the food is cooked very thoroughly, that is, thoroughly dried-out. The only other method used by the Cuiva to cook food is to place it directly on the fire, a roasting method which is much quicker but which leaves the food half-cooked, that is 'a little juicy' or 'a little raw'.

After five or six hours, when all the food is thoroughly cooked, the meat and vegetables are mixed together by pounding them in a mortar. The food is then placed on mats on the ground and left there for at least a day. This ensures its final dehydration, during which the mixture of meat and vegetables which was at first called *kwané*, becomes *akwéro* — perfectly dried. In this use, the term *akwéro* seems to be more than just phonemically related to the term *akwé*, the cover kinship term for grandmother. Cuiva men say that old women become 'dried-out' once they no longer menstruate and that their skin is like the bottom of dried-out lakes during the dry-season.

During the four or five days of the ritual, both the girl and her husband (in Cuiva society a girl marries between the ages of ten and twelve, or in any case always before puberty) must refrain from eating 'wet' foods like meat, honey, and fruit, and are allowed to eat only 'dry' food — vegetables. Husband and wife should also refrain from sexual intercourse during this period. Failure to comply with these food and sex taboos is believed to cause cavities in the teeth.

More evidence could be cited to support the claim that through the puberty ritual Cuiva society attempts to prove that it is able to transform what is naturally 'wet' into something that is 'dry'. Many details from the ritual are attempts to achieve 'dryness': cooking the food most thoroughly, drying one's body through drugs and dancing, eating by the couple of only 'dry' food, etc. More important perhaps is the fact that this interpretation of the ritual corresponds to that expressed by many adult Cuiva (both sexes). First of all, the Cuiva see a very direct relation between puberty and fertility; when news of the first menstruation is made public, the most common reaction is to say 'Now she can have children', and parents claim to be delighted at the coming of their daughter's puberty as it will make it possible for them to have grandchildren. Similarly, it is also clearly stated that without going through the ritual a woman would be unable to have children. It is also expressed openly that what society is doing during the ritual is proving that anything 'wet' can in fact be dried' and that the purpose of the ritual is to dry the girl who is in a state of 'very wet'.

The manner of ordering physiology and sex means that the normal development of a Cuiva woman is to evolve from a 'dry' child into a 'very wet' person at puberty, to become a 'wet' woman after the ritual, and to be transformed, through marriage and fecundation, into a state of 'dry' pregnancy.

There is a striking analogy — but one which the Cuiva themselves do not draw — between the transformations a woman passes through during her life cycle and the way in which fish is transformed into food. The Cuiva hunt fish with bow and arrows, usually from a standing position in a canoe or on the river bank. This technique requires that the fish be seen by the hunter, and consequently whenever fish remain in deep water hunters are unable to approach them. (The deep part of a river or lake, which the Cuiva distinguish by the name *ôwubo*, is the source of less than 2% of all meat produced by hunting.)

Similarly, whenever a woman is in a state of 'very wet' her husband cannot approach her and intercourse is not allowed. Practically, fish can only be killed when they venture into the shallow part of a river or lake (called *tséwa*, and the source of roughly 28% of all meat produced). Again, it is when a woman leaves the state of 'very wet' for that of 'less wet' common to all adult women during the days between menstruations, that her husband can approach her and intercourse occurs. Finally, it is through cooking that a fish is transformed from 'raw meat' to 'cooked meat' by becoming 'dried'. In the same way, it is through becoming pregnant that a woman is transformed from 'wetness' to 'dryness'.

The Cuiva with whom I discussed this point agreed to the logic of my argument, although they had never drawn this analogy. I can suggest two possible explanations for this. First, the analogy made with fish is not applicable to other foods which are equally important economically but which are caught in other ways. Secondly, the analogy presents women in a rather negative, passive role, and this certainly does not correspond to the general Cuiva view of the relationship between males and females. Thus, the only analogy which is openly expressed by the Cuiva is that between fire as an agent of transformation of raw meat into cooked meat and marriage as an agent of transformation of pubescent women into pregnant women.

Fire and Marriage as Agents of Transformation

Let me now return to the original question of why, during menstruation, it is forbidden for a woman and her husband to have sex or to eat honey and sweet fruit. It is now possible to understand the kind of fit that exists between the set of ideas relating to sex and physiology and the set of ideas relating to food, and which allows connections and convertibility between elements belonging to each domain. The logical ordering of the two domains can be summarized as follows:

	Very Wet	*Wet*	*Dry*	*Very Dry*
Food:	Honey Sweet Fruit	Meat	Vegetables	Drugs
Physiology and sex:	Women when menstruating; at puberty or in childbirth	Women of childbearing age when not menstruating	Women before puberty or after menopause. Pregnant women. Men and children	

The logic behind the puberty ritual is already clear: a) men are considered 'dry' in opposition to women who are 'wet'; b) a woman periodically becomes 'very wet' and 'wet'; c) a menstruating woman, or a woman in childbirth, is considered 'very wet' and any man coming into close contact with her would suffer from *awapa* which would make him vomit all his food. Following this logic, during the puberty ritual, the girl and her husband are forbidden all food classified as 'wet'. In the case of menstruation, the restriction is more limited and both are allowed to eat meat. What is forbidden is only the 'very wet' food, specifically honey and sweet fruit, which are eaten raw and which are in a perpetual state of wetness since they cannot be dried by fire. It is as if, during the puberty ritual, proof has to be given that society is capable of drying by fire what is naturally wet; thus, the couple is allowed to eat only the kind of food which is naturally dry (vegetables). Once it is proven that fire can be used as an agent of transformation, and that as such it is analogous to marriage, subsequent menstruation does not impose restrictions on the couple against consuming food which can be dried by fire (meat), but only those foods on which fire has no effect (honey and sweet fruit). This assumes, of course, the existence of a direct link between puberty and all subsequent menstruations: the Cuiva refer to puberty as 'a first menstruation' and the origin of both puberty and menstruation is found in the same myth telling how a small lizard once made love to a young girl.

Thus the connection between honey, sweet fruit, and menstruation results from the fact that honey and sweet fruit constitute exceptions to the general principle that fire can transform 'wet' food into 'dry' food, while menstruation represents the exception to the principle that 'wet' women are made 'dry' by marriage. By abstaining from eating honey and sweet fruit, husband and wife reassert the principle that food is indeed transformed by fire. It seems logical that the restriction should apply to both husband and wife since it is the very effect of their marriage which is being questioned by the menstruation.

A Further Proof

The food preferences of a pregnant woman are the exact opposite to those of a menstruating woman. Women say that during pregnancy they prefer to eat primarily honey and all varieties of sweet fruit. It is a common Cuiva joke to say of a woman who eats a large quantity of honey or fruit that she must be pregnant. Pregnant women are said to eat little meat or vegetables since these foods, it is believed, would painfully inflate their bellies which are already pressed by the baby. On the whole, pregnant women are supposed to eat less than usual; in support of this practice, the Cuiva point out that female turtles (a particular species) defecate less at the beginning of the dry season, at the time when they are carrying eggs, and therefore must also be eating less. Pregnant women are said to have their insides pressed by the embryo, so that they rarely feel very hungry and prefer to eat mostly liquid food which is not as filling and easier to pass than solid food. In other words, and in opposition to a menstruating woman, a pregnant woman, who is in a 'dry' state, can indulge as much as she wishes in consuming 'wet' food without danger. As the living proof that marriage successfully transforms women from 'wet' to 'dry', a pregnant woman has nothing to fear from eating the 'very wet' food which cannot be dried by fire.

Cavities

Failure to comply with food and sex taboos during menstruation is believed to bring cavities in the teeth. Besides being painful and very annoying, the Cuiva say that cavities create an infection of the gum which makes it practically impossible to eat any solid food: there are stories and myths about people suffering from cavities (and I saw two persons suffering from them). In all cases, the person affected is reduced to consuming only fruit juices, claiming to be incapable of chewing anything. Thus, when a woman is in a 'very wet' state during menstruation, she and her husband must avoid 'very wet' foods, or else be forced afterwards to eat nothing but this type of food and become incapable of eating 'dry' food. This would mean that, by failing to re-affirm the principle that fire does transform food, the couple later deprives itself of all the food on which fire does have an effect (and it could be shown that in the wider context of Cuiva culture to deprive oneself of fire is to deprive oneself of culture). It would have been equally valid for the Cuiva to say that failure to comply with the sex and food taboos would result in a perpetual menstruation, a rejection of the principle that marriage does transform women. Obviously, however, the end of a menstruation period is an easily verifiable empirical fact, while cavities in the teeth, besides being more common, are said to appear months, years, or even decades after the actual breach of the taboos.

Conclusion

The problem was to attempt to explain how some elements from the conceptual domain of food can be linked to elements from the domain of sex and physiology. Taking honey, sweet fruit, menstruation, and sexual intercourse as the starting point, a number of other linkages between the two domains later appeared: meat and vegetables associated with a woman at puberty, pregnancy and the eating of liquid food; fire and marriage as agents of transformation. It soon becomes obvious that there is a perfect fit between the two sets of ideas, so that elements from one domain become translatable into elements of the other, and thus the cooking of food can mean something about the physiological changes of a woman, meat and vegetables can be substituted for the young girl during the puberty ritual, honey and sweet fruit can be forbidden together with sexual intercourse, etc.

The essential point for an understanding of these symbolic statements is a consideration not of the elements themselves but of the relationships which exist between them. The logical ordering of the two domains forms a systematic structural arrangement which can be summarized as follows:

$$\left[\begin{array}{c} \text{Honey} \\ \text{Sweet fruit} \end{array} \right] : \left[\text{Meat} \right] : \left[\text{Vegetables} \right] :: \left[\begin{array}{c} \text{Women when} \\ \text{menstruating} \\ \text{at puberty or} \\ \text{in childbirth} \end{array} \right] : \left[\begin{array}{c} \text{Adult} \\ \text{women} \end{array} \right] : \left[\begin{array}{c} \text{Pregnant} \\ \text{women} \end{array} \right]$$

which also includes the transformational rules:

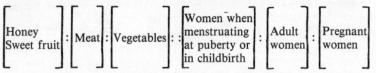

$$\left[\text{Fire} \right] : \left[\begin{array}{c} \text{Meat} \\ \text{Vegetables} \end{array} \right] : \left[\text{Fecundation} \right] : \left[\text{Women} \right]$$

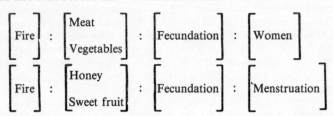

$$\left[\text{Fire} \right] : \left[\begin{array}{c} \text{Honey} \\ \text{Sweet fruit} \end{array} \right] : \left[\text{Fecundation} \right] : \left[\text{Menstruation} \right]$$

It is the existence of this structure which allows the Cuiva to make meaningful statements about sex and physiology while talking of food. Meaning is found in the system of relations when taken as a whole, rather than in the limited semantic content of single elements considered in isolation: it is because of the relationship of honey and sweet fruit to fire is identical to the relationship of menstruation to marriage that these foods are forbidden during the days of menstruation.

Viewing any social fact as a relation internal to a system and concentrating on the discovery of the structure of that system constitutes perhaps the most basic rule of structural analysis — one which Lévi-Strauss borrowed from linguistics and introduced into anthropology some thirty years ago (1945). This essay was intended as a further demonstration of the validity of this general rule.

A second and perhaps more original conclusion is that the preceeding analysis corresponds to the explanation given by the Cuiva themselves; it forms what is usually referred to as 'a conscious model' and indeed a Cuiva could very well have written this essay. This would suggest that structural analysis is an approach to understanding reality which is not necessarily limited to modern anthropology. I intend to argue this point at length later and expect it to be confirmed by other field reports. As Tyler (1969:91) pointed out, in all scientific investigation it is axiomatic that the kind of question asked determines the response. Anthropologists have only recently turned their attention to this approach and are only beginning to ask the relevant questions. The level of awareness shown by the Cuiva might well be typical of the kind of answers a new generation of ethnographers will receive.[3]

NOTES

1 Much of Lévi-Strauss' second volume of his *Mythologiques* has been given to a demonstration of the validity, for a large area of South America, of what the Cuiva express openly: that honey and menstruations are symbolically related. To test Lévi-Strauss' complete thesis in the light of information provided by the Cuiva would require more space than is available here. However, it is openly stated by the Cuiva that honey is 'la matière par excellence des prestations dues aux alliés' (Lévi-Strauss 1966:243), but not 'ce qui doit passer du mari aux parents de la femme' (1966:340) but rather the opposite.

2 This approach, of course, is not new and merely follows the analyses suggested among others by Lévi-Strauss (1962), Leach (1964), Douglas (1966) and Tambiah (1969).

3 I wish to express my gratitude to Sharon Bohn and George Gmelch for their assistance in rendering the English text.

BIBLIOGRAPHY

Arcand, Bernard 1972a: 'Documento — Los Cuiva', in Grünberg, Georg (ed.), *La Situacion del Indigena en America del Sur*, Montevideo, Tierra Nueva, Biblioteca Cientifica, 121-4.

_____ 1972b: *The Urgent Situation of the Cuiva Indians of Colombia*, Copenhagen, International Workgroup for Indigenous Affairs, Document 7.

_____ 1973: 'Notes pour une étude de l'ethnocide' in Université de Montréal, *L'Amérique Latine: développement et société*, Montréal.

Douglas, Mary 1966: *Purity and Danger*, London, Routledge and Kegan Paul.

Leach, Edmund R. 1964: 'Anthropological Aspects of Language: Animal Categories and Verbal Abuse', in Lenneberg, Erich H. (ed.), *New Directions in the Study of Language*, Cambridge, Mass., M.I.T. Press.

Lévi-Strauss, Claude 1945: 'L'analyse structurale en linguistique et en anthropologie', *Word, Journal of the Linguistic Circle of New York*, 1, 2, August.

_____ 1962: *La Pensée Sauvage*, Paris, Plon.

_____ 1966: *Du Miel aux Cendres*, Paris, Plon.

Moser, Brian and Arcand, B. 1971: *The Last of the Cuiva*, 65mm. documentary film, 'Disappearing World' series, Manchester, Granada Television.

Tambiah, S.J. 1969: 'Animals are good to think and good to prohibit' in *Ethnology*, VIII, 4.

Tyler, Stephen A. 1969: *Cognitive Anthropology*, New York, Holt, Rinehart and Winston.

The Invading Guest:
some aspects of oral transmission

PIERRE CRÉPEAU

This paper has three purposes. First, it aims at introducing the reader to a specific example of Rwandan lore, namely a Rwandan proverb which has been heard in 70 different variants or versions. Second, an analysis of this particular item is proposed from which some conclusions can be drawn as to the principles which seem to regulate its oral transmission. And third, it makes some very tentative suggestions as to how oral transmission operates in general. But, before coming to the point itself, I feel it necessary to set forth some of the theoretical assumptions underlying this essay.

Theoretical Assumptions

As the item under study is a proverb, one might expect some clarifications about the problem of the definition of the proverb. Unfortunately, I have none to propose for the moment. Whether a proverb is essentially a metaphoric saying (Forster 1936) or a statement in which the symmetry of content is reproduced in the symmetry of form (Milner 1969:54) is not a crucial issue for the present study. Suffice to say that the Rwandan people can easily distinguish their proverbs from other genres of their verbal arts although they cannot provide clear criteria for the distinction. Sometimes one will hesitate when another is sure that the item is or is not a proverb. But those cases are rare. Most of the time, a proverb is introduced with the stereotyped formula *Abanyarwanda baca umuganí bati:* 'The Rwandan people chisel a proverb saying', or in elliptical form *Bacu umuganí bati:* 'One chisels a proverb saying'. This way of identifying a Rwandan proverb is for the folklorist of another culture the only sound criterion for deciding which product of Rwandan verbal art is a proverb and which is not. Holding to this one criterion is the only way of avoiding ethnocentrism and of deciding within the Rwandan cultural matrix.

This being said, I would however agree with Greimas (1970:310) that a proverb necessarily implies connotation. It functions at two levels of signification: one referential or denotative, and the other connotative. The two levels of signification are bound together in such a way that the first level is the very expression of the second. This can be figured as:

second level	F	R	C
first level	F R C		

In this figure F stands for form, C stands for content and R for relation between form and content (cf. Barthes 1964:130). At the first level of signification, content is determined through an immediate though arbitrary relation between *designantia* and *designata*. At the second level, content is determined through a mediate relation between *connotantia* and *connotata*. This relation is mediate, that is to say, it is established by the aid

11

Level of change	Object of change	Kind of change	Result of change
Linguistic	Terms	Variation	Variant
	Grammatical structure		
Semantic	Terms	Permutation	Version
	Functions	Transformation	New items of folklore

Fig. 1

of the socio-cultural context and of the enunciative process. The enunciative process includes the situational context and the intentional or functional aspect of the proverb. This brings us to the second assumption.

A new trend is spreading among the folklorists which tends to conceptualize folklore as event rather than as item (Bauman 1971). According to this conception, studies of folklore should consider the happening rather than the objects of folklore. That folklore is a communicative process rather than an aggregate of the traditional materials and that it should consequently be dealt with as such, is a point no one will argue. But one should also bear in mind that if analysis of folklore items cannot pretend to explain the whole of folklore, it nevertheless constitutes a necessary step towards a full comprehension of this cultural phenomenon. Psycholinguistics, sociolinguistics and ethnolinguistics are all necessary complements to descriptive and structural linguistics, but the study of language cannot be reduced to these fields. So it is with folklore. Of course folklore is performance and as such it cannot be fully explained without any attention being paid to its process.

However, in folklore as in language, there is no performance without underlying competence. Folklore is a communicative process of its own, with its own structuring rules. There is the folkloristic *parole*; there is also the folkloristic *langue*. No one would question the legitimacy of descriptive or structural linguistics which are the study of items of language. Why then should one question the legitimacy of analysis of items of folklore from which can be drawn at least some of the rules of its process? The present essay is based on this legitimacy.

The words 'variant' and 'version' will often be used here. If there is any distinction between the two terms, it is a subtle one. One might venture to say that a variant is nothing but a different way of saying exactly the same thing, whereas a version is saying something related to but different from another version. A variant is a change in form at the pure linguistic level; a version on the contrary implies a switch in semantics. Referring to the above mentioned distinction, one might say that a variant is a change in form at the first level of signification only, whereas a version is a change in content at the first level of signification and consequently in form at the second level. It must be kept in mind however that not all changes in content at the first level of signification are versions. Indeed some of these changes may go as far as to generate a new item of folklore.

Lévi-Strauss, in his *Mythologiques* has made a constant use of such words as variant, version, permutation, and transformation. As far as I know, he never gave a formal definition of these terms. One is left to figure out the meaning through the uses of the words. If I understand properly, variant and version in the *Mythologiques* are interchangeable although version tends to be used more naturally when changes in the myths seem to have more analytical value. 'Permutation' is a change of terms which leads to a switch in semantics and to a version. As for 'transformation', it means a change from one item to another, from one myth to another. It comes at the end of a long series of permutations. Myth A permuting from version to version finally becomes Myth B. The Bororo, for example, transform their myth of the genesis of the cooking fire into the myth of the genesis of water through a long series of permutations of the terms (Lévi-Strauss 1966:18). In fact, transformation occurs when a new function is assigned to opposed terms. As long as the functions remain unchanged there is no transformation. Referring to Lévi-Strauss' canonical formula, changes of *a* and *b* are permutations as long as *x* and *y* remain untouched; 'transformation' is a change in *x* or *y* and it generates a new item of folklore. This interpretation seems to be shared by Elli Köngäs Maranda for riddles (1971:54-55). It seems applicable also to many other genres of verbal art, if not all. One can briefly say: a variant is the result of variation at the linguistic level only; a version is the result of semantic variation in terms only; a new item of verbal art is the result of variation in functions. Figure 1 summarizes all these.

'Oral tradition' is often used either for the traditional materials of verbal art or for the process of transmitting from mouth to ear. For the sake of clarity in the present essay, oral tradition will be used exclusively for the products of verbal art, the process itself being termed 'oral transmission'.

A Rwandan Proverb

First, here are the different variants and versions in which the proverb was heard. All 70 of them were actually heard. I feel necessary to stress this point as the reader might be inclined to think that some of them are nothing but my logical deductions. There are logical possibilities that a lot more versions or variants might be acceptable to Rwandan culture. We will see later what the restrictions are. Of course, the variants and versions were not heard in the order they are presented here. I arranged them in such a way as to make it possible for the reader, even without knowing the language, to discover at least some of the features of the variational matrix.

The Rwandan text is written according to the rules established by André Coupez (1961 and 1962). The phonetic units, consonants, vowels and semi-vowels, follow current orthography and generally correspond to the *Africa* system of the International African Institute except in some details as, for example, the voiceless front fricative which is written sh instead of ʃ. Consonants and semi-vowels also admit many allophones which are not written. Quantity and tone follow the rules of Africa to which are added particular rules required by specific Rwandan tonal system. Quantity is usually indicated with a double vowel except when found in determined positions. Tone is indicated by the aid of diacritical signs. The Rwandan language has four tones: one low tone which is indicated by the absence of diacritical sign and three high tones which are distinguished by the position and the form of the diacritical signs ['] and [ˇ].

1 *Umutuutsi umusembereza ikwéru akaguca muu mbere*
   The Tuutsi you lodge him in the ingle-nook and he throws you out of the front-room.[1]

2 *Umutuutsi umusembereza ikwéru akaguca ruguru*
   The Tuutsi you lodge him in the ingle-nook and he throws you out of the upper-room.

3 *Umutuutsi umusembereza ikwéru akaguca ku buriri*
   The Tuutsi you lodge him in the ingle-nook and he throws you out of the bed.

4 *Umutuutsi umusembereza haakwéru akaguca muu mbere*
   The Tuutsi you lodge him in the ingle-nook[2] and he throws you out of the front-room.

5 *Umutuutsi umusembereza haakwéru akaguca ruguru*
   The Tuutsi you lodge him in the ingle-nook and he throws you out of the upper-room.

6 *Umutuutsi umusembereza haakwéru akaguca ku buriri*
   The Tuutsi you lodge him in the ingle-nook and he throws you out of the bed.

7 *Umutuutsi umusembereza mu muryángo akaguca muu mbere*
   The Tuutsi you lodge him in the lobby and he throws you out of the front-room.

8 *Umutuutsi umusembereza mu muryángo akaguca ruguru*
   The Tuutsi you lodge him in the lobby and he throws you out of the upper-room.

9 *Umutuutsi umusembereza mu muryángo akaguca ku buriri*
   The Tuutsi you lodge him in the lobby and he throws you out of the bed.

10 *Umutuutsi umusembereza ikwéru akagukuura muu mbere*
   The Tuutsi you lodge him in the ingle-nook and he forces you out of the front-room.

11 *Umutuutsi umusembereza ikwéru akagukuura ruguru*
   The Tuutsi you lodge him in the ingle-nook and he forces you out of the upper-room.

12 *Umutuutsi umusembereza ikwéru akagukuura ku buriri*
   The Tuutsi you lodge him in the ingle-nook and he forces you out of the bed.

13 *Umutuutsi umusembereza haakwéru akagukuura muu mbere*
   The Tuutsi you lodge him in the ingle-nook and he forces you out of the front-room.

14 *Umutuutsi umusembereza haakwéru akagukuura ruguru*
The Tuutsi you lodge him in the ingle-nook and he forces you out of the upper-room.

15 *Umutuutsi umusembereza haakwéru akagukuura ku buriri*
The Tuutsi you lodge him in the ingle-nook and he forces you out of the bed.

16 *Umutuutsi umusembereza mu muryángo akagukurra muu mbere*
The Tuutsi you lodge him in the lobby and he forces you out of the front-room.

17 *Umutuutsi umusembereza mu muryángo akagukuura ruguru*
The Tuutsi you lodge him in the lobby and he forces you out of the upper-room.

18 *Umutuutsi umusembereza mu muryángo akagukuura ku buriri*
The Tuutsi you lodge him in the lobby and he forces you out of the bed.

19 *Umutuutsi umusembereza ikwéru akaguteera muu mbere*
The Tuutsi you lodge him in the ingle-nook and he intrudes on you in the front-room.

20 *Umtuutsi umusembereza ikwéru akaguteera ruguru*
The Tuutsi you lodge him in the ingle-nook and he intrudes on you in the upper-room.

21 *Umutuutsi umusembereza ikwéru akaguteera ku buriri*
The Tuutsi you lodge him in the ingle-nook and he intrudes on you in the bed.

22 *Umutuutsi umusembereza haakwéru akaguteera muu mbere*
The Tuutsi you lodge him in the ingle-nook and he intrudes on you in the front-room.

23 *Umutuutsi umusembereza haakwéru akaguteera ruguru*
The Tuutsi you lodge him in the ingle-nook and he intrudes on you in the upper-room.

24 *Umutuutsi umusembereza haakwéru akaguteera ku buriri*
The Tuutsi you lodge him in the ingle-nook and he intrudes on you in the bed.

25 *Umutuutsi umusembereza mu muryángo akaguteera muu mbere*
The Tuutsi you lodge him in the lobby and he intrudes on you in the front-room.

26 *Umutuutsi umusembereza mu muryángo akaguteera ruguru*
The Tuutsi you lodge him in the lobby and he intrudes on you in the upper-room.

27 *Umutuutsi umusembereza mu muryángo akaguteera ku buriri*
The Tuutsi you lodge him in the lobby and he intrudes on you in the bed.

28 *Usembereza umutuutsi ikwéru akaguca muu mbere*
You lodge the Tuutsi in the ingle-nook and he throws you out of the front-room.

29 *Usembereza umutuutsi ikwéru akaguca reguru*
You lodge the Tuutsi in the ingle-nook and he throws you out of the upper-room.

30 *Usembereza umutuutsi ikwéru akaguca ku buriri*
You lodge the Tuutsi in the ingle-nook and he throws you out of the bed.

31 *Usembereza umutuutsi haakwéru akaguca muu mbere*
You lodge the Tuutsi in the ingle-nook and he throws you out of the front-room.

32 *Usembereza umutuutsi haakwéru akaguca ruguru*
You lodge the Tuutsi in the ingle-nook and he throws you out of the upper-room.

33 *Usembereza umutuutsi haakwéru akaguca ku buriri*
You lodge the Tuutsi in the ingle-nook and he throws you out of the bed.

34 *Usembereza umutuutsi mu muryángo akaguca muu mbere*
You lodge the Tuutsi in the lobby and he throws you out of the front-room.

35 *Usembereza umutuutsi mu muryángo akaguca ruguru*
You lodge the Tuutsi in the lobby and he throws you out of the upper-room.

36 *Usembereza umutuutsi mu muryángo akaguca ku buriri*
You lodge the Tuutsi in the lobby and he throws you out of the bed.

37 *Usembereza umutuutsi ikwéru akagukuura muu mbere*
You lodge the Tuutsi in the ingle-nook and he forces you out of the front-room.

38 *Usembereza umutuutsi ikwéru akagukuura ruguru*
You lodge the Tuutsi in the ingle-nook and he forces you out of the upper-room.

39 *Usembereza umutuutsi ikwéru akagakuura ku buriri*
You lodge the Tuutsi in the ingle-nook and he forces you out of the bed.

40 *Usembereza umutuutsi haakwéru akagukuura muu mbere*
You lodge the Tuutsi in the ingle-nook and he forces you out of the front-room.

41 *Usembereza umutuutsi haakwéru akagukuura ruguru*
You lodge the Tuutsi in the ingle-nook and he forces you out of the upper-room.

42 *Usembereza umutuutsi haakwéru akagukuura ku buriri*
You lodge the Tuutsi in the ingle-nook and he forces you out of the bed.

43 *Usembereza umutuutsi mu muryángo akagukuura muu mbere*
You lodge the Tuutsi in the lobby and he forces you out of the front room.

44 *Usembereza umutuutsi mu muryángo akagukuura ruguru*
You lodge the Tuutsi in the lobby and he forces you out of the upper-room.

45 *Usembereza umutuutsi mu muryángo akagukuura ku bururi*
You lodge the Tuutsi in the lobby and he forces you out of the bed.

46   *Usembereza umutuutsi ikwéru akaguteera muu mbere*
You lodge the Tuutsi in the ingle-nook and he intrudes on you in the front-room.

47   *Usembereza umutuutsi ikwéru akaguteera ruguru*
You lodge the Tuutsi in the ingle-nook and he intrudes on you in the upper-room.

48   *Usembereza umutuutsi ikwéru akaguteera ku buriri*
You lodge the Tuutsi in the ingle-nook and he intrudes on you in the bed.

49   *Usembereza umutuutsi haakwéru akaguteera muu mbere*
You lodge the Tuutsi in the ingle-nook and he intrudes on you in the front-room.

50   *Usembereza umutuutsi haakwéru akaguteera ruguru*
You lodge the Tuutsi in the ingle-nook and he intrudes on you in the upper-room.

51   *Usembereza umutuutsi haakwéru akaguteera ku buriri*
You lodge the Tuutsi in the ingle-nook and he intrudes on you in the bed.

52   *Usembereza umutuutsi mu muryángo akaguteera muu mbere*
You lodge the Tuutsi in the lobby and he intrudes on you in the front-room.

53   *Usembereza umutuutsi mu muryángo akaguteera ruguru*
You lodge the Tuutsi in the lobby and he intrudes on you in the upper-room.

54   *Usembereza umutuutsi mu muryángo akaguteera ku buriri*
You lodge the Tuutsi in the lobby and he intrudes on you in the bed.

55   *Umutuutsi umusembereza muu mfúruká akaguca muu nzu*
The Tuutsi you lodge him in the corner and he throws you out of the house.

56   *Umutuutsi umusembereza mu kirǎmbi akaguca muu nzu*
The Tuutsi you lodge him in the living-room and he throws you out of the house.

57   *Umutuutsi umusembereza muu mfúruká akagukuura muu nzu*
The Tuutsi you lodge him in the corner and he forces you out of the house.

58   *Umutuutsi umusembereza mu kirǎmbi akagukuura muu nzu*
The Tuutsi you lodge him in the living room and he forces you out of the house.

59   *Umutuutsi umusembereza muu mfúruká akaguteera muu nzu*
The Tuutsi you lodge him in the corner and he intrudes on you in the house.

60   *Umutuutsi umusembereza mu kirǎmbi akaguteera muu nzu*
The Tuutsi you lodge him in the living-room and he intrudes on you in the house.

61   *Umutuutsi umusembereza mu muryángo akaguteera mu kirǎmbi*
The Tuutsi you lodge him in the lobby and he intrudes on you in the living-room.

62   *Umutuutsi umusembereza ihéeru akaguca ikámberé*
     The Tuutsi you lodge him in the second house and he throws you out
     of the main house.
63   *Umutuutsi umusembereza ihéeru akagukuura ikámberé*
     The Tuutsi you lodge him in the second house and he forces you out of
     the main house.
64   *Umutuutsi umusembereza ihéeru akaguteera ikámberé*
     The Tuutsi you lodge him in the second house and he intrudes on you
     in the main house.
65   *Umutuutsi umusembereza ikwéru akaguca ikámberé*
     The Tuutsi you lodge him in the second house and he throws you out
     of the main house
66   *Umutuutsi umusembereza ikwéru akagukuura ikámberé*
     The Tuutsi you lodge him in the second house and he forces you out of
     the main house.
67   *Umutuutsi umusembereza ikwéru akaguteera ikámberé*
     The Tuutsi you lodge him in the second house and he intrudes on you
     in the main house.
68   *Umutuutsi umusembereza mu isămbu akagukuura muu ngo*
     The Tuutsi you receive him on the estate and he forces you out of the
     dwellings.
69   *Umutuutsi umusembereza mu muryángo agakwimura muu mbere*
     The Tuutsi you lodge him in the lobby and he chucks you out of the
     front-room.
70   *Umutuutsi umucumbikira mu kirămbi akaguteera nó muu mbere*
     The Tuutsi you put him up for the night in the living-room and he
     intrudes on you even in the front-room.

Contextual Analysis

Let us take No. 1 as the basic text. This choice is of course arbitrary as I
have no means of nor interest in finding which is the *textus princeps*. The
particularity of text No. 1 is that it is found in the oldest important corpus
of Rwandan proverbs (Kagame 1953: No. 1409) and that its form seems
rather archaic. Recourse to socio-cultural context in this case implies the
knowledge of house-building as well as of socio-political structure of
traditional Rwanda. First, here is a ground-sketch of an average Rwandan
compound (fig. 2) and of an average Rwandan house (fig. 3).

Rwanda is a country of hills and mountains. Flat surfaces are almost
unknown so that compounds and houses are mostly built on hill-sides, the
gates and doors usually perpendicular to the hill-side at some angle, the hill
being on either side of the compound indifferently. The area of the
compound is flattened sometimes as a result of laborious terracing. To a
certain extent this geographical situation is reflected in the naming of the
different sections of the compound. The back is called *haruguru* or *ruguru*:
'up there' and the front part is called *epfó:* 'down'. The same applies to the
different sections of the house, the remotest part being called *ruguru* which
I translate as 'upper-room'. The more people reside in the compound or

the house, the more they go up. This also has some bearing in seating the guests inside the house, the more important being given the 'upper' places.

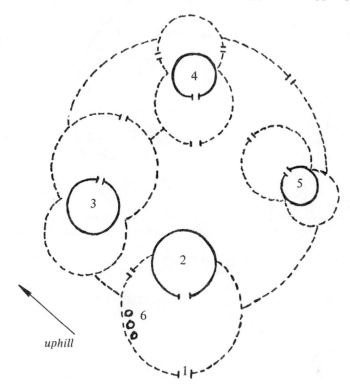

Fig. 2 Ground sketch of a traditional compound
(adaptation from Sandrart 1939:38-9)

- - - limits of the fences
——— limits of the houses

1. *ku irémbo*: at the gate
2. *ikámberé*: at the main house
3. *ihéeru*: up there
   Kagŏndo: Proper name (first secondary house)
4. *igihisí*: Proper name. Name of the hill on which the house is built (second secondary house)
5. *urutéekero*: the kitchen
6. *ibiráaro*: the byres

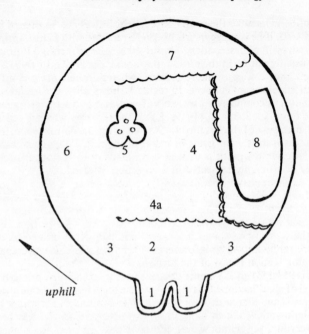

Fig. 3 Ground sketch of a traditional house
(adaptation from Sandrart 1939:40)

～～: plain partitions
≈≈≈: adorned partitions

1.	*ibitabo*:	door-steps
2.	*mu muryángo*:	in the lobby
3.	*muu mfúrukä*:	in the corner
4.	*mu kirämbi*:	in the living-room
	muu nzuugi:	inside the partitions
4a.	*mu ruugi*:	inside the partition
5.	*ku zíiko*:	by the fire-place
6.	*mu mugendo*:	in the passageway
	mu rubúmbiro:	by the fire-place or in the goat-fold
	mu ruhŏngore:	in the calf-fold
	mu mukúbo:	in the fold
	mu ndugú:	in the goat-fold
7.	*muu mbere*:	in the front-room
	haruguru or *ruguru*:	in the upper-room
8.	*ku buriri*:	on the bed

The compound includes the main house in which lives the 'master of the compound' and, if he is polygynous, his preferred wife with her offspring. His other wives live in secondary houses with their offspring. Intimate guests are usually put up in the most important secondary house (No. 2 in fig. 2) where they can enjoy more privacy, whereas others are put up in certain sections of the main house. In regard to hospitality, the traditional Rwandan house is composed of two sets of sections: one set which guests are allowed into (No. 2, 3, and 4 in fig. 3) and the other set which is strictly reserved to members of the family (No. 7 and 8 in fig. 3). As for No. 6, it is usually used as a shelter for goats or calves at night in compounds which have no byres. Otherwise, it is used as a passageway to the upper-room. Guests may occasionally be seated in this section, as needed.

As one can see from the ground sketches, some sections of the compound and of the house have one fixed name whereas other sections are given different names. This indeterminacy raises some difficulties in the interpretation of the proverb at its first level of signification. For example, the terms *ikwéru* and *haakwéru* although often quoted in the proverb, are rarely known to informants. There are also some discrepancies in naming section No. 6 of the house.

Kagame (1953:155) gives a comprehensive note to explain the proverb at its first level of signification. This shows that the form in which he quotes it must be archaic and that he expects many a Rwandan reader, for whom his collection is intended, not to understand it properly. Had the text been clear to everyone, the author would not have felt the need for such an explanation. Now, according to Kagame, *ikwéru* means a narrow place near the fire-place between *muu ndugú* and *muu mbere*, respectively No. 6 and 7 in fig. 3. Moreover, people of the upper class speak of *mu mukúbo* and *haruguru* whereas people of the lower class speak of *muu ndugú* and *muu mbere*, *muu nduguú* being the section of the house where people of the lower class fold their goats for the night.

I checked Kagame's interpretation among many informants, Tuutsi as well as Hutu. None of them confirmed what Kagame had written 20 years ago. First, all of them use indifferently both expressions *muu mbere* and *haruguru* (or *ruguru*). Secondly, *muu ndugú* was known only to informants from the northern region of Rwanda, those from the south using *mu mukúbo*, *mu ruhŏngore* or *mu rubúmbiro*. *Mu rubúmbiro* is generally used when goats are folded, *mu ruhŏngore* when calves are byred and *mu mukúbo* when no herds are byred, the section being a passageway to the upper-room. Many a southerner would also use indifferently *mu mukúbo* and *mu rubúmbiro*. One informant separates section No. 6 of the house in two parts: *mu rubúmbiro* is the 'lower' part, next to *muu mfúruká* and *mu mukúbo* is the 'upper' part next to *muu mbere*. Important guests are seated in front of the upper part, the others in front of the lower part. Thirdly, very few of my informants ever heard of *ikwéru*. One could say no more than: 'it is a nice place which is good for people', probably deriving the term from the verbal radical *-éer-* which means to be white, to be good. In Rwanda as in many other African countries, white is a symbol of auspiciousness and black of woe. A lady identified *ikwéru* with the corner, another informant with the upper-room. Another placed it in the upper right corner of the living room, close to the upper-room and the bed, in fact opposite to Kagame's identification. This probably occurs when the entrance to the upper-room is on the right side. Finally another identified it with the main house, feeling at the same time that the term must be of foreign origin, probably from Burundi. All these informants were 55 years of age or more. Other informants, who were all under 55, corrected me when quoting the proverb in Kagame's form saying that I should rather say *ihéeru* instead of *ikwéru*. And not only for all of them but also for all my informants, *ihéeru* means at the second house of the compound (No. 2 in fig. 2), in opposition to *ikámberé* at the main house. A wife will also name the compound of her parents-in-law *ihéeru*. Whether this is related to the rule forbidding a wife to pronounce the names of her parents-in-law or any other word phonetically related, I could not establish with certainty, the information I gathered being contradictory. It is quite puzzling that although informants do not understand the term *ikwéru* and some even tend to discard it, it has been heard over and over again during collecting time. All that can be said for the moment is that Kagame's version is still nowadays very often quoted without being understood and is even sometimes questioned. People quote the proverb in its archaic form contenting themselves with its general meaning. But when asked the exact meaning of each term, they fail to provide a suitable explanation and tend to replace the term by another one which is better known to them. We will later see the significance of this fact in regard to oral transmission. Let us note meanwhile that the socio-cultural context of house-building and of rules as to places where guests are put up allows us to grasp the meaning of the proverb at its first level of signification. It means: if you let the Tuutsi in as a guest, he soon considers himself as master of the compound. All the different forms in which this general idea is expressed are variations or permutations of terms, the function of the terms remaining the same throughout. Their signification in regard to oral transmission will be studied in the next section of this paper.

At its second level of signification, the proverb provides a rule of behaviour in one's relations with the Tuutsi. This rule of behaviour is not clearly expressed: it is a conclusion anyone can draw from the description of the Tuutsi's attitude. It is suggested behaviour in anticipation of an expected behaviour. Better be cautious with the Tuutsi, because if you give him a foot he takes a mile. This connotative meaning can be understood only in the light of the socio-political structure of traditional Rwanda. The limits of this paper do not bear but a few remarks on the subject. For further details, the reader is referred to Maquet (1954) and d'Hertefelt (1962). I restrict my comments to what I feel necessary for the understanding of the proverb.

The Tuutsi were the rulers of traditional Rwanda. Although forming but a small minority, they succeeded in establishing a socio-political organization which gave them control over the Hutu peasants and the Twa. This socio-political organization was based on three structures: an administrative framework, a military force and serf bondage. The king was the supreme ruler whose authority was officially unchallengeable, although he was in fact submitted to some restrictions, especially from the queen-mother, the high chiefs and his two councils. Authority was delegated through the three structures so that political responsibility was often shared by two or more persons in one and the same field of action. This peculiar organization created a complicated network of relations which criss-crossed all along the social scale. It also enabled the subjects to play one master off against the other whenever they felt it was in their own interest. To keep his subjects from resorting to trickery, the ruler had to keep himself very well informed of all matters. This gave rise to a specific political attitude to which the proverb alludes, and which Maquet has called the 'diffuse authority'. That is to say that the ruler did not confine his control to political matters but extended it to all activities of the subject. There existed no field of competence nor time restrictions in the relation ruler/subject. It pervaded the whole life of the subject, down to the most intimate matters.

The Tuutsi was educated to rule. The tendency to pervade others' lives was consequently incrusted in the child's soul very early during the educational process. Thus it soon became a Tuutsi characteristic to interfere with others' lives no matter how private the issue may be. Although shared, to a certain extent, by members of the other two ethnic groups, this attitude is perceived by all as specifically Tuutsi. Of course, this political attitude met with resistance. Anyone would tend to protect his privacy. Therefore the Tuutsi needed to develop specific qualities in relation to their political attitude. Sheer force would have been useless in this case, whereas astuteness, shrewdness and doggedness were very effective. That is why the educational process of the Tuutsi child insisted upon those 'qualities' which soon become characteristics of the group.

This partly explains the political success of the Tuutsi. It also partly explains the recent events in Rwanda. As late as last February, the Tuutsi were ejected from secondary schools and from higher educational institutions as well as from most civil servant and clerk jobs. The reason given by the young Hutu generation who were responsible for the deed is that after 13 years of Hutu power, the authorities have not reached what had been proclaimed as a revolutionary goal, namely that the number of Tuutsi in schools and in good jobs should be in proportion to their demographic importance. In fact, close to 100% of the clerk jobs in the private sector were held by Tuutsi. They also numbered near 50% of the civil servants and of the students at the secondary and higher level. Such an achievement is due to the fact that they resorted to all kinds of devices such as falsification of their ethnic origin, exploiting the corruptibility of some Hutu officials, and blackmail. But the most fruitful means they used was marrying their daughters to Hutu officials, thus weaving a powerful network of reciprocal obligations and forcing the new masters to subvert one of the main goals of the revolutionary manifesto. What they could no longer obtain with their long-horn cows, they secured with their 'nice-legged' women. As for the foreigner becoming acquainted with Tuutsi, he is soon forced to fight for his last bit of privacy sometimes at the cost of friendly relationships. The proverb alludes to all this and that is why it is so real even nowadays. This might also be one of the reasons why it is so often used and its form subject to so many changes.

Structural Analysis

The proverb under study may be divided into two segments *A* and *B*. The two segments are ordered in a consequential unit: assuming *A, B* follows, which can be written *A→B*. Each segment includes two terms *a* and *b*, *a* expressing an action *v* exerted by an agent *s* on some other, *o*, and *b* expressing a local determination *p*. These terms are ordered in such a way that *Aa* is in opposition to *Ba* and *Ab* to *Bb*. The action in segment *A* is one of receiving a guest whereas in segment *B* it is one of forcing someone out of his own place. Moreover, the agent in segment *A* is object in segment *B* and the object in segment *A* is agent in segment *B*. This structure can be represented as in fig. 4.

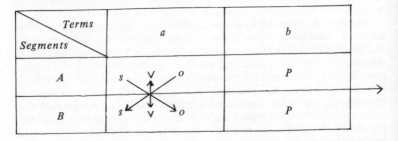

Fig. 4

Applying the basic text to the structure, one would read as in fig. 5.

You – lodge – Tuutsi	in ingle-nook	and
He – throws out – you	of front room	

Fig. 5

Change may affect any of the four terms. Let us list all the changes:

Aa1. *Umutuutsi umusembereza*: The Tuutsi you lodge him
Aa2. *Usembereza umutuutsi*: You lodge the Tuutsi
Aa3. *Umutuutsi umucumbikira*: The Tuutsi you put him up

Ab1. *ikwéru*: in the ingle-nook
Ab2. *haakwéru*: in the ingle-nook

Ab3. *mu muryángo*: in the lobby
Ab4. *mu kirămbi*: in the living-room
Ab5. *muu mfúruká*: in the corner
Ab6. *ihéeru*: in the second house
Ab7. *mu isămbu*: on the estate

Ba1. *akaguca*: and he throws you out
Ba2. *akagukuura*: and he forces you out
Ba3. *akaguteera*: and he intrudes on you
Ba4. *agakwimura*: and he chucks you out

Bb1. *muu mbere*: in the front-room
Bb2. *ruguru*: in the upper-room
Bb3. *ku buriri*: on the bed
Bb4. *mu kirămbi*: in the living-room
Bb5. *muu nzu*: in the house
Bb6. *ikámberé*: at the main house
Bb7. *muu ngo*: in the dwellings

We can also add in term *Aa* the inversion: *ucumbikira umutuutsi* 'you put up the Tuutsi' (*Aa4*). Informants did not volunteer this form but upon enquiry they did accept it as correct. So that altogether we have 4 forms in term *Aa*, 7 in term *Ab*, 4 in term *Ba*, and 7 in term *Bb*. Then the logical possibilities for change in the proposed forms are $4 \times 7 \times 4 \times 7 = 784$. There exist hundreds of other possibilities if we include all the different sections of the house and of the compound but their detailed analysis would not add anything to our purpose. I tested all the possibilities arising out of the phrases cited above, also a few of the others. Among all the forms which had not been volunteered, some were accepted as correct, others were firmly discarded as no good and a third group, though structurally correct were put aside in favour of more usual forms. We will look at all this later on. For the moment, let us keep on clearing the ground.

Referring to the distinction between variant and version, one might ask which of the forms are variants and which are versions or, in other words, which among all culturally acceptable forms imply a semantic change. *Aa2* is an inversion of *Aa1* without semantic impact, except may be a little stress on the *Tuutsi* in form *Aa1*. The same applies to *Aa4* in regard to *Aa3*. Therefore there are only two versions of the first term: the verbal radical *-semberez-* means 'to receive someone as a guest' without indicating any time limits whereas the radical *-cumbikir-*means 'to receive someone for the night or for a short period of time'. *Ab2* is a variant of *Ab1*: both words vary only in one formal element, namely in the locative class. They meant exactly the same thing. As for *Ab6*, grammatically speaking, it is a variant of *Ab1* for the same reason as *Ab2*: it is another locative form. But, as we have seen earlier, it implies a real semantic switch, at least for most of the informants. *Ab3, AB4* and *Ab5* are versions since they indicate different sections of the house. So it is with *Ab7* which indicates the whole of the estate. Therefore 6 versions must be retained in term *Ab*. The four forms of term *Ba* are versions. Indeed, as one can see from the proposed translation, the four verbal radicals differ at least in some nuances: *-ci-* means 'to throw out', *-kuur-* 'to force out', *-teer-* 'to intrude on' and *-iomur-* 'to chuck out'. Some of these nuances are subtle of course, but they do exist. The seven forms of term *Bb* are also all versions as they indicate different sections of the house or of the compound, or the whole of the compound. A difficulty may arise as to form *Bb2* which indicates the same section of the house or of the compound, or the whole of the compound. A difficulty may arise as to form *Bb2* which indicates the same section of the house as *Bb1*. Nevertheless, the cultural meaning of these forms is different, *Bb1* being in relation to the entering guest and *Bb2* being in relation to the geographical set up of the house.

It is time to turn to the reasons for the cultural acceptability of the different logical forms. I said earlier that some sections of the house are strictly reserved to members of the family. Consequently, any of those sections would be culturally unacceptable in term *Ab*. To say for example: 'The Tuutsi you lodge him in the upper-room' would be cultural nonsense. I tried it and was rewarded with a big laugh.

If some sections of the house are culturally unacceptable in term *Ab*, there is no such restriction in term *Bb*. Any section of the house or of the compound would suit. But there exists another cultural restriction. For the sake of brevity, let us call the sections reserved to members of the family *F* and sections opened to guests *G*. The opposition *Ab/Bb* can be of two types only: *F/F* or *G/G*, *F/G* or *F/F* being culturally unacceptable as we have just seen. There is no restriction as to *G/F*: any *G* in *Ab* can be in opposition to any *F* in *Bb*. But there exists a cultural restriction as to *G/G*. This opposition is correct on condition that *G* in term *Ab* indicates a section of the house closer to the entrance than *G* in term *Bb*, or that *G* in term *Bb* be more general than *G* in term *Ab*. When the opposition *G/G* is related to the compound, *G* in term *Ab* must be a secondary house and *G* in term *Bb* must be the main house. When related to the whole estate, *G* in term *Ab* must be more general than *G* in term *BB*. Thus any of phrases *Ab1*, *Ab2* or *Ab4* can be opposed to *Bb1*, *Bb2* or *Bb3*, *Ab3* or *Ab5* to any *Bb* forms except *Bb6* or *Bb7*, *Ab6* to *Bb6* only and any *Ab* forms to *Bb7*. For example, one cannot say: 'The Tuutsi you lodge him in the living-room and he throws you out of the lobby or of the corner'. When quoting the proverb in this form, I drew pitiful comments. As much as my informants were amazed at my knowledge of house-building and so many forms of the proverb, so were they astonished at my ignorance of the structuring rules. One even volunteered the structuring rule saying: 'Hey man! that is going backwards!'

It should be noted also that some forms are more common than others. *Ab7*, *Ba4* and *Bb7* for example appear only once among all proposed forms. I tried all forms 1-68 with the variant *umucumbikira*. My informants agreed as to the correctness of those forms but always immediately volunteered a more common form. Which means that although they were ready to accept these new forms as correct, they preferred forms more commonly used. In this case, we are faced with the weight of tradition. Some forms can be culturally acceptable but the proverb is generally

transmitted in other forms. It is a matter of preference, not of acceptability. Tradition is so strong as to transmit forms which are no longer
understood in their details. Such is the case, as we have seen earlier, of
forms *ikwéru* and *haakwéru*. Of course, the connotative meaning of the
proverb is still fully understood. But some references are lost: the
significatum is still alive in the tradition whereas the *significans* has been
partly lost.

Conclusions

There are two sets of conclusions one can draw from the above analysis:
rules for the oral transmission of the proverb itself and suggestions in
regard to oral transmission in general.

1 The structure of the proverb can generate a great number of logical
forms.

2 Not· all logical forms are culturally correct. There exist some
contextual and structural restrictions as to how the logical forms can be
applied. All house sections which are reserved to members of the family are
unacceptable in term *Ab*. House sections which guests are allowed into
must be in such a position that the more intimate is in term *Bb*.
Compound sections must be opposed in such a way that the main house is
found in term *Bb*. In reference to the estate, the more general section must
be in term *Ab*.

3 Among all culturally acceptable forms, traditional ones are preferred. New forms are accepted as correct but forms which have been heard
before are preferred. The preference is strong enough to favour traditional
forms in which some of the terms are no longer in common use or even
intelligible, rather than new forms in which all of the terms are fully
understood.

Our case study is very limited. It concerns one single item among
thousands of one genre of verbal art of one population. Its significance in
regard to oral tradition in general cannot be but suggestive. A great many
more small scale analyses of this kind are needed before case materials will
allow some conclusions of cross-cultural significance. The following are
hypotheses for further research.

1 The materials of folklore are usually conceptualized as traditional.
They constitute a body of knowledge inherited from the past which
accordingly is transmitted with a certain fixity. But the materials of
folklore are also mobile and manipulative. Our case study is a clear
example of this truism within the same cultural group. When it comes to
transcultural transmission, we may expect greater mobility and manipula-
tiveness and less fixity.

2 Change can affect oral tradition in many ways. A new situational
context may completely change the connotative signification of an item
whereas the denotative signification remains untouched. Materials of
folklore may change in form without changing in content. They may also
change in form and content. Change may lead to a variant or a version but
may also generate a new item of folklore. The variational matrix proposed

in fig. 1 is of course very general. It needs to be qualified in the light of other case studies. But it can be useful as a starting point in classifying the different modes of change in oral transmission.

3   Many factors are at play either in orienting or limiting variation in oral transmission. One is tempted to distinguish external factors and internal factors. External factors would be the different kinds of pressures exerted on oral transmission from outside the communicative process itself such as for example social change, political turnover, economic development, cross-cultural contacts, religious missions and so on. Internal factors would be all the possibilities for change inside the communicative process such as the structure of the language, logical appositeness, structural inventiveness and limitation, the weight of tradition and so on. In regard to internal factors, our case study allows us to suggest four rules of change: (*a*) the tendency of oral transmission is to explore as many linguistic and logical forms as possible within each of its genres; (*b*) the structures of the materials of folklore which are determined by the aid of socio-cultural context maintain this tendency within certain limits; (*c*) the weight of tradition operates a choice among all structural possibilities; (*d*) the more an item of folklore is 'alive', the more it is subject to change.

Needless to repeat that these are not conclusions but hypotheses which need to be tested by other case materials. Their significance might extend not only to folkloristic research but also to all fields of anthropology related to systems of representations such as cognitive anthropology, educational anthropology, anthropology of religion and so on. Such studies can also be of some importance in applied anthropology and in all cross-cultural contacts be they diplomatic, economic or religious in nature. Foreign aid bodies and international boards as well as missionary groups would also profit by a better knowledge of educative processes which can be gained from studies of this type.

NOTES

1   This is a very literal translation meant to keep the original image. What the Rwandan call the front-room (or the front of anything) is always in regard to the person concerned. Here it means the section of the house which is in front of the entering person. As it is the farthest away from the entrance, the section should have been called the back-room. But the original image would have been lost.

2   *ikwéru* and *haakwéru* vary only in the locative classification (*i vs haa*), the meaning of which is the same. Both words are consequently translated into the same English word.

BIBLIOGRAPHY

Barthes, R. 1964: 'Eléments de sémiologie'. *Communications* 4:91-135.
Bauman, R. (ed.) 1971: 'Toward New Perspectives in Folklore', *Journal of American Folklore* 84, special issue.
Coupez, A. and Meeussen, A.E. 1961: 'Notation pratique de la quantité vocalique et de la tonalité en rundi et rwanda', *Orbis* 10:429-33

Coupez, A. and Kamanzi, Th. 1962: *Récits historiques rwanda*. Tervuren, Musée royal de l'Afrique centrale.

d'Hertefelt, M. 1962: 'Le Rwanda', M. d'Hertefelt, A.A. Trouwborst and J.H. Scherer, *Les anciens royaumes de la zone interlacustre méridionale: Rwanda, Burundi, Buha*, Tervuren, Musée royal de l'Afrique centrale, 9-112.

Forster, E.A. 1936: 'The Proverb and Superstition Defined', unpublished Ph.D. thesis, University of Pennsylvania.

Greimas, A.J. 1970: *Du sens: essais sémiotiques*. Paris, Seuil.

Kagame, A. 1953: *Imigani y'imigenûrano*. Kabgayi, Editions royales 7.

Köngäs Maranda, E. 1971: 'Theory and Practice of Riddle Analysis', *Journal of American Folklore* 84:51-61.

Lévi-Strauss, C. 1966: *Du miel aux cendres*. Paris, Plon.

Maquet, J.J. 1954: *Le système des relations sociales dans le Rwanda ancien*. Tervuren, Annales du Musée royal du Congo belge.

Milner, G.B. 1969: 'De l'armature des locutions proverbiales: essai de taxonomie sémantique'. *L'Homme*, 9:349-70.

Sandrart, G. 1939: 'Cours de droit coutumier', unpublished m.s., Astrida.

Observers as Participants:
a note in anthropology and social theory

RODNEY CROOK

The starting point for the present discussion is located in the view of social science as a form of social activity. Thus the peculiar feature of the thought of social scientists lies in the logical necessity of the application of the thought style to the activity itself as an instance of social action. It is a measure of the success of the professional socialization of most contemporary social scientists that in self-consciously taking the posture of observers we fail to realize, or at least devote attention to the realization that in observing we are also participants.

There is of course an ultimate absurdity in the continuous questioning and reinterpretation of our activities. However, it is in the management of this tension generated by the continuing attempt to do so that intellectual awareness develops. The avoidance of such tension through the premature adoption of observer categories tells us perhaps more about the moral, or indeed cultural, bankruptcy of modern society than about the object of scrutiny — man himself. It is in the analysis of the historical circumstances — the social situation of modern social scientists, that we understand anthropology rather than the objective correctness of the resulting analysis.

Positivistic Assumptions about Knowledge

While the primary purpose of the present paper is not to enter into a discussion of the methodological issues concerned with the status of social scientific knowledge, some attention to these issues is unavoidable. Two assumptions are selected for comment in the context of our attempt to indicate the implications of social scientific thinking when applied to social science itself as a form of activity.

These basic assumptions behind positivistic social science are as follows. First, knowledge and ignorance are viewed as being poles on a continuum, such that as scientific observers we have either greater or less knowledge, and thus inversely greater or less ignorance. The criteria for knowledge involves amenability to disconfirming evidence and the capacity for replication of results by other trained observers. Assuming the preferability of truth as a value in our society, it becomes relatively easy to make a transformation whereby truth becomes equated with scientific knowledge. Thus empirical social science tends to be seen by its practitioners as the sole basis for moving from ignorance to awareness.

Given this generalized conception of knowledge, the second assumption follows. Knowledge, because it is empirically based, is value neutral. Thus, inasmuch as the social scientist is engaged in empirical investigation, his own values should not, and in principle do not, affect his analysis. Clearly within these assumptions, the greater the precision of the observer categories and the 'instruments' developed for research the less the distortion is likely to be. In this attempt, words with distinct value colouration, e.g., cruelty or exploitation, will be strenuously avoided in the search for neutral neologisms which admit of operational definition.

The Social Scientist in Action

As all beginning students of social anthropology know, men's activity is to be understood in terms of the assumptions within which the activity occurs. In other words we begin analysis through attempting to locate the actor in his location in social space — a space made up of meanings and interlocking obligations and expectations. Taking an observer posture, we attempt to unravel the complexity of social structure by first coming to terms with the language, symbolic systems and assumptions of the society concerned. Although there are variations in method, we further tend to examine the life history of the actor, his trajectory through social space, and the significant impingement of others on him. It is quite basic to such analysis that in the study of social institutions such as religion, we concern ourselves not with the ultimate truth or falsity of the beliefs but rather with the consequences which flow in action from holding such beliefs. Similarly our analysis leads to an examination of the ritual activities and associated sanctions which stabilize beliefs and activities. We need, I submit, to apply such basic assumptions to our own activities as social scientists.

Of course if our objective is to do more than ethnography, such that we wish to develop explanations having comparative applicability, it is necessary to go beyond the lived-in realities of participants, what Alfred Schutz termed the 'first-order abstractions,' (Schutz 1962) to develop second-order abstractions for analytic purposes. The purpose in this context is not to examine the procedures for doing this, or to analyse alternative positions taken towards that objective. The immediate issue concerns the implications of social scientific approaches to the social world in terms of both the social conditions under which such a view of reality arises, and also the consequences of social activities generated from such a world view (albeit unintended) both on other societies and also on our own.

The secularization of modern society, what Max Weber termed the process of the 'disenchantment of the world,' fits well the specific orientations and assumptions of modern science. The impressive success of that science and its relation to the technological transformation of the world has led not surprisingly to the assumptions of empirical science being applied to human activity. The very rapidity of technological change and the ramifications of such change throughout the institutional structure of relatively modernized societies hastens the breakaway from traditional beliefs and practices, and poses problems of human adaptation which necessitate new solutions.

Yet the view of man as an object and thus in principle open to the development of social technologies is not simply a matter to be viewed in terms of the explanatory power of alternative theoretical frameworks. Such a view of man with its explicit attempt at demystification involves unavoidable moral issues and consequences, and is ultimately absurd within its own assumptions. 'Absurd' in this context merely means that inasmuch as the object of investigation is defined as man, or as social action, then the investigator himself and his scientific activity, is necessarily an instance of the more general class of events to which the assumptional framework applies. Yet in everyday life, including the decision to be involved in intellectual activity, quite different assumptions need necessarily to be made. It is perhaps surprising that many social scientists remain in fact committed to the human values of freedom and dignity while adopting a view of man which is necessarily nihilistic.

The deterministic assumptions about human conduct, if applied in everyday social life, would rapidly render such daily activity impossible. In other words, fundamental ideas of reciprocity and justice hinge precisely on a willingness to view the other as indeed a moral agent. Only the very young, the old, and those defined as mentally ill are managed in this technical and non-reciprocal way. Interestingly enough, it is this refusal to admit reciprocity which precisely prevents the emergence and stabilization of 'normal' human conduct. In other words, men who are not treated in interaction with others as responsible and free cannot in fact develop or maintain their humanity.

The demythologization of man is a modern cultural product which may be viewed as itself a short-run destructive myth which is an expression of the fundamental moral or ideological crisis of the modern world. Its consequences may readily be seen as the destruction of human relationships and indeed the possibility of meaningful conduct, although allowing for a relatively pacified population which fits into bureaucratic structure. While it is suggested that such models of man are destructive within Western society itself, it is hopefully clear that the consequences for other societies, the relatively non-modernized, are doubly destructive.

The anthropologist working within such assumptions carries into his research situation, as a form of social relationship, his own basic categories concerning man. While, within his own assumptions, he may be a neutral observer concerned to expand the frontiers of the discipline, he is engaged, in fact, in an intrusion, in which he is whether intended or not an agent for the diffusion of disenchantment. This refers not merely to the possible manipulation or use of the observed for scientific purposes, but to the simple fact of an alien orientation which expresses in its very presence and purposes, the assumptions of modern society.

It is not necessary to follow the arguments of Lévi-Strauss to make the claim that the modern world is involved in a maladaptive relation with the environment. We have all become increasingly aware of the essentially short-run possibilities attached to continued exponential growth and thus to the institutional context which supports such a maladaptive set of activities. It is necessary, however, for present purposes to underline that modern assumptions about man, and in particular the assumptions of a positivistic social science, are an expression of that maladaptive mode of social organization. It is such assumptions which constitute the categories of thought of modern men including anthropologists and other social scientists. Behind the myth of demythologized man lurks truly alienated man.

Directions in Structuralism

Two possible directions appear to be present in the structuralism of Lévi-Strauss. The first involves the essentially trivial task of proceeding with a potentially endless series of technical games. The second involves an intense concern with the self-destructive, and indeed globally destructive, implications of modern culture. It is entirely within the framework of the present paper to reject the first and support the second of these directions.

The preparedness of anthropologists to engage in technically complex and intellectually trivial pursuits is surely an expression of the worst features of modern culture. Similarly the absurdities of a radically social scientific view of human action compound the meaninglessness of modern man. A science of man which becomes a technical game has reached the point of bankruptcy. What begins as an attempt to understand becomes nothing more than a further instance of what Jacques Ellul, in his astute analysis of modernity, has termed 'technique.' (Ellul 1964). That such activity may periodically delude its practitioners into believing that they are indeed engaged in something other than trivial suggests only that professional socialization in graduate schools is effective and that the nature of bureaucratic control strategies in modern societies and their universities have more or less successfully removed the possibility of effective social criticism.

The second and important direction for development in structuralism lies in the analysis of modern society. Lévi-Strauss working from quite different assumptions has arrived at the same general conclusions as Weber, Marx, and other social theorists concerning the humanly destructive directions of modern social change (Lévi-Strauss 1971). The directions for anthropology, and indeed for the social sciences generally, are apparent, and they could hardly be less trivial or more intellectually pressing.

In recognizing the maladaptive system of technologically advanced societies, it is essential to question rather than to merely express the assumptions of that society. Our concern is thus to analyse the range of alternative structural possibilities for the future directions of change. We need then to examine the range of possible planned social action to move in the directions indicated by such analysis. In this way political action and social theory begin once again to converge.

There is no suggestion here of nostalgic visions of a return to pre-technological society, nor any suggestion of an optimistic certainty regarding human possibilities for the future. What is essential, however, is that our knowledge of alternative structural possibilities be considered in relation to the finite possibilities for alternative modes of adaptation under modern technological conditions. Such analysis necessarily involves not merely the structure of modern societies themselves but also the limitations set by such societies on the future possibilities for all other societies.

Implications for Anthropology

It has been suggested that the analysis of our own activities, including social science as a form of social activity, indicates the absurdity of positivistic assumptions. The resolution of this paradox does not lie in the rejection of the attempt at systematic analysis and observation. What it does involve is a realization that the paradigm of a social science modelled on natural science assumptions needs to be rejected. It is, of course, far easier to remain comfortably within the assumptions of that paradigm limiting one's analysis to those events in the world which more or less fall within the framework, and thus dismissing all other questions as either metaphysical or simply too complex for present theoretical developments — while assuming that at some future date, our science will be developed to that stage. This confidence is nothing more than the myth of progress through technical rationality, itself a major element of modern mythology.

The beginning of such new possibilities — a new paradigm — does not, I repeat, involve rejection of systematic comparison and analysis. It does, however, require a recognition of the human reality with which social science deals. Human society is not merely a system, albeit highly complex, to be analysed through analogy to other natural systems and within the same deterministic assumptions. Social structure is thus a moment (a slice through micro time) in human history, expressing the creative response of people to their historical situation. Systematization need not remove our attention from this human reality, but should operate within assumptions which indeed correspond to our awareness in everyday social life, of human activity as meaningful conduct.

In moving away from deterministic assumptions, the social consequences of social scientific models becomes apparent and may be seen not simply as unanticipated consequences but rather as moral choices on our part. Precisely because we ourselves are unavoidably social beings, in recognizing both the logical paradoxes in our own thinking and the moral consequences of our activities, we are free to turn our attention to those issues which are of immediate and indeed long-run human concern. We have no choice but work with the repertoire of cultural possibilities which constitute our reality and within the limits of our social situation. However, we have the possibility of directing our creative energy towards new syntheses. One dimension of such choice is found in the decision concerning which elements of our cultural tradition we wish to reject and which we wish to work with. The second order abstractions, or observer categories with which we seek to develop a genuinely comparative sociology are precisely a function of these choices. Under conditions of the limited possibilities for modern society and the minimal implications of our models and activities for the direction of our own and other societies, these choices are not merely assumptions made for heuristic purposes in terms of a conception of natural science explanation, but are total human choices.

To be indeed the science of man, anthropology must concern itself with the possibilities for man, i.e., the possibilities for human social organization. Comparative analysis of other societies which are technologically less complex can provide at least a set of possible realities which have the potential for informing our choices for the future. However, movements within anthropology (and, of course, other social sciences) which have become mere technical exercises need to be viewed as maladaptive responses within the paradoxes of our own historical situation, in which technique replaces thought and intellectual concern has become equated with playing bridge, reading professional journals, and *Time* magazine.

As social scientists, we intervene in the social process of all stages of our activities. The social scientific models and assumptions of today become the coinage for social interaction and social policy tomorrow. Our choice is thus whether to continue to intervene apparently unconsciously and destructively, or consciously and constructively.

In closing, I can do no more than quote directly from Max Weber whose writing has been so seriously trivialized in modern Sociology. Writing at the end of *The Protestant Ethic and the Spirit of Capitalism* and referring to the 'iron cage' of modern industrial society, he says:

> No one knows who will live in this cage in the future, or whether at the end of this tremendous development entirely new prophets will arise, or there will be a great rebirth of old ideas and ideals, or, if neither mechanised petrification embellished with a sort of convulsive self-importance. For of the last stage of this cultural development, it might well be truly said: 'Specialists without spirit, sensualists without heart; this nullity imagines that it has attained a level of civilization never before achieved' (Weber 1958:182).

BIBLIOGRAPHY

Ellul, J. 1964: *Technical Society*. New York, Alfred A. Knopf.

Lévi-Strauss, C. 1971: *Mythologiques IV: L'Homme Nu*. Paris, Plon.

Schutz, A. 1962: *Collected Papers: I. The Problem of Social Reality* (edited M. Natanson). The Hague, Martinus Nijhoff.

Weber, M. 1958: *The Protestant Ethic and the Spirit of Capitalism* (translated by Talcott Parsons). New York, Charles Scribner's Sons.

The Averted Gift:
the Lau myth of the seeker of exchange

ELLI KÖNGÄS MARANDA

The field of myth, ritual and religion seems nevertheless to be one of the more fruitful for the study of social structure; though relatively little has been done in this respect, the results which have been obtained recently are among the most rewarding in our field.

Claude Lévi-Strauss (1963:313)

The problems, being existential, are universal; their solutions, being human, are diverse.

Clifford Geertz (1966:5)

This article is about one myth; and there never being a myth that is *the* myth, this is a discussion of one version of a Melanesian sacred narrative. At the same time, as this rendering expresses the singer's view of the meaning of his culture, I will have to draw in things to which his text only alludes. To understand this one manifestation of one 'theme' we have to refer to various aspects of Lau ethnography and Lau thought. These references are given only as translation aids. The main portent of this discussion is the view that *myth is a reflection on culture;* that it is more than a charter of land tenure (cf. Malinowski 1926), more than a precedent established to block away probing and inhibit further questioning (cf. Cohen 1969).

I can make no claim that understanding one myth (or one version of one) is an open-sesame for all mythologies of all cultures at all times. It can, however, hopefully give a new view of the meaning of myth, a minimal opening into a world of meaning. The world is complex, but then it is far less complex for those who share a culture; although alien myths can be made intelligible to outsiders, they were not meant for the outsiders.

The analysis of myth is, in my opinion (and experience), a series of translations. The stream of speech — recitation or song — has to be rendered into a string of words in the original language; the text thus created has to be faithfully translated into another language (the intended reader's). The semantic differences between the languages must somehow be bridged. Further, the semantic differences between the two cultures must be clarified; otherwise, the reader follows his own and may interpet concepts, signs, events in a way alien to the original context. In writing the text down, I noted where the storyteller made pauses, and treated the segments thus isolated as verse lines; in the translation, I again followed these units. The verses were then numbered, and the summary of the myth indicates what lines are condensed into each of my summary statements. The purpose of this tedious exercise is to give the reader as close an outline

37

of the text as is possible. The principle of translation was, moreover, that the best service is rendered to the original text by a word-to-word translation, which may seem strange in the beginning but will show the original style and structure better than any free rendering would.

The rationale behind this passion for the 'letter' of the original text — puritanical fundamentalism as it were — is that it is utterly wrong to impose Western aesthetic principles on other literary traditions. Each oral literature develops its own aesthetic principles, and its carriers, passive as well as active, are often quite articulate about their 'native' or 'ethno'- aesthetics. The Lau are. They also have a theory of the meaning and proper uses of the different named literary genres which they have developed and foster (I have indicated some of this native theory in earlier articles, Köngäs Maranda 1971, 1974a, 1974b). Hence, since people do what they do quite knowingly and by a social contract, as it were, the translator must have a commitment to the rules of the poetry he is presenting.

For most myth-translators, the hardest thing to yield is that the repetition in the original text is meaningful. The Lau say explicitly that it is so. Especially important in all their prose renderings of myths are the descriptions of the characters' wanderings from one ancestral place to another, their meetings with the 'great men' in each community, and their exchanges with their hosts. These descriptions take much of the space of the narrative. They are meaningful because the theory that the Lau hold of the functions of myths is that they teach the history and geography; even more than that, they *are* the history and geography of their known world. A myth well told will be so detailed 'that a man can travel where he has never been and always know where he is.' What for us appears distracting and interminable is in fact invaluable airing of basic knowledge, stored in the sacred epics of the Lau.

Consequently, I retain all the references to villages and all the genealogi- cal information given by the myth teller. A more difficult thing for me is to know when to make something out of the meanings of place and personal names. I will detail those as much as I estimate necessary for the understanding of this version, and I will let the rest lie; the same places and persons are activated in other myths for other purposes. A Lau audience may have all the allusions under control at all recitations; we cannot utilize them all at once.

A Note on the Lau

Lau are Melanesian lagoon-dwellers who live off the coast of Malaita in the British Solomon Islands Protectorate. Their own name for themselves is 'sea people', *toa i asi*, as opposed to the hill groups, *toa i tolo*. The traditional religion, still vigorously alive, is ancestor worship, conducted by specialists, sacrificial priests *fata abu* or *ngwane ni foa*, literally 'holy speech' or 'man of worship'. In the traditional order, which is under missionary and other Western pressure crumbling at the corners, the eldest son was a chief, the second, a priest, and the third, a war chief, *ramo*. Pax Britannica forbade warring; it may be that 'fighting with feasts', *maoma*, has taken on some of the functions of feuding (cf. Maranda 1975).

Lau social life has two dimensions. Within the patrilineal clan, ancestor worship cultivates a vertical exchange between the two halves of the clan, the ancestral spirits, *agalo*, and the living (male) members of the clan. In this exchange, chiefs are mediators because they organize the great clan feasts to commemorate the ancestors; and the priests are mediators because they officiate in the feasts. The feasts consist of many phases, among which are myth singing sessions to celebrate the great deeds, *gesta* so to speak, of the most famous ancestors; other elements of the feast cycle are sacrifices of pigs (we saw feasts in which 96 pigs were 'tied' and distributed to the guests); further, magnificent dance pageants form parts of the *maoma* cycle. This vertical exchange is sacred, and the ancestors are seen as the protectors and supporters of the clan; if they withdraw their protection, sickness, death, famine will follow.

Exchanges between clans are secular. They consist of alliances cemented and symbolized by intermarriages between clans. Women reside virilocally and thus become important mediators in the exchange between clans (cf. Köngäs Maranda 1970). The fathers of a married couple are said to be *roongwairuana*, a pair of exclusive friends. The same term is used of trade partners. In both cases, a lifetime relation of reciprocity is implied.

A very important economic institution is the native, traditional market system. Lau, who produce a surplus of fish, trade it for vegetables at 18 market places where hill peoples bring their produce. For feasts, large orders of taro are placed beforehand; and the taro is then delivered on the agreed-on market place. These exchanges are thus public; they are also binding and solemn. A native 'monetary' system exists, utilizing shell strings and dolphin teeth; each unit has a fixed value, as have marketable items. An exchange is not supposed to bring interest to either of the parties involved. The ideology is one of balance, not one of gain; this point will become important in the understanding of the myth. (For more on Lau markets, Maranda 1969.)

Definition of Myth in Malaita

The Lau term which most closely corresponds with our term myth is *'ainimae*. Literally, *'ae* means 'reason for', 'cause of', *ni* means 'of' and *mae*, 'death.' The whole term then yields 'the reason for death,' and conveys such connotations as that myths are primarily concerned with death and that they are thought to be true. When sung at the memorial feasts of ancestors, they are sacred. They can, however, also be recited in prose form for information and pastime, for the education of the young and the aesthetic satisfaction of their elders. A stated function of myth is, as mentioned above, to instruct people about history and geography. Even today, this function is so well fulfilled by the myth tellers that we saw a young person travel where she had never been and name landmarks and villages unerringly. To our question how it was possible — we were travelling on a ship with her — she simply said that she knew myths. In the same vein, the most famous present-day genealogists and arbitrators of land disputes attribute their expertise directly to the knowledge of myths. Mythology in Malaita thus functions as a reservoir of knowledge.

It has been said of Malaitans, indeed, of the closest neighbours of the Lau that 'Primitive Man is a poor ethnographer' (Ross 1973:10). Perhaps so, but maybe ethnographers have not been preliterate enough to read the native ethnography. Furthermore, purely ethnographic matters might interest participants of the culture only slightly, since they are immersed in them. What does interest people is what events and relations mean, and this is not taken for granted. Unlike Napoleon's Josephine (or Napoleon's perception of Josephine), 'primitives' *do* reflect. The Lau have a special term for people whom we would call intellectuals: *lio too*, 'fitting mind,' that is, people with a sharp mind. Their ethnography may appear sloppy, but their ethnology is excellent. Locked in the language of concrete events, Lau myths, and possibly all myths if we could find the means of understanding them in their proper setting, discuss principles of social life. Like Malinowski (1926), I believe in myth as a charter; unlike him, I expect symbols to be a language, at times a metalanguage. It seems only reasonable to assume that myths, cherished by members of a culture as valuable, venerable, sacred, restricted in presentation to sacred or otherwise serious occasions, owned by clans, should have something to say.

Meanings of Names in Lau Usage

Since the analysis is going to also refer to the names of dramatis personae, we must understand the system of naming in Lau. There is — as in all cultures — a relatively limited pool of names. Each person has a name, and in principle only one name (although variants of the name are used). The name is transferred from a suitable ancestor. The 'one' or basic name is said to be the person's *hata baita*, 'the great name'. This name is not for everyday usage, for fear that ancestral names be taken in vain, furthermore, for fear that children who have a great liberty of language, utter the name in a curse. To avoid the use of the great names, layers of secondary names or nicknames have been developed.

One way of creating nicknames is by reference to the manner of the death of the previous owner of the name. Hence, a person may be called Rakefii, 'stomach ache', because the previous owner of the great name died of a stomach ache. Some of the most modern nicknames based on this principle would be Mae'anadoketa, 'died of doctor', and Teolatigi, 'slept in the dinghy' (a person who died abroad and was brought back to the lagoon in a dinghy of a ship).

Another key to nicknames is the personal characteristics of a carrier of a name. Hence, the mythsinger who was my informant for the myth considered here is called *Bobongi*, approximately 'mañana', the procrastinator. He is not so called because of his own character — a more fitting nickname for him would indeed be 'the go-getter' — but because of the manner of his ancestor who carried his great name.

It is because of the second principle that personal names in myths are significant: they refer to the characteristics of the ancestors who are thought to be the very sources of the great names. They are the first known carriers of names; thus their names are central signs in a semiological sense. A short name, *kurihata*, or a nickname, *hatafolo*, is the key to the personality. This is why the name of the most important person in the myth, Iirofoli, 'the seeker of exchange', can be taken as a clue to the understanding of the myth: the very name of the myth is a vehicle to carry meaning.

The Myth and its Teller

The myth was told to me by Timoti Bobongi, chief of Sikwafunu clan, resident of Kwalo'ai village, a man active in politics — he was one of the nine chiefs of the Marching Rule — as well as in economic and religious exchange (for more on Bobongi, see Köngäs Maranda 1971). Bobongi recited for me, for purposes of archiving, about 30 myths during the first months of 1968. He has a great admiration for the character of Iirofoli of Asiningwane, ancestor who is thought to have been cunning and clever; one of his pet descriptions is 'double-faced Iirofoli'. Bobongi tends to elaborate on Iirofoli's cleverness and competence. Storytellers of several Malaitan tribes refer to Iirofoli's power and political influence; for example, To'aba'ita singers of tales describe Iirofoli as one of the ancient heroes of Malaita. Yet, he was of another tribe altogether.

The myth was given as a prose rendering by Bobongi. Perhaps a little bizarre for an outside reader, the myth embodies a native rule-book of proper social conduct in exchanges. An illustrated catechism of the religion of reciprocity, a Lau *essai sur le don*, the text elaborates a whole typology of possible exchanges, positive and negative, vertical and horizontal, successful and unsuccessful.

Outline of the Myth

The following is a linear summary of the narrative. The numbers after the sentences refer to the lines of the text.

1   Iirofoli thinks it is time to go ahead with his ancestral feast (1-8). He calls on his clansmen to collect and contribute shell spans and dolphin teeth (9-22). The valuables collected form a *rau*, treasure, (23-24). Iirofoli visits all the villages of Talakali district to place an order for taro needed for the feast; none of the villages has enough taro (25-155). Iirofoli returns to Asiningwane and reports to his clan (156-73).

2   In another attempt to place the taro order, Iirofoli goes to the market of Fakanakafo and sees his friend Ilisau of Foubala (174-234). The two friends chew betel and talk, and Iirofoli tells of his problem (235-58). Ilisau accepts the order (259-63). The exchange is to take place at the market of Fakanakafo (264-71).

3   The contract is overheard by two girls, Ilisau's crosscousins Buagali and Takanagwaraa of Bina, Gwanu's sisters (272-83). The girls are impressed by the *rau*, hug each other in excitement, and decide to convince Gwanu to intercept the exchange, since he has four gardens, two of which

they think sufficient for the feast of Bina (284-311). They return home and roast fish bought at the market (312-17). Gwanu is carving war clubs and plaiting combs; he smells the fish and asks his sisters for some (318-38). They tease him about not going to markets and thus not having fish and missing the news (339-44). Gwanu threatens to beat them if they do not tell him the news, and they tell about Iirofoli's and Ilisau's planned exchange (345-68). Gwanu decides to interfere (369-84).

Ilisau returns to Foubala and tells his clansmen about the exchange (385-84).

4   In Bina, Gwanu and his younger brothers go to the market early on the day of the preliminary exchange (394-433). Iirofoli arrives with his *rau*, is sitting in his canoe and waiting for Ilisau (434-48). Gwanu approaches Iirofoli, offers betel, and asks what brings such an important man to the market (449-62). Pressed, Iirofoli explains, and pressed on, he shows his *rau* (463-84). Gwanu grabs the *rau* and declares he himself is going to cut taro for it (485-93). Iirofoli objects (494-6). Gwanu says that he and not Ilisau will complete the transaction (497-501). Iirofoli refers to the existing contract (502-5). The two men dispute, Gwanu takes an oath to go ahead with the exchange, and leaves Iirofoli in great distress (506-31).

5   Ilisau arrives with a preliminary delivery of the taro and with additional gifts, taro-and-canarium-nut puddings and areca nuts; Iirofoli is ashamed (532-46). He attempts to refuse the delivery, and speaks of raising another *rau* (547-71). Ilisau asks him not to tax his men again, since valuables are not limitless; he will gather his compensation in another manner (572-92).

6   Ilisau returns to Foubala, takes an oath of revenge, and summons his clansmen to intercept Gwanu's taro delivery (593-668). His brother Dangi'ania is married to Gwanu's sister Sigilitoo, who learns from Dangi'ania what the men intend to do (669-88). In the night, Sigilitoo goes to Gwanu and betrays Ilisau's plans (689-723). Gwanu says if his taro delivery is intercepted, he and his men (real and classificatory brothers) will fight with Ilisau and his men (724-8). His father Nutoa warns him: equals, cross-cousins should not fight, Gwanu could deliver the taro at Manu market instead (729-60). Gwanu decides to follow this advice (761). He collects a taro-carrying party of 200 men and 200 women (762-88). Sigilitoo returns to her husband and boasts about Gwanu's cleverness, thus betraying Gwanu's new plans (789-801). Ilisau's men take note of the news (802-8).

7   Ilisau makes a distribution of wealth to his men (as if he had received Iirofoli's *rau*) and plots additional revenge against Gwanu (809-62). He visits a hermit woman Keningwaroabu and asks her for a supernatural means to play a trick on Gwanu (863-920). Keningwaroabu offers to destroy Gwanu's village, to cause its stones to split, to cause its trees to wither, its streams to flood (921-5). Ilisau refuses that, saying Gwanu is his crosscousin; he only wants to teach him a lesson (926-9). The supernatural woman has an assortment of monstrous frogs and lizards as her famililials, and she agrees to lend the most frightening frog lizard to play the trick (930-98). Ilisau and his men are to be introduced to the monster before-

hand so that they can witness the trick without harm (999-1023). They follow her instructions and are ready (1024-89).

8   Gwanu's party, 200 men and 200 women, are carrying the taro order along the trail to Manu market (1090-3). Gwanu arranges four unmarried girls, his sisters Buagali and Takanagwaraa and his classificatory sisters (parallel cousins) Tagesau and Tagefata to walk at the head of the line, without carrying anything, in a honorific position (1094-1117). The frog lizard spits upon the party and causes all 400 to fall down 'dead', or rather, unconscious (1118-32). Ilisau and his men watch it (1133-9). Then she opens the women's legs and wakens the men (1140-9). All men see their wives exposed; everyone is mortified, and no one knows the reason for the scandal (1150-60). The women are wakened (1161-2). Tagesau and Tagefata declare their chastity and weep (1163-82). The taro is delivered, but the two innocent girls hide themselves under pandanus mats, lament all day, and hang themselves in the evening (1183-97).

9   The news is brought to the girls' father Lumakofu who, although he is Gwanu's 'second father' (father's brother) surrounds Gwanu, declares war on him, and demands compensation (1198-301). Gwanu makes a large payment; Lumakofu repeats the demands twice more, receives two more payments of compensation, and declares peace (1302-69). Lumakofu distributes the wealth gained to his clansmen who have formed his war party (1370-81).

10   Ilisau is satisfied with Gwanu's punishment (1382-95). Sigilitoo overhears the talk and goes again to report to Gwanu (1396-437). Having learned what caused the scandal, Gwanu declares war on Ilisau (1438-56). Ilisau makes a counterdeclaration (1457-70). Gwanu's father Nutoa suggests the two crosscousins make an exchange (1471-5). Ilisau and Gwanu exchange valuables of exactly the same kinds and amounts in the course of the day (1476-85).

The Dramatis Personae, Their Relationships, and Their Names

Three patrilineal clans enter the narrative. One is that of Asiningwane, where we meet an ancestral feast in preparation, with the direction of Iirofoli, the leader. His clansmen are also enumerated: Beli, Gaofanua, Mola'iolo, Kwalukona, and Forekwao. Later enumerations add Kobirobo and Fouabula.

As mentioned above, Iirofoli's name means 'the seeker of exchange', and this is the capacity in which he acts in the course of events described. He is preparing a clan feast and seeking to place a taro order. He is in a position of obligation to his ancestors, as the leader of their descendants; he is in position to call on his kinsmen to contribute; and when he receives payments from his trade partners, he distributes them to his men.

Iirofoli's *ruana*, friend, that is trade partner, is Ilisau of Foubala clan. Ilisau's brother Dangi'ania is married to his crosscousin Sigilitoo, Gwanu's sister, member of Bina clan. Between Foubala and Bina, the following network of relationships is described.

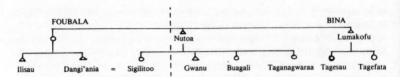

They key person between the clans is Sigilitoo, a young married woman who owes her greatest loyalty to her husband's clan; indeed, since she has only one child, and that one nursing, she is not yet, according to current Lau practice, supposed even to visit her natal village. She is and will remain a member of Bina; but she resides in Foubala, and her proper function would be to act as a tie between the two clans. Her name means 'the confuser of people', and we will see her in this ominous role.

Sigilitoo's sisters and classificatory sisters bear names referring to flowers, especially so her parallel cousins Tagesau and Tagefata. The word *tage* is a contraction of *tagana* 'flower of'. The word *sau* is in Lau an archaic form of *hau*, 'sago palm', *fata* means *Vitax cofassus* (Fox 1974:59). We will meet these girls in the role of innocent victims.

Nuto means 'squid'; the meaning becomes clear when we know that a Lau simile refers to backing out: *dudu mala nuto* 'to back out like a squid'.

I know of no etymology for Gwanu's name, except that his whole name is Gwanuomea and *omea* means 'war party.'

The only supernatural who appears in the text is a hermit woman Keningwaroabu. The word *keni* (archaic for *geni*) means 'woman', *gwaro* 'armlets', and *abu* 'taboo'. Hence, the woman who has tabooed her place for all men (lines 905-7) bears testimony of that in her name. The monster who is her most terrifying familial and here plays the trick, also has a transparent name, *'oru* 'widow', *bila* 'smelly'. The name may refer to the sexual pollution of women.

The general conclusion to be drawn from this partial investigation of the names of the dramatis personae is that they offer clues to the understanding of the myth. What we see here is the seeker of the exchange, the warrior who becomes the intruder; the woman who should bind but who confuses; the peacemaker who calms tensions; the victims who are innocent. This much for the meanings of the proper names. This is, I freely admit, the area of analysis that is the hardest to document, for the simple reason that as soon as a proper name is established, the word tends to lose meaning. It loses its general meaning because it now has a specific reference. In this myth, I believe the constellation of names which have fitting meanings to be too large to be incidental. I also believe that the Lau naming — or rather re-naming — system elucidates the way that meanings of names may be worth investigating. And I want to finally remind the reader that one of the epoch-making studies of myth, Lévi-Strauss' first article (1955) used names as if they were in themselves minimal narrative units, such as the name of Oedipus, that this has been criticized (Leach 1970:63-5); whether Lévi-Strauss could back it up or not, his intuition seems valid and valuable.

Under the influence of Vladimir Propp (1968), it has become fashionable to look at events only when seeking to describe narrative structures. Rather in line with Lévi-Strauss, I would maintain that several kinds of structure appear in a narrative: the sequence of events, for sure, that is, Lévi-Strauss' *linear* structure or, as he would also term it, *parole* (1968:87). In addition, the very setting of a narrative, the laying out of social relations with their accompanying obligations and tensions, such as here the position of a young wife, the setting up of an ancestral feast, the expectations of trade relationships, also is part of the structure of the myth: the framework in which the events will take place. These roles, relationships, this social setting will give the meanings to the events the structure of the schemata; thus, it is itself the *langue* which Lévi-Strauss believes to carry the main structural weight.

Levels of Reciprocity and Types of Exchange

Several levels of reciprocity within several exchange groups can be distinguished in the narrative. The first and foremost in Lau ideology is that within the clan, between the two halves of the clan, the ancestors and the clansmen alive. This exchange I term vertical. A clan sacrifices to its ancestors, the ancestors reciprocate by granting health and wealth to the clan. The sacrifices are most importantly presented in public grand-scale feasts, *maoma*, in which large distributions of food are combined with dance and myth performances.

Two of the clans referred to are preparing feasts: Iirofoli's and Gwanu's. Iirofoli is in the beginning of the story thinking of the next phase of his *maoma* cycle and decides that its time has come. He calls his men together and announces his intentions. The clansmen respond by contributing valuables, shell spans and dolphin teeth, necessary for the purchase of 50,000 taro.

The number of taro is of legendary proportions, but there is an exact correspondence between the *rau*, treasure collected and the market value of the taro, as follows:

> 20 *malefo* (shell strings) is equivalent of 20,000 taro (current value)
> 2,000 *lifoia* equals 10 *malefo* equals   10,000 taro (current value)
> 1,000 *robo* equals 10 *malefo* equals   10,000 taro (current value)
> 1,000 *unubulu* equals 10 *malefo* equals   10,000 taro.

The total adds up to 50,000 taro. We must, however, note that Bobongi attributes a value to a unit *unubulu* which is not currently used in exchanges, but only as ornaments. Yet, the equations yield a modern day market equivalence between the taro and the *rau*. Since according to the oldest Lau, at least malefo has changed in value within their memory, the point shows that, as I have argued elsewhere (Köngäs Maranda 1974a), fixed texts are figments of collectors' imaginations: a storyteller builds his narrative as he goes.

Whether the values are 'historical' or updated, the narrative makes clear that Iirofoli's feast is to be a grand one. This is also emphasized by his long wandering in all the villages of Talakali (lines 41-173); the amount of taro needed is so great that it cannot be found just anywhere. Moreover, the proper place to place a large taro order and to receive it is an established market place, such as Fakanakafo (literally, 'the mouth of the river', but a proper place name which pertains to a certain market area). The setting must be public because of the magnitude of the transaction.

In all his dealings, Iirofoli and his men behave properly. Gwanu, on the contrary, is doing wrong. His clan Bina is also preparing a feast. For this purpose, he has planted four gardens. Hearing of Iirofoli's *rau*, Gwanu decides to avert his gift to the ancestors, to sell the produce of two of the gardens. This is a 'mortal sin', for to avert a sacrifice from its intended ancestral receiver is to invite sure disaster. We witnessed the miseries of a man who in 1968 averted a pig whom he had dedicated to a given ancestor, and sacrificed it to another. In his own words, the act was *nue*, stupid. The health and welfare of this own children was immediately endangered; indeed, several of his children became sick.

Gwanu is thus breaking a contract with his ancestors, a promise made by him when he dedicated all four taro gardens to their feast. At the dedication, made with prayer before the ancestors, they are made fully cognizant of the contract, and thus the contract is inviolable.

Such are then the vertical exchanges within the narrative. One is described in the affirmative, that of Iirofoli: he behaves properly, and the blessings are his. Gwanu behaves improperly, and before the action ends, he has squandered the valuables of his clan. In the words of the myth,

and the shell spans are finished,
And the dolphin teeth are finished,
and the pigs are finished,
and the feast of Upper Bina has fallen (1417-20).

Gwanu's ancestors reciprocate negatively downwards, since he has committed the greatest folly known to the Lau, changed the address of his sacrifice. Gwanu's exchange with his ancestors is negative. But if there is, as I believe, a general statement in this narrative about the proper conduct in cult, it is stated twice:

1 Do as Iirofoli did; he worshipped properly, and he received blessing;
2 Do not do as Gwanu did: he did not worship properly, and he received punishment.

The horizontal exchanges discussed in the myth are of various orders: between leaders and their men, between different clans between trade partners, between marriage groups, between sets of brothers. The things that circulate are *words*, such as promises, oaths, war declarations, peace declarations, accusations, counteraccusations, gossip. They are also *goods*: betel nuts, shell spans, dolphin teeth, taro, fish, pigs. A betelnut is comparable to a greeting, a small symbol of friendly approach, preliminary to a friendly exchange of words and perhaps objects. Shell spans and dolphin teeth are not consumables but measures of value carrying a great symbolic weight. The consumables discussed here are not to be consumed in a trivial context: they are feast goods, taro and pigs, and as such subject to taboo regulations.

There is also horizontal circulation of *services*: leaders receive contributions, and they give distributions, men rally around a leader to wage war and receive compensation for their efforts; women are married to reside among their husbands' clans.

The reciprocities can again be negative: oaths, curses, quarrels, blows, war parties, and deaths. That death is thought of as a negative exchange of persons is made quite clear in the description of the suicides of Tagesau and Tagefata: the two innocent girls die as a result of other people's wrongdoings, and no blame is directed to them; instead, the guilty party, Gwanu, has to compensate their father for their deaths.

The typology of exchanges then is the following; I label them positive or negative, vertical or horizontal, according to definitions above, and show their interrelations:

1 Iirofoli works to fulfil his contract with his ancestors, to complete his *maoma* (positive vertical upwards, from descendants to ancestors).

2 Iirofoli and Ilisau enter into an exchange contract (positive horizontal between trade partners).

3 Iirofoli delivers his *rau* (positive horizontal, between trade partners, to follow 2).

4 Gwanu grabs Iirofoli's *rau* (negative horizontal; intrusion in a trade partnership, intercepting 3).

5 Gwanu averts his taro from his *maoma* (negative vertical upwards, breaking a contract between descendants and ancestors).

6 Sigilitoo betrays her husband to her brother (negative horizontal, between marrying groups).

7 Sigilitoo betrays her brother to her husband (negative horizontal, between marrying groups).

8 Ilisau delivers his taro to Iirofoli (positive horizontal between trade partners, to cancel 3).

9 Gwanu delivers his taro to Iirofoli (positive horizontal, as if between trade partners, to cancel 4).

10 Note that 8 and 9 constitute double value for Iirofoli's treasure. This can be treated as proof that his ancestors are indeed pleased with him (positive vertical downwards, from ancestors to descendants, to reciprocate for 1).

11 Ilisau plays a trick on Gwanu (negative horizontal, to counteract 4).

12 Gwanu causes the suicide of Tagerau and Tagefata, his classificatory sisters (negative horizontal, within a clan).

13 Lumakofu declares war against this classificatory son Gwanu (negative horisontal, within a clan, to counteract 12).

14 Gwanu gives compensations to Lumakofu (positive horizontal, to compensate for 12 and counteract 13).

15 Lumakofu declares peace (positive horizontal, to accept 14 and cancel 13).

16 Gwanu and Ilisau exchange equal valuables in one day (positive horizontal, to reestablish balance and cancel 4 and 7).

As is easily seen, the exchanges work from the distrubance of balance towards the reestablishment of balance. At the end of the narrative, all tricks are balanced out, all war is resolved, and the social order is totally restored, with the exception that Gwanu has learned his lesson, that he has experienced the wrath of his ancestors caused by his averting his gift to the ancestors.

Discussion

We have seen the setting of the myth where individuals are groups were poised in the network of their social roles and obligations: the clan of Asiningwane busying itself with the preparation of a great feast, its leader Iirofoli moving from village to village in a vain quest for fifty thousand taro, the 'deniers denying'; his men hurrying to and fro to compile the treasure needed for the exchange. We saw Gwanu, war chief of Bina, also preparing for a feast, but not active: puttering about with his carving and comb plating, in his craving for fish falling prey to girlish gossip, and in his craving for valuables concocting a foolish scheme to avert a gift to the ancestors. We saw the old man Nutoa, Gwanu's father' warn his son too mildly to prevent disaster. The young wife and mother Sigilitoo forgot her allegiance to her husband's and child's clan; instead of uniting and strengthening relations between her natal and conjugal groups, she divided and confused, so much so that finally even her brother asked warily: 'What do you want now?'.

All Lau now living would know the rules of proper conduct for all the situations depicted in the myth. Why should they then tolerate, indeed, cherish narratives in which so many of the actors do wrong things? The Lau are coolheaded people: they are the ones who call the aversion of a sacrifice 'stupidity', and, in the same vein, adultery *oengwanea*, 'madness'. Why would they care to listen to narratives describing follies?

Perhaps Marcel Mauss gave at least a partial answer to such questions when he wrote: 'In society there are not merely ideas and rules, but also men and groups and their behaviours' (1969:78). The ancient Greeks also were cool, analytic, and intellectual; yet their mythology is akin to that of the Lau: people, even gods are drawn to violate 'ideas and rules' and suffer for it.

For the Lau, as for the Greeks, as for all of us, there is also a pleasure in the meditation of things that are perfectly understood. We do not want only to ponder mysteries. And in the things understood there may always be something mystifying. We all know the 'thou shalt nots' of our catechisms, yet we are quite taken by stories of breaches of the commandments: killings, adulteries, thefts. We may ask why people who know better commit forbidden and foolish deeds, but our knowing the rules and their knowing the rules only provides the framework for the understanding of the events. It does not prevent such events from happening.

In listening to a narrative like the myth of Iirofoli, the Lau may then have an occasion to ponder human nature. It is human nature as molded by the rules of proper conduct developed in Lau society in the early times and known and followed now. The narrative touches on the rules: the audience knows a contract is inviolate, the audience knows a woman's chastity is protected, the audience knows fathers advise their sons and sons obey their fathers, that classificatory 'fathers' regard their brother's sons their own and do not declare wars on them, that sisters do not tell brothers what to do. Such things are known from childhood, learned in the daily interaction within and without kin groups; they are learnt when a quarrel between brothers is resolved by a sacrifice of reconciliation, when deaths caused voluntarily or involuntarily demand compensation, when quarrels end in a symbolic payment. To understand the myth, the audience must know the rules. This does not mean that the narrative should appear dull to the listeners: for with all its strife, its descriptions of disasters and their resolutions, or proper behaviours and their rewards, it is a reflection on Lau culture, the way of life the Lau follow.

There is a further dimension to the validity of myth in Lau. It is thought to be *mamana*, sacred; when sung, it is charged with mana. But the Lau have come to the conclusion that what is sacred is also true; the word *mamana* has a double meaning, *true and sacred*. Valid would perhaps be a good translation: a man's word can be *mamana* if he speaks the truth; and because he speaks the truth, his word has power. We come here quite close to Christian semantics, as in the statement, 'Truth will make you free'. Or, we come close to what Lévi-Strauss said twenty years ago about the 'non-lineal' structure of myth, the validity of the French Revolution to the French: not only was it an historical event but it is an event still valid in the minds of Frenchmen, still a model for their behaviour and their interpretation of the present as history; and we need only to think of the rhetoric of the revolution of 1968 to know that this observation is true.

One of the most exotic features of Lau myth telling and myth singing is the insistent repetition. This is partly due to the general nature of oral communication: if a text is on paper, the eye can flip back and reiterate, and we tend to reject repetition as unnecessary. But in oral communication, scanning back is not possible, and all oral styles tend to be repetitious or not successful. Furthermore, as said above, Lau myths are expressly the vehicle to carry factual information about places and people, and hence have to list their names. Boas called myth 'the autobiography of a tribe'; at first encounter, we were inclined to call Lau myth the travelogue of the Lau. Yet the places and genealogies are not rattled off in a random fashion: the repetition serves to emphasize the difficulty of the quest (as in Iirofoli's travels for the taro), or the magnitude of the gathering (as in the women repairing to the market of Fakanakafo).

Another feature hard for Westeners to grasp is the ideology of balance, when we are accustomed to thinking in terms of gain. The whole exchange system works against disturbed balance and for reestablishing balance. Words, goods, services, and people must circulate, for otherwise there would not be social life; but this circulation must not result in accumulation. Lau houses have few goods in them, only what is necessary; the definition of a rich man is not he who has but he who gives. An influential man knows where he will find assistance, he does not collect surplus. A large prestation is soon redistributed.

The difference between the ideology of gain and the ideology of balance is perhaps made clear by the anecdote of New Guinea Melanesians playing football: they would play as many days as it took for the two teams to score equal. This is also the Lau idea, and such ideology is reflected in this myth and reflected on by this myth.

NOTE

1 Versions of this paper have been read and commented on by Ira Buchler, Clifford Geertz, Claude Lévi-Strauss, Pierre Maranda and David Schneider. To all of them I owe thanks and a promise to elaborate elsewhere in a greater depth; this paper is still only a sketch.

BIBLIOGRAPHY

Cohen, Percy 1969: 'Theories of Myth,' *Man,* 4(3) 337-53.

Fox, Charles E. 1974: *Lau Dictionary*. Pacific Linguistics Series C, 25. Canberra.

Geertz, Clifford 1966: *Person, Time, and Conduct in Bali: An Essay in Cultural Analysis*. Yale University Southeast Asia Studies, Cultural Report Series, 14.

Köngäs Maranda, Elli 1970: 'Les Femmes Lau (Malaita, Iles Solomon) dans l'espace socialisé,' *Journal de la Société des Océanistes, XXVI* (27), 155-62.

_____1971: 'Towards the Investigation of Narrative Combinatories: Introduction'. Köngäs Maranda, Elli, and Pierre Maranda, Structural Models in Folklore and Transformational Essays. Mouton, The Hague, Paris, 11-15.

_____ 1974a, 'Individual and Tradition,' International Congress of Folk Narrative Research, Helsinki.

_____ 1974b: 'Lau Literary Genres', unpublished ms.

Leach, Edmond 1970: *Claude Lévi-Strauss*, New York, Viking Press.

Lévi-Strauss, Claude 1955: 'The Structural Study of Myth,' in Thomas A. Sebeok (ed.), *Myth: A Symposium*, Bloomington, Indiana University Press, (1968), 81-106. Also published, with minor stylistic corrections, as Chapter XI of C. Lévi-Strauss, *Structural Anthropology*, 206-31.

_____ 1968: *Structural Anthropology*. New York, Basic Books.

Malinowski, Bronislaw 1926: *Myth in Primitive Psychology*. New York.

Maranda, Pierre 1969: 'Lau Markets'. Unpublished ms.

_____ 1975: 'La Dynamique des Mythes: Contrats et échanges semantiques', Lectures given at the Collège de France, Paris.

Mauss, Marcel 1969: *The Gift*, London, Cohen and West.

Propp, Vladimir 1968: *Morphology of the Folktale* (2nd ed.) University of Texas Press, Austin.

Ross, Harold M. 1973: *Baegu: Social and Ecological Organization in Malaita, Solomon Islands*. Illinois Studies in Anthropology No. 8, University of Illinois Press, Urbana.

Burning our Trees:
metaphors in Kewa songs

JOHN LEROY

This essay examines some metaphorical songs, known as *rupale*, performed in connection with the pig kills of a Highlands people of Papua
New Guinea.[1] The songs, sung by groups of men to an audience of
villagers assembled in a large men's house, are about the procedures and
exchanges in the feast of the pig kill. A literal reading of the songs would
not suggest this, however, for the songs refer not to exchange partners nor
to exchange objects but to cultivated plants, trees and their fruits, birds,
marsupials and young girls. My purpose here is to analyze this imagery.

Metaphor rests on a similarity between domains of experience. It is, as
Barth puts it (1975:210) 'an expression that uses the more familiar and
evident as a model to grasp and clarify the less evident and elusive'.
Fernandez (1974:123) likewise asserts, as part of a complex definition, that
'the semantic movement accomplished by metaphor is from the abstract
and inchoate in the subject to the more concrete, ostensive, and easily
graspable in the metaphoric predicate'. With some qualifications, this idea
of a movement from the less defined to the more defined is applicable to
the *rupale* corpus. An important analogy here is between the killing of pigs
and the clearing and planting of a new garden under slash-and-burn
cultivation. For example a song might have this as its meaning. 'We have
prepared the ceremonial ground and now you should bring your pigs' but
be expressed as: 'We have burnt the tree bases and now you should bring
plant cuttings.' Although these two statements would appear to be equally
graspable and concrete, I shall argue that these and other metaphors
accomplish a movement from the less explicit and poorly understood to the
more explicit and better understood. This shift occurs in two ways. First,
the substitution of metaphorical language for ordinary language is a
rhetorical strategy: that becomes more explicit is the certainty or truth of a
message. Second, the bringing together of two domains of experience, the
gardening cycle and pig killing, clarifies some value conceptual or affective
problems encountered in each.

There are questions of form and questions of content, and there are
different levels of abstraction for dealing with both. I have organized my
study as follows: In Parts IV and V I shall take up the question of what
certain *rupale* metaphors, such as pig killing = gardening may mean when
considered apart from their actual verbal form. The discovery of metaphorical meaning here is not unlike the discovery of meaning in ritual
operations: metaphor is treated as a form of expression and an act of
partial comprehension of certain underlying or non-verbal ('unconscious')
perceived realities. Part III takes up the problem of form: the difference
between metaphorical language and ordinary language and the relationship
between form and social function. Before dealing with these problems one

51

must first have a sample of metaphors to work with and some idea of what they mean: the translation of selected metaphors is found in Part II, which presents the material in a direct, ethnographic manner. I begin in Part I with a sketch of Kewa society, of the pig kill, and of the manner in which *rupale* are sung, and I conclude in Part VI with some comparable metaphorical materials collected from Kewa women.

The Context

The Kewa are a population of roughly 40,000 persons of the Southern Highlands District. Though most of their land is a plateau of grassy valleys separated by forested ridges, the southern portion of Kewa territory is entirely forested except for scattered patches of secondary growth near habitations. In this rugged limestone country, some 4,000 Kewa live in clustered settlements or villages, practise shifting cultivation of sweet potato and taro, and raise pigs. The South Kewa are organized into patrilineal clans known as *repa*. Several different clans are represented in each settlement, and most clans have segments in two or more settlements. Regardless of his residence, a person of one's own clan and generation is known as a sibling, and intra-clan marriage is forbidden. Nor may one marry into the mother's or father's mother's clan; in addition, any descendent of a remembered marriage into one's own clan is unsuitable as a marriage partner. Kewa say that these consanguineal relatives are not to be married because of exchange: a man does not marry a classificatory sister or a female cross-cousin because he may be in a position to receive a portion of her husband's marriage payment, child payment, and eventually wife's mortuary payment. A spouse may be found either within the village or in another village provided he or she is not one of the prohibited kin. The effect of the prohibitions is to widen the number of affines with whom one may interact, but this is counteracted by a tendency to make a spouse from a clan segment into which a sibling or collateral has married.

Exchange obligations lie, in the main, to one's own wife-givers; these are the men who must be compensated when their married sisters give birth or die. With groups that gave wives to one's father or father's father (i.e., with MBS and FMBSS), on the other hand, exchanges are of a more equal or balanced nature. Male cross-cousins are more equivalent and brother-like than are their fathers, and in the next generation the second cousins (FMBSS and FFZSS) are even more like brothers; both kinds of cousins are, nevertheless, 'affines' and therefore in a position to exchange valuables. If he is active in exchange, a Kewa man may therefore have three sets of kinsmen to whom he may be making affinal payments (the clans of his WB, MB, and FMB) as well as any number of true or classificatory ZH, FZS, and FFZSS.

Many of these exchanges are accumulated and discharged at the event of a pig kill. Village pigs are killed ceremonially every eight years or so (the interval varies). Nearly every adult male, with the exception of the aged and the occasional Christian convert, takes an active part. The pig kill itself is a two- or three-day event. On the first day there is an exchange of pearlshells among the pig killers. On the second day the pigs are killed, butchered, and cooked; then the pig killers make return gifts of pork sides to the donors of shells. A side of pork today is generally worth about two pearlshells. If the exchange is being made with a wife-giver, the latter will be given one or more shells 'freely' (*kode*), i.e., without expectation of a return of pork. To put it differently, before the shell exchange each pig killer has at his disposal a number of live pigs and a number of his own pearlshells. After the shell exchange he will be left with a number of other persons' shells. The donors of these shells will be the recipients of his pork, and he in turn will receive pork from those who have kept his shells. The transactions are of considerable complexity and therefore are not left to chance; pig killers begin to work them out well in advance.

The pig killers are mainly residents of the sponsoring village. Kinsmen residing elsewhere may be drawn into the pig kill in either of two ways. First, they may simply be called upon by their pig-killing relatives to loan a shell. Making visits to one's distantly residing relatives in the months preceding the pig kill is a commonplace means whereby one's stock of shells is increased. Alternatively, kinsmen may be invited to participate as visiting pig killers — that is, to kill their own pigs in the host village. The relationship between host and visiting pig killers is both an arrangement between immediate kin (cross-cousins or brothers-in-law) and an alliance between clans. According to the custom known as *kaberekale*, shells, pork, and sometimes shoats are given to outsiders to reward them for killing their pigs in the host village. Since men are reluctant to kill pigs in any place other than the ceremonial grounds of their own villages, the number of such persons who can be drawn in reflects the political and economic strength of the host group. Furthermore, since killing one's pig in another village increases that village's prestige, this is a favour which should be returned eventually when the visitor becomes host and the host visitor. Through these reciprocal obligations Kewa pig kills establish a network of political and ceremonial ties between allied groups.

Villagers begin actively preparing for the pig kill about half a year ahead of time. Each pig killer is responsible for building a section of the accommodation and cooking shelters, or *neada*, which enclose the ceremonial ground. During the several months when the *neada* are being built, and when the cooking stones and supplies of firewood are accumulated, the village pig killers hold sessions of *rupale* singing.

The singing takes place inside the communal men's house (*tapada*) between dusk and dawn. In late afternoon while it is still light the pig killers put on their ceremonial finery. Soon after sunset they gather outside the men's house and announce that the singing is about to get underway by uttering some marching chants, *yasa* or *mata* (cf. Franklin 1970). When enough men have assembled they form groups of four to six each. One group enters the house through the veranda (*polo*) and, tramping heavily and in unison on the floor boards, marches along the central corridor (*pukama*), until the first pair of hearths are reached. There the group forms into two rows of two or three abreast. Stationary now, they continue

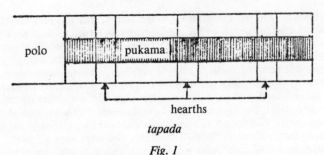

hearths

tapada

Fig. 1

to strike the floorboards with their heels; some shake rattles in the same steady rhythm. The singing begins.

Rupale are responsorial in form. The leader, usually the composer of the song, begins with a phrase and then the others in his group then join in a refrain. The final vowel of the song is altered into an 'o' which is sustained at the same pitch through subtle crescendo-diminuendo patterns, dies, out, and returns after some ten seconds of silence in a single repetition of the same note.[2] After another silence, during which the foot-tramping and rattle-shaking are kept up, the song is repeated with some slight variation in wording, perhaps a substitution of one named tract of land for another. A second song is sung and repeated in the same manner. Then the group marches to the second pair of hearths. Here the whole process is repeated, as it is for the third pair and however many other pairs of hearths there may be in the men's house. Once the singers have left the first hearths, a second set of singers enters from the *polo*, and begins its own songs in precisely the same way; later a third group enters. When a group has sung at all the hearths, it leaves the men's house by the back entrance, decides upon two new songs and re-enters from the front, repeating the whole cycle. In a three-hearth men's house there are, then, three groups of singers in the house at any one time, each with a different set of songs, and sometimes a fourth group outside waiting its turn. The singing of different groups may overlap, and this is said to yield a pleasing effect.

The singing of the *rupale* is one of the few occasions in which women enter the men's house. Normally only males go inside but during the festivities women and children, as well as men who are not killing pigs, pack the sleeping quarters on either side of the *pukama*. Some spectators remain the entire night, if the singing lasts that long, but the women and children often begin to drift back to their own houses when the coolness of early morning sets in. Then only the men remain, either singing or sitting and watching by the light of low fires or kerosene lamps.

The Songs

R1   *abi go nainuna kololu wiru poloameyada sipalurai rudusi ya, kisi naya lawa.*
Now I will cut down these youths' hoop pines of Kololu land: the

stone ax is short and there is no hand (help).

R2 *abi gonuri nainuna pukiara wiru poloameyada na aga pu pi pare, ki naya lawa.*

Now I will cut down the youths' hoop pines by the Puki stream; I would do (sharpen) the ax blade, but there is no hand (help).

R3 *semoko edali yago so go kari mada okane nai ya lawale kololu mari ...,kubi adasi para none bana lawa pare ...*

Bow-and-arrow friend, a youth from the north up there on the mountain ridge said, 'let's go down there to the bark-walled house of Kololu land,' but ...

R4 *oranu ya pare nonosalisina naripi palesi kupu kia pirua none koneda dia la.*

These are true things, but the brush turkey of Nonoalisi's Naripi land is staying making a nest, and there is no thought of down there.

R5 *melapasina rakunapi palesi kupu kialo pirina kapa kusalo pirina.*

The brush turkey of Melapasi's Rakunapi land is continuing to make a nest and to bury eggs.

The songs are seemingly about trees, tracts of land, birds, eggs, and axes, but in reality they are metaphorical statements about the forthcoming pig kill. With the help of informants I was able to find more or less definite meanings for many of these statements. The main theme of the first five songs is the insufficient number of pig killers in the village. In R1 and R2 the village men, who call themselves youths (i.e., unmarried men) state that they cannot cut down the trees on their land. This actually means that others are not coming to help them by bringing pigs to be killed. The metaphors here are based on an analogy which appears often in the song corpus: between killing pigs on the ceremonial ground and clearing the forest for a new garden. In R1 the blade of the stone axe is too short (after repeated sharpening) to cut down the trees; men without supporters are likewise 'short'. In R2 the blade cannot be sharpened for lack of help: just as one man alone does not sharpen a stone blade, but summons the help of others, so a single clan or village does not kill its own pigs. The next two songs recount how an invitation to the pig kill was made (R3) and turned down (R4): the man (or men) who was asked to come said that he was saving his pigs for a pig kill in his own village.

The main image of the fourth and fifth songs is a wild bird called *pale*, or brush turkey.[3] The unusual thing about this bird is the way it makes a nest. The brush turkey nests on the ground, building a large mound of dry leaves gathered from the forest floor in the vicinity of the nest. Eggs are buried about a foot deep in the mound, and here the heat of the rotting vegetation incubates them. This nesting behaviour is a metaphor for pig killing. The forest floor cleaned of dead leaves bears some similarity both to a new garden and to a ceremonial ground. The bird itself 'is' the pig killer, the egg 'is' a pig.[4] In R5 the singer states that a *pale* of a certain tract of land is making a nest in order to bury its eggs, but what he actually announces is that a man known as Melapasi, a resident of a distant village, is preparing to kill pigs in his own place.

The following metaphors have appeared:

unmarried youth	married man
felling trees and making new garden	killing pigs
cleared garden	
cleared garden 〱	prepared ceremonial
cleared area around *pale's* nest 〱	ground
egg	pig

R6　*mopo nane mopo pira aya adapolosi waneme mata epalia paleme, mea epalia paleme.*
　　The Adapolosi daughter staying down there would carry and come, would bring.

R7　*mopo nane mopo porara subusi wane epalia la, adalu pawa kama, yolayo pawa kama.*
　　The Porarasubusi daughter down there will come, she said; I made long, I pulled out.

R8　*sopo nane sopo tagata walusi wane go epa pirina, ora waru pa pirina.*
　　The Tagatawalusi daughter up there has come and stays here, truly still stays.

R9　*ainya bali nu isu matalo alenumi page ana na pi, nogo ya lawale, ni laliya lawa.*
　　Brother, your sister cannot make a woven net bag for carrying many things; she is just a girl; will you talk of me?

Three of the four songs quoted above refer to daughters. The names *adapolosi* and *porara subusi*, which designate the Pololo and Porarepa clans, tell us that the daughters are not of the host village: the 'daughters' are in fact men from other villages who come to kill pigs with the sponsor group. The first two songs convey the hosts' chagrin that the invited pig killers are not coming. This means that they will not be bringing pigs (R6) and that their absence will leave an empty place in the *neada* (R7). In R8 the visiting pig killer is praised for coming. In R9 one of the pig killers sings that he does not know the skills of net-bag weaving (killing pigs);[5] he tells others that he is just a girl and wonders if others will talk disparaginginly of him. Here the singer is alluding to the uneasiness that may be experienced by a newly married woman in her husband's village. Indeed the metaphorical daughters are considered to be 'married' by the host group. A single verb (*lamu mea*, probably 'to say and take') can be used both for marriage and for the contract of a visiting pig killer (*kaberekale*). The association is confirmed by a comparison made during a discussion in the men's house: the embarrassment experienced when an invited pig killer refuses to come is likened to that which is suffered when a marriage offer is refused. Both bring shame. On the other hand, when a girl takes the initiative and 'comes to stay' in a youth's village (R8), she desires betrothal. These new associations are:

male youth	host pig killer
daughter of other clan	visiting pig killer
marriage	contract of pig killer
woman's skill (weave net bag, etc.)	man's skill (kill pigs)

R10 *penoada apana suli yawi re kiru wiala pia, ma mula wai wasa piada,
mea puala pema.*
Because they were burning and leaving the bases of the yawi trees of
Penoada's father's Suli land, and were looking for cuttings of mula
taros, we took (the cuttings) and went.

R11 *werepe nane nainuna kololu pai re kiru wia minya kadu wai wasa pula
pira, mea epalia paleme.*
Later on when we were to burn and leave the youths' pai trees because
of the Kololu stream, and look for the cuttings of kadu pitpit, they
would take (the cuttings) and come.

These two songs refer to the burning of tree bases and to the cuttings of
two cultivates, taro (*Colocasia*) and highland pitpit (*Setaria*). The two
songs are therefore about making gardens. At this point a brief summary
of south Kewa cultivation techniques is in order.

The people living in the northern part of Kewa territory practice
intensive horticulture with grass fallow. The south Kewa, who live in a
warmer and more humid environment of extensive lower montane forests,
practise shifting cultivation with forest fallow. The gardener begins by
cutting away the undergrowth, chopping down the smaller trees, and
pollarding some of the larger ones. The brush is allowed to dry out, and
then it is heaped at the tree bases and burnt. The burning gets rid of the
debris by turning it into ash, and in doing so it releases nutrients for the
cultivates. Most of the ash is concentrated around the tree bases and these
areas are, as the Kewa gardener knows, the best places to plant his crops.
With a few exceptions crops are reproduced vegetatively through cuttings.
The cutting may be a bunch of runners (sweet potato), the top of a corm
(taro), or a shoot or sucker (banana, 'pitpit'). The cuttings are placed in
holes made with a digging stick.

We may turn now to the metaphorical meaning of the songs. When the
youths of a village are said to burn a garden, this actually means that the
host pig killers are building the *neada* and preparing the ceremonial
ground. When the daughters are said to bring the cuttings of various
cultivates, this means that the visiting pig killers are bringing pigs. The
associations are:

cuttings   pigs
burning the tree bases preparing the ceremonial ground and
                        constructing *neada*

The metaphorical planting of a new garden follows the metaphorical
marriage. Bringing the cuttings is the task performed by daughters who
have married into the host village; preparing the garden by burning is the
task of their husbands. Or in reality: men from other villages bring pigs
which are killed in the *neada* of the host village. In R10 and R11 these
metaphors are used to criticize men of another village. The singers recall
that they had gone to help that village when pigs were being killed there
(R10), and they express their regret that men of that village did not return
the favour as expected (R11).

R12 *nena nainumi kololu yawi kili moke pilimi, ado mea puenya lalo, remo abe na puape.*

Ghost, your sons are sharing out the nuts of the yawi trees of Kololu stream; having looked, go; go not quickly.

R13 *Naripinu ama nena tomena kamareke yawi kili moke ouluri anya kone wilida, ageme pada liape.*

Mother of Naripinu, since you are sharing out the nuts of your sweetheart's *yawi* trees of Kamareke ground, because you are thinking of your brother, kick some over.

R14 *arabona naisimi nene nemaya yawi kili talamea komenu giliada, goi tabamea poloa.*

Son of my father's sister, when you have given me one or two nuts gathered from the *yawi* trees of your Nemaya ground, I shall take them and go.

R15 *Ali nakinumi apitayake to pumea tatamea yabala yasasiri wasalo piri lawa.*

The men and boys have climbed the trunks of the Apitayake tree and are searching for and collecting yabala mushrooms.

R16 *nena amana orake ya wili ma para wiape ora yamu irisiri meda abe epa giape.*

On your neck you wear the beak of your mother's bird of Orake land; come and quickly give me one of the yamu parrot's feathers.

The *yawi* tree mentioned in three of these songs (R12-14) is one of the several species of aercoid palms ('black palm' or *limbum* in pidgin) that grow in the surrounding forests. This tree, along with the hoop pine and the casuarina among others, associates with men, with the continuity of a lineage of a settlement, and with the strength of the co-residential group. It is a male image, and *Yawi* is not uncommon as a man's name. The *yawi* palm bears clusters of inedible nuts which, in the songs, are gathered and shared among kinsmen much as in real life, the nuts of the pandanus tree are shared.

In the *rupale* idiom the nuts or seeds of several trees, especially the *yawi* palm and the hoop pine, represent the pearlshells exchanged at the pig kill. Other forest things may represent pearlshells as well, such as red parrot feathers or white mushrooms, but tree nuts are the most frequent. It would appear that trees (or birds) associate with men, and that nuts (or mushrooms and feathers) associate with their possessions.

A number of different messages are conveyed. R12 is addressed to the ghost of a dead wife; it informs the wife's kin that a death payment will be made. R13 is directed to the singer's married sister, reminding her to think of her brother when she gives away the nuts of her husband's trees; in other words an affinal payment is asked of the sister's husband through the sister. In R14 a similar affinal payment is requested, but the parties are this time the descendants of brothers-in-law, cross-cousins. Again it is the wife-giver who solicits the payment.

The following associations were found in the sixteen songs discussed here:

felling trees and making new garden	killing pigs
cleared garden; cleared	prepared ceremonial
area around *pale*'s nest	ground
tree base	*neada*
cutting, egg	pig
youth of resident clan	host pig killer
daughter of other clan	visiting pig killer
marriage	contract of pig killer
woman's skill (weave net bag)	man's skill (kill pigs)
palm tree, hoop pine	man
nuts and seeds, mushrooms,	pearlshells
bird feathers	

The Structure of Metaphor

I shall now turn from the translation of specific metaphors to a discussion
of the role of metaphors in communication. The question here is, why
should metaphorical discourse and not normal language be used to convey
messages about pig killing and exchange? Why say 'daughter' or 'tree nut'
instead of 'visiting pig killer' or 'pearlshell'? To answer this we need to
understand the general structure of metaphor. In view of the fact that
rupale metaphors can provisionally be considered an alternative language
replacing the normal one,[6] a linguistic or semiotic theory can be applied.

To begin with, there is the Saussurean distinction between the signifier
(*signifiant*) and signified (*signifié*). In linguistic systems the signifier is an
acoustic (phonemic) image and the signified is the concept to which it
refers. In addition there is a third term, the *sign*, which is the relationship
between the other two. The sign is the concrete entity, the *word*; it is what
experience encounters, whereas the distinction between signifier and
signified is an analytical one (Barthes 1973:112-3).

Language is not the only content for these formal terms. To quote
Barthes (*ibid*, 113),

> Take a bunch of roses: I use it to *signify* my passion. Do we have here,
> then, only a signifier and a signified, the roses and the passion? Not even
> that: to put it accurately, there are only 'passionified' roses. But on the
> plane of analysis, we do have three terms; for these roses weighted with
> passion perfectly and correctly allow themselves to be decomposed into
> roses and passion: the former and the latter existed before uniting and
> forming this third object, which is the sign.

The same formal system can be applied to metaphor. In metaphor as in
ordinary language, the sign is a word (for instance, 'daughter'). The
important difference between a linguistic sign and a metaphorical sign is
the nature of the signifier. The metaphorical signifier is not simply an
acoustic image, but this in conjunction with a meaning; it is, in other
words, already a *sign* in ordinary language. The metaphorical system is
constructed from the pre-existing linguistic one; signs of the one become
mere signifiers in the other. Metaphor is therefore an example of what

Barthes calls a 'second-order semiological system'. (114)

As an example consider the word *wane*, which has the normal meaning of 'daughter' and the metaphorical meaning of 'pig killer'. In the linguistic system the acoustic image /*wane*/[7] is the signifier, and a category of kin that we may translate as 'daughter' is the signified concept. In the metaphorical system the acoustic image /*wane*/ again appears, but this acoustic image by itself is not the signifier for the new signified ('pig killer'). Were that the case 'daughter' and 'pig killer' would be alternative meanings of the same acoustic signifier and the system would not be recognized as metaphorical. It is rather the unity of the acoustic image /*wane*/ and the meaning 'daughter' or 'category of female consanguineal kin' that is the new signifier. Following Barthes (115), the relationship between the two systems can be diagrammed in Table 1.

	1. SIGNIFIER /*wane*/	2. SIGNIFIED kin category of daughter	
LANGUAGE {	3. Sign		II. SIGNIFIED Visiting pig killer
METAPHOR {	I. SIGNIFIER /*wane*/ – daughter		
	III. SIGN (or SIGNIFICATION) /*wane*/ – daughter-like visiting pig killer		

Table 1

In the metaphorical system, then, what is grasped (i.e. the sign) is a combination of the sound /*wane*/ and a meaning which is itself the association of two categories, daughter and pig killer.

As a 'second-order' semiological system, metaphor departs from language in an important respect: whereas in language the signifier stands in an arbitrary relation to the signified, in metaphor it clearly does not. The arbitrary mature of the linguistic sign, it will be recalled, derives from the fact that no *a priori* relationship can be demonstrated between a sound form and a particular semantic content. What happens in metaphor is that a content in the linguistic system, e.g. *wane*/daughter, functions as form in the metaphorical system. When *wane*/daughter passes from meaning into form, only certain qualities are kept, those pertaining to the status of daughterhood; other qualities are lost, those imminent in the female person(s) to whom someone may refer as his *wane*. The qualities retained make up the basis of an analogic (non-arbitrary) association with other contents. In the case of daughter-like visiting pig killers the association between daughter and pig killer is based in part on the way both are brought into the village from the outside in return for an outlay of valuables (the marriage payment or the *kaberekale* payment), and in part on the wider analogy between gardening and pig killing.

Having defined how metaphors mean, we can return to the original question: why communicate in metaphors? One can argue that it is the very fact that metaphorical words are *not* arbitrary but rather have a motivated form that gives them greater persuasive weight. The words of normal discourse are transparent; one sees through them as through a pane of glass to the intended meaning.[8] Because the words themselves offer no resistance, as it were: one's attention turns entirely to what they mean, with the result that this meaning may be taken as itself permeable, concealing a different meaning. That is, the discourse may not be believed: it may be accepted as imaginary. This is where metaphorical speech may be strategic. Metaphors are mythical, but the metaphorical relation refers to what is taken to be incontestably real. Hence, in a society where myth is the major source of knowledge, metaphorically phrased speech is less likely to be disbelieved, i.e. less likely to be considered imaginary as to its (semantic) content. Unlike normal speech, then, metaphorical speech is protected by the slight 'opacity' of its signs. In support of this I have noted that Kewa frequently use metaphorical language when they want to lend added force to utterances directed to persons, groups, or other agents. The language or spells offers many examples of metaphorical usage, and the same is true for oratory. For example when a Koiari elder, *Gie*, endeavoured to instruct the younger men of Koiari about their responsibilities in exchange, he did not say:

> Will you give your shells in the proper way to the visiting pig killers, who are many? Are you young men prepared to do well by them, as you promised? Some of us are old and cannot help you ...

He said rather:

> What will you do with seeds of the hoop pine? Will you look at the many daughters who stay outside? You showed your bailer shells and your headbands of nassa; but now that the daughters have come, what will you orphan boys say to them? The leg-bands have slipped down over our calves and rest at the ankles. I do not know ...

In the first version, the use of non-metaphorical speech leaves the opinion open to question; it may be dismissed as one old man's querulous misgivings. In the second version, I suggest, the words offer a slight resistance even to those who may be certain about their meanings, and as a result the statement is more likely to be accepted as a certainty.

Formal Considerations

So far I have considered metaphors at the ethnographic level and at the level of semiotic theory. I shall now situate the argument at an intermediary level and discuss metaphors in terms of Kewa culture and experience.

In the preceding section we saw that metaphorical signs are not arbitrary but motivated. This motivation can be understood in two ways.

The first is the question of categories of thought. Here we want to know what motivates the choice of metaphors, such that a pearlshell is represented by a tree nut and not, say, but a pebble. Answering this sort of question requires some idea about where tree nuts, cuttings, brush turkeys and other things are found within the conceptual order.

The second question is about the relationship between homologous structures at the 'unconscious' level. Two basic analogies have already been noted, one between pig killing and gardening, and another between bringing in pig killers and marrying-in women. These analogies are based on an awareness of practical and structural similarities between related parts of Kewa culture: between two kinds of subsistence activities and between two forms of social or political contracts. Ultimately the two analogies rest on pairs of contrasting elements: animal/plant, and male/female. The question which may then be asked is: If pig killing 'is' gardening, and if visiting pig killers 'are' women married to their host-husbands, do these identities modify experience at all? Are metaphors nothing more than the product of an intellect at play with logic and resemblances, or do they also accomplish some more practical or affective function?

These two aspects of metaphors are discussed in this section and the next. In this section, then, I am concerned with the culturally conceived form of *rupale* images.

The following generalization may be made about *rupale* signifiers: they are taken from things or activities situated outside the confines of the village, and they refer to things and activities situate within. 'Wild' things signify 'domestic' ones.[9] The term 'wild' has both an objective and a moral dimension. On the one hand it refers to that part of the environment not modified by man: the primary forest, the rock outcrops, the sinkholes in the limestone, and the streams. On the other hand it evokes, through the ghosts and wildmen that reside in these parts, unconstrained or non-reciprocal conduct.

The wild is removed from the domestic or moral by horizontal and vertical space: horizontal when the ceremonial area and the *neada* are likened to the cleared earth and the burnt tree bases of a forest garden, and vertical when men and their shells are associated with things of the above: birds and bird feathers, tree nuts, ghosts and stars. It must be stressed that these oppositions have contextual and not absolute meanings. The tree base is 'wild' when forest opposes to village, but 'domestic' when tree base and earth oppose to sky. When Kewa affirm that ghosts and wildmen live in tree bases or rock outcrops, they are seeing these abodes as the wild counterparts of human habitations. But when, in some *rupale*, men say that they sit down together at the base of a tree, they are not likening themselves to wildmen but rather to cultured and cooperative beings, to men that sit together in the *neada*.

Three parts of the wild are used in *rupale* metaphors: trees and other plants, birds and other animals, and water and other natural phenomena. Different referents can be found for the same metaphor and, more commonly, one thing may be represented by two or three metaphors. For example, a possum may represent a pig in one song and a man in another. Likewise, the *neada* in the ceremonial ground may be represented in one song by a burnt tree base with the cleared earth around it, and in another by the brush turkey's nest with its own clearing. These multiple meanings are easily explained: the association between an image and its referent is based on a quality or feature both are perceived to embody, but obviously each also has other qualities which linked it independently to other images or referents. Pearlshells, for example, are evoked by tree fruits, parrot feathers, and celestial bodies. They are like tree fruits because of the association between tree trunk and men, because both are aggregate entities, and because tree fruits are sought by birds the way shells are sought by ghosts. Pearlshells resemble the features of certain parrots because of their irridescence and red colour, and because men are likened to birds. Finally, pearlshells are like the stars or the sun because they shine even in dark interiors or glint with the reflected light of the sun.

One can identify a number of contrastive qualities, such as hard/soft, wet/dry, lustrous/dull, which modify metaphorical predicates in the same way that adjectives modify subjects. A wrinkled old man is like a dried-up tree-fern stalk. Or a thin, sickly pig is like the wilted taro cutting. Beyond a simple listing of these oppositions, one could go on to discover associations between opposing pairs. There seems to be a definite association between the wild, the hard, and the male: the forest is the abode of wildmen and ghosts of patrilineal ancestors which either inhabit or leave their traces in rocks and trees. Spells and rituals coax maleficent ghosts into returning to the tree bases, rock outcrops, stones, lithic artifacts, or fossils where they are immobilized. The tough inedible nuts of palm tree inflorescences represent shells, and it is not the ripe tuber of fruit but the cutting or sucker of 'male' plants that stand for pigs.

In a similar manner mortality and impoverishment are represented by soft and weak things: rotting trees, wilted leaves or cuttings, banana plants. On the evidence of Kewa myths, one can assert that weakness of body, either in infancy or old age, is related to female influence.

Structure

One structuralist argument proposes that myths and rituals deal with practical or cognitive problems within a culture. It proposes that the real meaning of a myth is an unconscious one. We have seen that at one level the referents of *rupale* images are quite explicitly or consciously known. Yet at another level, the level sought in a structural analysis, metaphors point to less easily verbalized or understood domains of experience. I shall argue that some of the songs discussed above point to practical and affective difficulties in Kewa experience and that metaphors provide a way of rethinking the logical relations on which practice and affectivity are based.

The songs I have in mind are those about gardening: village youths who burn the tree bases and daughters who bring the cuttings. Though I am not discussing them for this reason alone, I should point out that these songs are quantitatively the most important in the corpus (see Appendix to this article). Of some 400 songs collected, 45 mentioned tree bases, cuttings, or both, and 33 others mentioned daughters. Next in frequency were palm nuts, signifying pearlshells; there were 32 of these. There were some 20 occurrences of the pandanus leaf, signifying 'barbed' talk or dispute. The remaining metaphors appeared 8 or fewer times.

A possible explanation for frequency of gardening songs is that these songs faithfully reflect cultural priorities. Although Kewa society is ideologically oriented toward 'pigs and shells', (*mena sekere*), both pig husbandry and the ritual or ceremonial use of pigs rest on the society's horticultural base. Pork is highly valued, but it forms a small part of the diet; the gardening metaphor is conceivably a recognition of this fact. Furthermore, one might want to argue that when, in Kewa songs, men metaphorically become women, the message is something similar: although men possess and to a great extent control cultural property, and although they dominate the ceremonial and ritual productions, they recognize nonetheless that it is only through the voluntary productive and reproductive labour of women that they can occupy this ascendant position. Through the metaphors the pig killers seem to say: 'We are doing all this with our pigs because the women work hard in the gardens; therefore we, too, are women in our gardens'.

There is a difficulty with this argument: metaphors are drawn not from gardening in general but from one phase of it — burning the tree bases and planting the cuttings. I shall now take another look at this phase of the garden cycle and attempt to find its intellectual and symbolic significance.

Let us begin with firewood. Cooking fires, either of the hearth or of the earth oven, are made of dead, dry wood usually collected outside the village. Nowadays, when every male as a steel axe, the usual mode of producing firewood is to find a suitable live tree in the forest, ringbark it, and wait for a couple of years until it is thoroughly dry. By contrast, when a garden is cleared, all but the largest trees are chopped down immediately, since this allows a maximum amount of sunlight to reach the forest floor. The fallen trees rot and are thus useless for firewood, though they prevent erosion, provide humus and contribute to the recovery of the forest. There is good reason to think that with stone-axe technology the procedure was different. Because the axes were less efficient, much of the firewood probably came not from the forest but from the gardens. Firewood-size trees were left standing or only pollarded when the garden was cleared, and these trees were killed when the gardener fired the dry debris piled at their bases. The trees were harvested after the garden was harvested.

So in stone-axe times much of the firewood came from new gardens; today much of it comes from the forest. I shall argue that the metaphor of 'burning the tree bases' must be understood in the light of the earlier techniques. Burning trees 'alive' was then the most effective mode of clearing the land for gardens and for producing firewood.

But firing is just the beginning of the garden cycle. Since the cuttings of various cultigens, sweet potatoes excluded, are planted in the ashes around the tree bases, the base (*re*) of the tree becomes the source (*re*)[10] of the mature crops that are later consumed. It is as if the Kewa cultivator were aware of the fact that both the food he cooks and the firewood he cooks it with, required the preliminary killing of a tree. If this is so, we might assume along with Lévi-Strauss (1969:151) that there is a 'vague feeling of guilt attached to this agricultural process, which makes a certain form of cannibalism the precondition of civilized nourishment'.[11]

If this interpretation is correct, gardening imagery is a way of thinking about killing pigs because consuming village pigs is also a form of cannibalism. Pigs receive until their death a solicitous treatment. Piglets are sometimes suckled by women and may be weaned on premasticated cooked food; throughout their life all domestic pigs receive a substantial portion of their diet from human hands. Some pigs spend the night indoors in the women's houses, respond to their owners like dogs, bear names, and have character traits. It is not surprising, therefore, that owners become attached to their pigs. Grown men and women have been seen to weep when a pig they have reared is killed. (The owner does not kill his own pig; the person who has a claim on the pork does.) Yet some men and women express a desire to keep for themselves at least one side of pork from their pig or pigs. It is a wish, which men usually ascribe to their wives, that a pig on which so much time and labour has been spent should not escape completely through the exchange system; it should rather be possessed in the most final and pure sense, by consuming it.

It would appear that there are two forms of cannibalism, a vegetarian and a carnivorous, and that the metaphors express the idea that the one can be thought in terms of the other. There is a reason for this transposition: killing and consuming a household pig is difficult from the affective point of view, but killing and 'consuming' a tree is not, through there is a cognitive similarity between the two acts.

Yet the two are, if one compares them closely, slightly 'out of phase', and here as well the metaphor may, in a sense, think away a conflict. The fact that most of the village pigs are killed at the same time means that the size of the pig herd undergoes a cyclical growth and decline. Cyclical change is also found in the horticultural system. But the exact point or points at which the two cycles correspond to one another is not so clear. It would be easy to be misled by certain external resemblances. One is tempted to see a similarity between burning the bark off a tree and burning the bristles and outer skin off a pig (as is done before butchering). Cognitively the two are much the same. But since metaphors tell us that burning the trees is like preparing the *neada* and that planting the cuttings is like killing the pigs, the stress is on pig killing as a kind of *planting* activity, i.e., conceptually at the beginning of a cycle rather than at its end (Table 3).

Table 3

| Vegetarian | *Re* burnt | *Wai* brought | Planting |
| Carnivorous | *Neada* built | Pigs brought | Killing |

To make a garden one first burns or cuts the trees, clears the area of bush, and prepares the soil by pulling up vines and grasses; then the cuttings are planted, and once this is done it is only necessary to wait until the crops mature. To make a pig kill one first prepares the ceremonial ground and builds the *neada*; then one plants the pigs, metonymically at least, when one plants the stakes to which pigs are tied the morning they are killed. Planting the pig-stakes in the ceremonial ground is analogous to planting the taro or *Seataria* cuttings in the garden.[12]

The pig kill, then, initiates the growth of the pig herd the way planting starts the growth of crops. One sees now a second way in which *rupale* metaphors modify the affective or emotional problems raised by killing pigs. In the first place, one must assume that affective phenomena are secondary to intellectual ones, that affective responses arise when the intellect alone can not resolve the conflicts posed by some aspect of the world in terms of which the intellect operates.[13] Killing and eating a pig that one has raised is a situation difficult for the rational consciousness to comprehend (and one may therefore choose to live the experience emotionally instead of rationally) only because pigs are conceptually known in terms of domesticity and culture. *Rupale* metaphors serve to mitigate the gravity and immediacy of the conflict by discovering a similar conflict elsewhere on a reduced scale and with different meanings (Lévi-Strauss 1971:621). Either the ceremonial ground at the centre of the village is likened to the distant clearings of the forest, and the consumption of pigs reduced to the consumption of garden crops, or the metaphors think the end of a cycle in terms of its beginning, and destruction in terms of productivity and creativity.

The metaphor of the brush turkey, mentioned earlier, can be viewed as a more accentuated expression of the same tendency. We have seen that this bird does its own 'gardening': it heaps up mounds of dead vegetation in which it buries its eggs. The 'burning' here results from the process of decay, and this 'fire' from rotting vegetation is the obvious precondition for the generational cycle (incubation and hatching of the egg). The brush turkey therefore represents a final attempt to think away the conflict of killing and eating pigs: repetitions of its cycle are continent on an activity which, while being strikingly 'cultural' in appearance, occurs through non-destructive natural processes. Natural behaviour in culture (men who kill their pigs) is known in terms of cultural behaviour in nature (the nesting of the brush turkey).

Conclusions

I have argued that metaphorical expressions have two practical results in Kewa society. First, metaphors have à rhetorical function: the non-arbitrary relation between image and meaning results in an 'excess'[14] of significance that increases the persuasive power of the metaphorical sign. Second, metaphors perform an ideological function by rethinking a predatory act in terms of a productive one. Gardening is an apt metaphor for pig killing in that the predatory phase of gardening, the burning of trees, is more a 'logical' predation than an actual one.

My final comments are about women in Kewa metaphor and life. The meaning of marriage used in *rupale* metaphor is the jural one, marriage as an alliance between kin groups and, by extension, between villages. We have seen that the *kaberekale* contract and marriage are alike in that both effect a movement of a person between kin groups through the transfer of wealth. There is another similarity between the two institutions, though: both the pig killer who kills a pig in another village and the woman who marries outside her natal village are refusing the possibility of 'staying' — that is, killing the pig or marrying within his or her own village.

There are good reasons why both the pig killer and the unmarried girl might well prefer to stay within the village. Killing pigs in another village confers prestige on that village, not on one's own, and it means that the pig killer has one less pig in his herd (though he does return with pork). In a like manner, it is often with reluctance that a young woman leaves her natal place and takes up residence in her husband's village; she might have preferred marrying some youth whom she had known with affection since childhood.

The latter sentiment is expressed in metaphorical songs, known as *mata*, which girls were singing during the several months prior to the Koiari pig kill.[15] Like *rupale, mata* are responsorial, but they have a different melodic line. The leader is an older married woman.[16] She stands inside a circle of some half-dozen girls, who form the chorus. Each girl holds a digging stick and joins hands with others. When a song is in progress, the circle of girls rotates slowly, the caller remaining immobile.

There are two types of subject matter in the *mata* genre. The first is the forthcoming pig kill. The theme is not the transaction of shells and pork, for that belongs to the men; it is rather the actual killing, cooking, and eating of pigs. The second theme is courtship and marriage. As one might expect, the meaning of marriage for unmarried women is not the same as for married men. The girls' songs emphasize not the exchange of wealth which legalizes the alliance, but rather the emotional and sexual ties of courtship. For example in one *mata* the girls sing: 'The Kololu stream tree-fern seemed to want to take, then turned about'. Here the tree-fern is a youth, 'taking' is marrying, and turning about is a reversal of his affections. As other songs make clear, it is actually the leafless trunk of the tree fern which stands for the man, while the fern leaves are metaphors either for the young woman or for the apron (*kura*) which conceals her sex.

Though these metaphors are only indirectly sexual, the meaning is sometimes more explicit: 'The wind is blowing my apron away, young boy cast your eyes down'; or (also to a boyfriend) 'I have no apron, let us go down to Wari stream where the wild taros grow', ostensibly to cut the grass for an apron. Another song compares a penis to a sugar cane cutting, and asks that it be given to eat.

These are not songs of innocence; traditionally women had little pork to eat,[17] yet it is they and not the men who sing about eating it. The metaphorical but nevertheless explicit reference to sex is intentionally provocative. The men are embarrassed and annoyed, or at any rate make a show of being annoyed. 'Sing about killing pigs!' they call out, but the girls and women laugh and continue with the same themes.

It would seem that through the *mata*, women are expressing a certain opposition, though a socially acceptable one, to the male-dominated order; and, more important in the present context, it would appear that this opposition carries over into an alternative interpretation of the very metaphors men use. I have argued that likening the killing of pigs to the planting of a garden underlines the productive or, more properly, the reproductive significance of killing pigs. The *mata* metaphors which refer to sexual intercourse have a similar message. Men sing about making gardens, women sing about intimate sexual affairs, yet the context for both sets of songs is the same, the pig kill, and both imply fertility and productivity. Furthermore, the correspondences are really triadic (Fig. 2) because planting cuttings (especially taro tops) is a metaphor for the sexual act, because gardens in the forest are a favourite spot for both licit and illicit sexual encounters, and because there is a less explicit but more pervasive association between eating and copulating.[18]

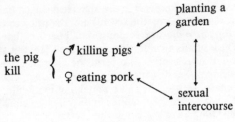

Fig.2

Those who favour psychoanalytic theory might be tempted to take the sexual symbolism as the 'real' meaning of *rupale* metaphors and regard the cutting = pig and tree-base = *neada* associations as improvisations concealing the more fundamental sexual imagery. That may be; but it would be more in line with the relation between the sexes in real life to see *rupale* and *mata* as complementary expressions. Men express the moral of 'cultural' view: an inter-village alliance between pig killers is metaphorically expressed as marriage, and the killing of pigs is seen as a productive act like the planting of a garden. Women, on the other hand, express the affective or 'natural' view: against the men's inter-village alliances based on the marriage of metaphorical daughters, the real daughters proclaim the importance of intra-village emotional bonds; and against the metaphorical productivity of the pig herd and the garden, they stress the more immediate and tangible satisfactions that both pigs and men afford them.

APPENDIX

RUPALE CONTENT

The table summarizes some 400 songs; when a metaphor appears in more than four songs the number or appearances is indicated within parenthesis; some songs could have been classified under two or more of the table headings, but were not.

I *Preparing the pig kill and killing pigs*

A *Cultural activities*

Burn bases of trees and bring cuttings (45); cut down tree; look for mushrooms; look for brush turkey eggs; look for rats in brush piles; secure or cut pig-tether (7); make armbands; make legbands (5); make bamboo knives; cut rattan for ceremonial hat; cut bark for weaving net bags; rattan piled in men's house; intention to eat possums; about to open earth ovens; hit pig with club; throw club in stream.

B *Natural phenomena*

Tree about to fall and cracks; palm nuts fall to ground with noise (7); thunder rolls; flashing of lightening; omen birds cry (7); brush turkey makes nest. (note: some imply disputes accompany the activity)

II *Exchanging Wealth*

A *References to wealth of other or of groups*

Palm nuts (32); hoop pine nuts (8); pearlshells wrapped in bark; stars shining; flowing stream; tree nuts shining in sun; bird feathers; climbing over mountain.

B *References to one's own poverty or that of one's group*

Ropes are cut (by death); stream dried up; pearlshell bands dry; moisture collected in wealth (5); dryness of cuttings; walk around outside of house; own body wrinkled like tree-fern stalk, like withered leaves; seasonal sickness; death of adult men (dry hoop pines, dry casuarinas, only saplings standing).

C *References to other persons*

Praise his thighs or femurs; as branch from mother's tree; carried in mother's net bag; thick wild pandanus of mother's group.

D *Dispute and barbed talk*

Speech of other or self like serrated edge of pandanus leaf (20); other's wealth as red nettle leaves; warning of harm caused by other's bad thoughts; other as liar or thief; argument with government over pig (5); argument beside tree bases.

III *Bringing non-resident repa members, pig killers, immigrants*

A *Metaphors for these men*

Cassowaries; cassowary young; cassowary wing quills; coming under cassowary (hornbill, quail) wings (8); following cassowary footprints; daughters (pig killers only) (33); one arm of fire tongs or one half of split fire-starting stick (6) immobile trees.

B *Motives for coming*

Sit badly in other houses; post-warfare sorcery accusations (eaten enemy's possum bones, eaten cassowary bone; drunk water from enemy's cordyline leaves) (6); pulled by agnates like possum by fur of neck; held in village like branch by bird's foot.

C *Demonstration of commitment*

Always looking for possums, sitting at base of tree, on tree-fern stalk; share pig ears as children; break pandanus taboo on movements (5); bring tree for pig posts and spirit cult house; paint spirit masks; drink water from stream with cup of leaves, drink water falling from trees of host village (8); put earth on skin (mourn 'death' of previous ties); put on cordyline leaves, share pillow of tree-fern stalk; go inside (share men's house; sit beneath headman's hair wig.

IV *Death*

A *Metaphors*

Cassowary sleeps in cave; remove man's armband, ceremonial hat or wig; remove woman's grass apron; plant cordyline leaves; pandanus thorns scratch; phosphorescent water; dove crying; egg breaks; darkness in house; tree top falls; water muddied; make marks on tree trunk with axe.

B *Social relations*

Procure possums for funerary feast; reference to burial ground; ghosts come to gather tree fruit or shells; expressions of sorrow for specified kin (total): wife (12), brother (5), sister (4), daughter (6), son (3), husband (woman's *remali*) (3), mother's brother (3), mother (1).

NOTES

1 The songs were collected in Koiari village, Kagua Sub-district, Southern Highlands District, in 1971. Eighteen months of fieldwork among the Kewa were undertaken with the aid of a doctoral fellowship from the Canada Council, whose help is gratefully acknowledged. I am grateful to Dr. Alan Gillmor for his comments on the musicological aspects of the songs.

2 The singing is monophonic. The higher pitches of the leader's phrase (F-sharp-E) are followed by a refrain built around a falling minor third (E-C-sharp). The final repetition of the tonic note (C-sharp), after a short silence, was said to be an innovation of the Koiari singers.

3 Three kinds of brush turkey are recognized by the Kewa at Erave. These are the *ealo*, *wa*, and *pale*. The *pale*, judging from descriptions given by Rand and Gilliard, is probably the wattled brush turkey (*Aepypodius arfakianus*) while one or both of the *ealo* and *wa* is probably the common scrub hen (*Megapodius freycinet*). The *rupale* may have chosen the wattled brush turkey because it is the largest of the three and lays white eggs rather than buff or brown ones. For mention of the Megapode's importance among the Mejprat of the

\Bird's Head peninsula of Irian Jaya, see Elmberg (1968:231-2). A. and M. Strathern (1968) mention that the Melpa use the bower bird in spell imagery because of the bird's 'cultural' activity. Barth (1975) discusses the brush turkey as a metaphor for gardening among Faiwol speakers.

4   These two associations are from informants. The preceding sentence is my own inference.

5   It may be observed that 'killing pigs', which includes the construction of the *neada* and other preparations, may seem a rather diffuse interpretation of some quite concrete images. One may wish to go further and associate the female task of weaving a net bag and the male task of braiding the rope of a pig tether, or with arranging shells in a net bag for display but these meanings were not offered by informants. Had I pressed them further I believe their answers would have been improvisations.

6   But the metaphorical language is not an *other* language; it is, as we shall see, constructed from normal language. This distinguishes it from the secret 'pandanus' language observed in northern Kewa communities by Franklin (1972).

7   The slashes indicate a phonemic representation.

8   The user of metaphor has something in common with the poet who, in Sartre's words, 'once and for all has chosen the poetic attitude which considers words as things and not as signs. For the ambiguity of the sign implies that one can penetrate it at will like a pane of glass and pursue the thing signified, or turn his gaze toward its *reality* and consider it as an object. The man who talks is beyond words and near the object, whereas the poet is on this side of them (Sartre 1966:5)'.

9   There are apparent exceptions, such as the metaphor 'daughter', but even here one can argue that among patrilineal Melanesians women are viewed as more natural than men (Forge 1972:536). For the most part the remaining 'domestic' images in the *rupale* corpus — bamboo knives, bark shell-wrappings, net bags, leg or arm bands, and the like — are, to be precise, metonyms and not metaphors. The knife refers to the pig to be butchered, the bark wrappings to the pearlshell, the net bag to the woman who carries it, and so forth.

10 *Re* indeed means base, basis, origin, source, cause, or owner.

11 In support of this horticultural cannibalism one can recall the metaphorical association between trees and men. It is interesting to note that the songs frequently refer to burning the bases of hoop pines and black palms, trees which are most commonly associated with men and which would not be burnt in practice.

12 This specific association occurred to me only after I left the field, so it could not be checked. I never inquired further than noting that informants thought the *wai* were pigs and that 'bringing the *wai*' was 'bringing the pigs to kill'.

13 The idea has been developed by J.-P. Sartre (1948:58*ff.*) and by C. Lévi-Strauss (1971:588, 596 *ff.*).

14 For the notion of 'excess' in myth, *cf.* Barthes (1973:126n.).

15 I observed *mata* sung only in Koiari, 1971, and at Erave Patrol Post on two occasions. I recorded only about thirty of them. I found their translation and interpretation even more difficult than the *rupale* and, unfortunately, I relied on male informants when translating them.

16 Although an older woman is the leader, in terms of content, *mata* are clearly girls' songs.

17 They were allowed some parts, such as the entrails, but I think it is quite likely that a certain amount of the more desirable cuts found its way to them. But in principle, if not in reality, they were not given pork.

18 In Kewa myths and insults.

BIBLIOGRAPHY

Barth, Fredrik 1975: *Ritual and Knowledge among the Baktaman of New Guinea,* New Haven, Yale University Press.

Barthes, Roland 1973: *Mythologies,* St. Albans, Paladin.

Elmberg, John-Eric 1908: *Balance and Circulation: aspects of tradition and change among the Mejorat of Irish Barat,* Stockholm, Ethnographical Museum.

Fernandez, James 1974: 'The Mission of Metaphor in Expressive Culture', *Current Anthropology,* 15:119-45.

Forge, Anthony 1972: 'The Golden Fleece', *Man,* 7,4,527-40.

Franklin, Karl 1970: 'Metaphorical Songs in Kewa', *Pacific Linguistics,* Series C, 13:985-93.

_____ 1972: 'A Ritual Pandanus Language of New Guinea', *Oceania* 43:67-76.

Lévi-Strauss, Claude 1969: *The Raw and the Cooked,* New York, Harper Row.

_____ 1971: *L'Homme nu.* Paris, Plon.

Rand, A.L. and Gilliard, E.T. 1967: *Handbook of New Guinea Birds.* London, Weidenfeld and Nicolson.

Sartre, Jean-Paul 1948: *The Emotions: Outline of a Theory.* New York, Philosophical Library.

_____ 1966: *What is Literature?,* New York, Washington Square.

Strathern, A. and M. 1968: 'Marsupials and Magic', in E. Leach (ed.), *Dialectic in Practical Religion,* London, Cambridge University Press.

Dan Kochhongva's Message:
myth, ideology and political action among the contemporary Hopi[1]

SHUICHI NAGATA

I

The Hopi Indians of American Southwest have long been known for their prophecy on the return of Pahana or 'White Brother'. This prophecy is derived from their emergence myth from the underworld that, very briefly stated, consists of the following features: association of Pahana with Machito, leader of the ancestral Hopi at the time of the emergence from the Underworld, his eventual parting with Machito to the east and his promise to return to Hopiland for the final salvation of the Hopi by bringing about the destruction of troublemakers and purification of the world and thus establishing the millennium. In the Third Mesa version, both Machito and Pahana were commissioned by the Great Spirit, Ma'asau, to keep a set of stone tablets, which contains the Spirit's message and instructions to the Hopi and which is to confirm the true identity of Pahana upon his return. The tablet is said to be in the hands of a leader of Hotevilla on Third Mesa at present.

There are numerous versions of this story, which have been recorded and published by many anthropologists on Hopi culture (see Goldfrank, 1948, for some references). As these anthropologists have discussed, the prophecy has been closely intertwined with political events in Hopiland, and the identification of the Pahana turned out to be a particularly painful political issue for the Hopi Indians. I shall give a few examples to illustrate the way the prophecy has become a political issue.

Jacob Hamblin, a Mormon pioneer renowned for his adventures in southern Utah and missionary work among the Paiutes, made his first visit to Hopiland in 1857 in a company of four Mormon friends. During their stay at Oraibi, the only village on Third Mesa at that time, he was told by 'a very aged man'

> that when he was a young man, his father told him that he would live to see white men come among them, who would bring them great blessings, such as their fathers had enjoyed, and that these men would come from the west (*sic*). (Little, 1909:66)

To Hamblin's delight the story was to match the Mormon theory of the Indians as the fallen tribe of the Lamanites, whom the Mormons had been attempting to convert into 'white and delightsome people'.

Unfortunately, though, the three members of Hamblin's party, who remained in Oraibi after his return north, were compelled to leave this village without achieving much missionary success. In Hamblin's own words:

A division arose among the people as to whether we were the men prophesied of by their fathers, who would come along with them with the knowledge that their fathers possessed.

This dispute ran so high that the brethren felt that but little or no good would result from remaining longer. Besides the chief men among the Moquis (Hopi) advised their return (Little, 1909:68).

The second example is related to the disintegration of Oraibi village about half a century after Hamblin's visit. In this event, referred to as 'Revolution' by a number of contemporary Hopi of Third Mesa, one main issue revolved around the identification of Pahana with the American government which, by the beginning of this century, came to play an ever increasing role in the lives of the Hopi. The 'Friendly' faction of Oraibi maintained then that the Americans as represented by the Indian Service were the legendary Pahana, while the 'Hostiles' accused them of an erroneous identification. The true Pahana, claimed the 'Hostile' leader, Yokioma, should be able to read the sacred stone table, jealously guarded by the village chief of Oraibi (Titiev, 1944:60, 75). The result of this turmoil was the withdrawal of the 'Hostile' faction from Oraibi and the establishment of another settlement, Hotevilla, in 1906 and Bacabi and New Oraibi in subsequent years.

The factionalism which precipitated in the above event, has continued, with slight modification, until the present time and with it, the question of Pahana. Thus, during the last war, some successors of the 'Hostile' faction claimed Hitler to be the White Brother (Talayesua, 1942:379; see also *Arizona Republic*, 25 May 1941). On the other hand, the view of the successors of the 'Friendlies' has been that the Pahana issue was closed by the arrival of the American government and they are critical of the leader of the other faction for his futile search for Pahana (Hopi Hearings, 1955).

As is clear from the above examples, the Pahana prophecy is strongly reminiscent of the Montezuma legend (Prescott, 1936:171, 899), which is widespread among the Pueblo Indians of the United States in various forms. A matter of some interest, however, is the manner in which this prophecy has been managed to further the political cause of a particular faction. In what follows, I shall discuss the mechanism of 'cultural management' (Fallers, 1961:677) of this prophecy by means of my personal experience with it.

II

Before presenting my experience, however, it is necessary to appreciate some structural features of Hopi factionalism.

Since 1934, when the Hopi Tribal Council was constituted as a result of the Indian Reorganisation Act, Hopi factionalism has been organised by the adherents of the Tribal Council and those against the Council, the latter occasionally being called *aiyave* (non-conformists, 'traitors', anti-

Council). Both factions include numerous survivors of the 'Friendlies'/ 'Hostiles' conflict of Third Mesa. The membership of the two factions, on the other hand, is not very stable and aside from a small number of leaders, individual commitment to either faction varies from almost total indifference to enthusiastic support.

This fluidity in faction membership is due largely to the lack of control by either faction over the access to such meaningful economic resources as government wage work employment, education and the general consumer market. In fact, there is some evidence to indicate that the more economically independent an individual is from his community, the less involved he is in factional issues on the reservation. This is not to deny the relevance of factionalism to issues of profound economic importance — such as, for instance, the use of land for residential, farming and grazing purposes and the disposition of the tribal land resources as a whole. Recently, the latter issue became a cause for a renewed factional conflict as the Tribal Council was involved in the lease of the reservation land to an American coal mining company and in a dispute over the reservation boundary with the Navajo Tribe. However, it is at the moment rather uncertain as to what degree these issues will contribute to the increasing control of the respective factions over their membership.

Of equal importance in Hopi factionalism is the participation in religious activities, which tends to be determined according to one's factional affiliation, although here again the degree of correlation is by no means perfect and I have seen a number of Hopi taking part in the ceremonies organised by the individuals of different political persuasions.

Throughout all this ambiguity in faction membership is one further factor underlying Hopi social structure. As Ellis pointed out (1951), Hopi society consists of numerous cross-cutting lines of cleavage — clanship, kinship, affinal ties, ceremonial society membership, *kiva* (semi-underground ceremonial chamber) membership, village and so on. In addition to these traditional lines of cleavage, generational differences, educational and military experiences, and occupational ties have been important in creating further contexts for interaction. In short, these cross-cutting ties made it impossible for the factions to establish neat and clear-cut boundaries in their membership composition and contributed to the weakening of their control. They also tended to increase the transactional nexus (Mayer, 1966:116) between the faction leaders and their followers and permitted a considerable degree of side-switching on the part of the followers.

The leaders of the two factions, whom I shall refer to as Council men and Traditionals respectively, legitimate their respective leadership on the recognition of the U.S. government of the Council as the sole representative of the Hopi tribe (Council) and on the traditional order (Traditional). Ideologically the Council has so far preempted a modernisation ideology ('white man's way') and the Traditionals have chosen one that justifies the return to the old ways of life. This is a very broad generalisation of the two positions but in reality, the ideological formulation is never so explicit and uncompromising as one would suppose it to be. While the Council ideology does not totally condemn the traditional way of life, the Traditionals are not averse to admitting some advantage of modern life. On the whole, though, it would appear that the existence of the rival ideology made it difficult for the Traditionals to come up with a syncretic solution such as that which characterised the Ghost Dance or Cargo cult ideologies.

This 'nativistic' orientation of the Traditional ideology creates serious disadvantages in mobilising a wide support for their cause. First of all, the source of the Traditional ideology lies in the traditions and myths of the Hopi, which vary from one village to another. The authenticity of the Traditional ideology is, in a way, enhanced by its closeness to the tradition of a particular village and thus the more authentic it becomes, the more parochial its appeal. Secondly, for a people who were recently exposed to the material amenities of American life, some aspects of the Traditional ideology are rather less attractive. As one Hopi mentioned, 'A true Hopi is poor', hardly an enticing proposition. Because of these characteristics, the Traditionals, more than the Council men, have been confronted with a serious problem of how to manage their ideology.

Two men have been important in dealing with this problem. One of them is Dan Kochhongva, a son of Yokioma quoted above, Born in the last century, he is the Sun clan of Hotevilla, Third Mesa, an important member of the One Horn society (Titiev, 1944:130ff.). During the 1940s, he was associated with James Pohgonyuma, who was Yokioma's maternal nephew and regarded as the chief of Hotevilla after Yokioma's death in 1929 (Titiev, 1944:211). In 1941, when several Hopi youths were imprisoned for their refusal to register for military service, Dan accompanied James to appeal their case as conscientious objectors to the office of the *Arizona Republic*, a newspaper in Phoenix. After James' move to New Mexico, Dan came to be recognised as a virtual leader of Hotevilla and Third Mesa Traditions.[2] His authority derives from his position in the traditional religious system, clanship, reputed knowledge of the Hopi tradition and his descent from Yokioma. On the other hand, his knowledge of the outside world seems relatively limited and he does not speak English, though he is fluent in Navajo. When he receives outsiders, therefore, he is invariably accompanied by interpreters. He is also remarkable in his adherence to the 'traditional' way of life and he does not work for wages nor does he drive an automobile. While I was in Hopiland, he went to hospital only when his daughter and her husband forced him to do so.

Dan's 'lieutenant' is Thomas Banyacya.[3] Born in 1902, he comes from a highly acculturated family in Noenkopi, a colony village of Oraibi. His brother has been quite successful in business in Noenkopi and one of his paternal sisters belongs to a group of the earliest Christian converts; Thomas himself is one of the first Hopi to receive college education, though he did not complete it. On the other hand, his roots in traditional Hopi society are not very significant. A member of the Coyote clan, which is not very important in the assumption of ceremonial roles, he is also a member of the Kachina society, which is a minimal requirement for entry to more esoteric ones. He has been residing in New Oraibi, a Council village of Third Mesa, where his wife was born.

Thomas' background thus tends to indicate his 'marginal' locus among the Traditionals. In fact, his early political career was oriented somewhat against the traditional authority and his initiative in establishing a self-governing organisation in separation from the Moenkopi chieftainship in the late 1920s is still regarded by many as a challenge to the traditional order. During the implementation period of the Indian Reorganization Act and the Second World War, he grew disillusioned by the Indian policy of the American government and was imprisoned for his campaign against compulsory military service. Soon he changed his English surname to one of the initiation names of the Kachina society. Through these experiences, Thomas emerged as a firm right-hand man to Dan and became the most articulate of the Traditional leaders. In acting as a Traditional leader, Thomas so far has refused to assume government employment and, like Dan, been engaged in farming and weaving, only occasionally working for wages in his village.

In contrast to Dan, Thomas' leadership lies in his ability to provide contacts with the outside world for the Traditional cause. Unlike Dan, he does not possess as strong a village identity and hence can manage to create supra-village consensus without much suspicion of domination by a particular village. On the other hand, the legitimacy of his Traditional leadership is supported by Dan, who provides Thomas' ideological basis and on whose behalf Thomas is said to be working. This mutual role articulation has been important for the Traditionals, who often splinter without ever achieving unity in opposition to the Council. I am almost tempted to characterise Dan as an expressive leader and Thomas as an instrumental one.

But Thomas' role has not been limited only to politics in Hopiland. He was able to establish contacts even outside Hopiland for the Traditional cause. The two most important contacts during the 1950s were one Mohawk Indian, who organised *American Indian Restoration Enterprises*, and a retired Army general, or organised *Constitutional Provisional Government of America*. Both men have been active in promoting the Indian cause in America and aired their views through numerous mimeographed pamphlets. They have all visited Hopiland in the past and came to know both Dan and Thomas intimately. The latter were in turn invited by them to attend meetings outside Hopiland. The linkage thus established resulted in Dan's visits, with Thomas accompanying him, to the United Nations in New York, Washington, D.C., Chicago, Six Nations Reserve at Brantford, Ontario, Canada, and numerous other places in North America as well as the publication of many obscure pamphlets, in which Dan's messages were propagated.[4]

III

Since my account involves my landlady rather intimately, it may be better to give a brief description of her family at the outset. During 1962-63, I was staying at a house in Upper Moenkopi, whose family members were the supporters of Dan and Thomas. The landlady and her husband had been on the Council side until the early 1950s, when they repudiated their connection with the Council as a result of a bitter court struggle against a Council man over a piece of farm land. The landlady's father also used to be on the Council side but during the 1940s, he was reinitiated to the Hotevilla Wuwuchim society and hence to the Traditional side. Incidentally, the landlady is Thomas' distant kinswoman. Her style of life, on the other hand, is quite non-traditional with numerous electric appliances at home and this 'white man's way of life' has invited in the past some criticisms even from other Traditional followers. Her husband has been a wage earner at the Bureau of Indian Affairs at Tuba City, a nearby town, after he quit being a policeman, a job obtained through his Council connection. The landlady's son is a veteran of Korean War and has had several years of college education. Though he is sympathetic to the Traditional politics, his more serious interest in life lies in the outside world.

I had been staying in this house for about two months when I first heard Pahana being discussed among the Third Mesa Traditionals. In September 1962, there was a meeting at Hotevilla, which not only Dan and other Third Mesa Traditionals but also many outsiders attended. Incidentally this type of meeting has been held frequently in Hotevilla in the past and so the September meeting was not an unusual event in itself. This particular meeting was organised by Thomas and an Eskimo Bahai'ist, who came to know Thomas through the introduction of the Mohawk mentioned above, and who had been staying in Moenkopi for missionary purposes. Thus at the meeting, there were a few Bahai'ists but also Zuni, Navajo and Ojibwa and a few Hopi from other villages. The meeting, the first day of which I attended, was rather desultory, though it was called to pray for World Peace. There were problems of communication among the attendants and of different interests in the meeting. At any rate, it went on for two days without, it seemed, accomplishing much for world peace.

I must add that a Chinese Buddhist priest and an American Japanese interpreter also attended the meeting, both of whom were invited from Los Angeles by the Eskimo Bahai'ist and the Hopi seemed to be rather intrigued by this priest in a standard Mahayana Buddhist monk's costume. But all he did at the meeting was to go around among the Indian audience and shake hands with them. Otherwise he remained silent, without addressing the meeting, sitting quietly and wearing an inscrutable smile.

Soon after the meeting, however, the landlady's father, who also attended the meeting, broke a rather surprising piece of news to her and her husband upon his return to Moenkopi. The old man recounted that Dan had decided this Chinese priest was the Pahana and now that Dan had met the real 'White Brother', he was handing over the job of protecting the Hopi to Thomas and others, while Dan himself retired. He further added that the priest as well as his Japanese interpreter were white of skin complexion and that the priest showed tattoo marks of the sun and swastika on his chest and belly. According to the old father, the priest also whispered into Dan's ear, saying that he came to help the Hopi. While recounting all this, the father showed to the landlady and her husband the swastika mark on a Hopi gourd rattle, which was hanging on the wall of our house.

In the afternoon of the day that we were introduced to this amazing news, the old father's sister's son visited us from Hotevilla and told essentially the same story but added that the priest had told the people he would come back in the near future. My landlady was obviously rather agitated with all this and in the next morning, at the breakfast table, she reported the news to her son and asked his opinion, whereupon the son made a rather strong response to her, adding that 'white' means only 'Caucasian'.

A few days afterwards, during which time nothing of consequence happened, Thomas visited our house and the landlady took immediate advantage of it by asking him about the authenticity of the story. Thomas was undisturbed and reassured the landlady by telling her that all Dan meant was only to support Thomas in what the Traditionals had been doing. According to Thomas, the Chinese priest never said he came to help but only that he was a friend of the Hopi.

About three months passed since this meeting but the priest did not return. The Eskimo Bahai'ist, in the meantime, left Hopiland and was no longer heard of. The Traditionals on Third Mesa appeared to be preoccupied with the more pressing matters of winter ceremonials and a government project that was going on in Moenkopi. They seemed oblivious of the Hotevilla meeting and the Chinese priest.

One day in December, two men came from Hotevilla to our house and told the landlady that they wanted me to write a letter to the general, previously mentioned. I must point out here that I have been helping various members of the Traditional faction write letters to various quarters and I acquired by this time sort sort of reputation which apparently spread to other villages in Hopiland. I am also a Japanese. These factors may have disposed Dan favourably toward me and induced him to enlist my service. In fact, some time ago, my landlady told me of Dan's comment upon my helpfulness. I have no means to determine, however, how much these factors contributed to the event that subsequently developed.

At any rate, Dan brought on this visit two letters, written by the general, in which the latter stated his determination to go to the Soviet Embassy in Washington, D.C., and secure their help to bring justice to the American Indians. As the landlady explained to me, Dan had recently come to identify the 'Red Ants' and 'Thin Eyed Ones' in Hopi prophecy with the Russians and the Chinese and held that they were to cause the Purification of the world prior to the reunion of the Hopi with the 'White Brother'.[5] Hence the general's plan. The two letters were dated June, 1962, and the landlady translated them to Dan. In the course of her translation, she asked me if the Japanese were on the side of communism, a difficult question to answer as there are some communists in Japan. I said the Japanese government is not communist and this she conveyed to Dan.

Then Dan wanted me to write a letter to the general supporting his plan, but the landlady somehow managed to dissuade him from this by suggesting to Dan that he should make sure if he did not possess any more recent communications from the general. All these conversations were mediated by the landlady as I could not speak Hopi.

That evening, at dinner, the landlady asked her husband about the identities of the two characters as well as Pahana but the husband said that the time was not yet ripe to reveal all these. My landlady seemed to be relieved to hear this and regretted the general's attempt to influence Dan.

Soon after this incident, I met Thomas in New Oraibi and told of our meeting with Dan. Thomas then said that all this talk about the Russians and the Chinese and the general's plan were due to some of the radical members of Dan's *kiva*, who always wanted to 'stir things up'. He also added that there were some points in the prophecy itself which have not been revealed yet, for instance, the identity of the 'Mother of the Hopi' and the 'White Brother'; that different variations of the prophecy from one village to another make the interpretation of the prophecy difficult. He mentioned finally that the ultimate test of the identity of the 'White Brother' should be the sacred stone tablet, since whoever is the 'White Brother' should carry a matching tablet and be able to read the Hopi counterpart of the tablet.

I did not see Dan until the next year. Since his first visit, Dan appeared in our house twice; once, when all but the son and myself were absent. Dan obviously wanted to know more about the exact nature of those letters but with the not-so-sympathetic son explaining, he did not seem to obtain any help for his own plan. The third time he showed up, he told the landlady that he was on his way to meet his friend in Moenkopi. I detected a bit of coolness on the part of my landlady and furtiveness on Dan's in this brief encounter. Half jokingly, I asked the landlady if she would be willing to follow Dan when he decided to become 'communist' and she said, with some emotion, 'No!'.

All this happened, I must point out, during Christmas and the performance of Wuwuchim and Soyal ceremonies. Soon after Dan's first visit, in fact, the landlady's family was busy with Christmas preparations and I, in turn, was asked by Thomas to distribute some sashes he had made to other villages. And when the new year began and winter Kachina dances started, Moenkopi was involved in a sudden conflict with the Navajo Tribal Council because the sewer lagoons of the latter at Tuba City were partially damaged and the sewer began to flow into Hopi farms, thus raising the fear of 'contamination'.[6] In these frantic times, Dan's concern appeared to lose any urgency and nothing seemed to emerge from his several visits to Moenkopi.

Then, one afternoon in March, Dan appeared to us unannounced. He looked more determined this time and after a somewhat impassioned exchange between him and the landlady, the latter asked her son and me to help him write letters — to, as she said to us, 'Khrushchev' and the *mongwi* (chiefs) of Japan and China. I brought out a Philips portable tape-recorder and Dan dictated his messages to the machine. Dan stayed with us until supper that day, and in the evening left for Hotevilla in a car driven by a Hopi from Shongopavi. Three days later, I asked the unwilling son to translate the message (see Appendix) but I did not compose any letter. Neither the landlady nor the son objected to my not writing the letters.

About a month passed before this tape was played back to Thomas on the occasion of his visit to Moenkopi. The landlady had told him of Dan's visit and asked him to listen to the tape. Later Thomas told me not to write the letters because, as he stated, Dan was being influenced by some members of his *kiva*. He said he would explain about these matters to Dan and repeated what he told me previously about the revelation. As for the general, Thomas said he had little to do with the Hopi.

I was not to meet Dan again personally and although I heard of his leading a struggle against the government's introduction of electricity to Hotevilla (see Clemmer, 1972:237-9 for its later development), all I saw of him was from a distance at two meetings in his village. I also sensed that Thomas and the landlady were not altogether happy about my association with Dan. Besides I felt guilty for not fulfilling my promise to Dan. Dan's position as the leader of Hotevilla and Hopi Traditionals, on the other hand, seemed secure enough as I left Hopiland in the fall of that year.

IV

I mentioned previously that the ideological orientation of the Traditionals is 'nativistic' because the Council preempted an ideology of modernisation. The symbols of the Traditional ideology are derived from Hopi cultural tradition and mark the boundary of the Traditionals from the Council men. An additional feature of these symbols, particularly that of Pahana, is that they direct the attention of the Traditionals in search of external support and thus alleviate their alienation from an otherwise hostile world. They define and legitimate the probable source of the external support.

I believe this sense of alienation and isolation among some old Traditional Hopi is quite real, especially when one reflects upon the possible psychological consequences of the experience, over half a century or so, of a growing discord in a small tribe of only 3,000 people. These people are being increasingly 'confined', as Dan's message says, in a tightly defined territory, by encroaching Navajo settlement and the presence of the powerful United States government, which have steadily been eroding the familiar basis of their very existence for a lifetime of these people. No words of admiration alone can do sufficient justice to the stubborn courage of these men in resisting the pressures of the environment so as to uphold 'Hopi way' and to await the return of Pahana. In this perspective, the search for Pahana appears to be a functional equivalent of the early Calvinist pursuit of this worldly signs of *certitudo salutis*, which according to Max Weber, is 'the origin of all psychological drives of a purely religious character' (1958:228, also see 109-12; Gerth and Mills, 1958:277-8). I submit this to be the basis for the psychological relevance of the symbols to the contemporary Traditions.

But the search for Pahana is dependent upon an empirical confirmation, which is not an easy enterprise in the case of the Traditional ideology. Geertz once suggested that the life of an ideology is dependent on the availability of not only scientific means to assess its empirical claims but also competing ideologies (1964:72-3). Dobyns and Euler showed, on the other hand, how, in the absence of an external threat of force, the Ghost Dance movement among the Pai Indians disappeared through its repeated failure to realise its supernatural claims (1967:3-35). As Festinger pointed out, a belief that compels flagrant contradictions with daily experience may be supported only through extraordinary social cohesion of the believers or through equally extraordinary, perceptive distortions (1956). On the other hand, a belief that may not overtly challenge mundane experience is generally difficult to refute. Thus Dostoyevsky's Grand Inquisitor postpones the millennium in order to avert the collapse of the church authority and to maintain the validity of the belief system. Worsley showed this to be the case in the more sober kinds of Cargo cult movements in Melanesia (1957a:149, 192; Mair, 1959). In short, for a belief and the symbols contained in the belief to be effective, they must be relevant to experience, but not so relevant as to invite obvious empirical disproof.

Such Traditional symbols as the swastika, 'sun', 'thin eyes', 'red ones' and 'White Brother' are, in this connection, all so vague as to be vehicles of any number of possible objects. The stone tablets, regarded as the ultimate check of Pahana, are, according to some outside observers and their descriptions (Titiev, 1944:60-1; Waters, 1963:32-3), also so obscure that they are an enigma even to the Hopi. All these symbols are thus pretty far removed from the possibility of any interpretation that can be agreed upon throughout the community. By so stating, I am in no way denying the significance of these symbols. In fact, I am inclined to believe that the Hopi tablets are just as genuine as those that supported the charisma of Moses and Joseph Smith. In the absence of such a charismatic leader in contemporary Hopi society, and the difficulty of unitary interpretation, however, it may also be understandable why they have become an object of political management for those involved in the factional conflict with the Tribal Council.

The political management of these symbols is necessary because, in addition to the interpretative question, they also provide the boundary of the Traditional faction, a point already stated, but at the same time because the symbols rely for their validity upon the tradition alone. This generates the question of the 'authenticity' of the meanings of the symbols which may vary among Hopi village communities. In contrast to the Cargo myths, which adopted symbols of a wider relevance and thus succeeded in the integration of the society beyond discrete segmental interests (Worsley, 1957b:348), the Hopi traditional ideology is confronted with the dilemma of becoming too parochial by becoming too authentic (cf. Fallers, 1961). To put it somewhat differently, overcommunication of the ideological message endangers its appeal to a wider constituency on the one hand, while its undercommunication jeopardises its cohesion. This question becomes more urgent to the Hopi Traditionals, who find themselves in the condition of contact I elsewhere called 'accommodation' (1968). The account given in the previous section illustrates it somewhat more precisely.

As previously pointed out, the leaders of the two factions do not control access to the resources to which many Hopi are attracted nowadays. Thus, although the Traditional leaders avoid assuming government wage work, the use of automobiles and electricity at home, they cannot coerce all the members of the faction to do the same. They are perfectly correct in arguing that one of the causes of the recent troubles in Hopi society is the introduction of money, but to live without it would call for superhuman efforts, even in present Hopiland, and only Dan has succeeded in doing so. Under these circumstances, the Traditional leaders are compelled to tread rather softly in their ideological discipline of the faction membership.

A delicate question emerges in this connection, regarding the relationship between the Traditional ideology and 'communism'. In some ways, the relationship is not so far-fetched when one reminds oneself of the communal features of Hopi traditional life and, in fact, Thomas once drafted a proposal for a Hopi money system (AIRE, 1961:24-6), which is somewhat reminiscent of a coupon system. The absence of private property in land in Hopi social institutions has been commented upon often enough. What is interesting to me is that these substantive similarities are expressed in Thomas' writings and in Dan's symbolic behaviours as a protest against the social system that has been confronting the Hopi for almost a century and that the source of this protest lies in their own cultural tradition.

But this very similarity poses itself as a threatening proposition to many other Hopi attracted to the material temptations of American society. Besides the access to American affluence has been for many Hopi through government employment, which they believe prohibits them from taking part in political activities. The experience in government employment also exposes the Hopi to the broad policy orientation of American government and its propaganda, which has, to everyone's knowledge, been anti-communistic. Thus, in Hopiland, to be called 'communist' has been one of the worst things that can happen to one's life and the Council faction has not hesitated to so characterise the Traditionals in the past, while the Traditionals call the Council a 'totalitarian dictatorship'. Although these exchanges do not demonstrate deep comprehension of the concepts used, there seems no doubt that a connection between anti-'communism', American government and government employment is clearly perceived by a majority of the Hopi. In this atmosphere, Dan's action, presented in the previous section, is impolitic to say the least and precisely because of its political implication, Thomas stepped in.

In a discussion on the definition of religion, Robin Horton described two ways of subscribing to a religion — commitment to a religious belief (Tylorian) and commitment to a social system symbolised in the brief (Durkheimian) (1960:203-4). It is our common experience that the two more often than not diverge and to us, familiar with a multiplicity of religions in contemporary society, my landlady's reaction is not unusual. Who, among us, would be prepared to abandon our familiar routine upon the arrival of the millennium here and now! If Dan was to be admired for his religious commitment, it was to Thomas' credit that the organisation of the Traditional faction was kept intact through this minor crisis in Hopi factionalism.

APPENDIX

The following is a slightly edited version of the translation from Dan Kochhongva's message, recorded in Moenkopi on March 8, 1963. It was addressed to the heads of Russia, China and Japan respectively.

I am from this village, Hotevilla, and I am a leader and I also know the instructions well. And so I shall tell about the path we are taking along with the dragging [suffering]. There is somebody who is standing behind us — our brother, our white brother. It is said that we get to a place where we are exploited and then we shall look for him. This is the way it is in the Hopi instructions and I have reached that point. And so I shall go by my knowledge of instructions and also in the name of Dan Kochhongva, which is my name, and also in the name of the one who is unseen and his instructions, namely Maasau and his instructions which I have never doubted and so I have come this far. And so going by his instructions, I now reach the point where I shall go look for him. And so I am here in Moenkopi, where I am telling this. I am not speaking at home, I am not speaking at a gathering as I am speaking confidentially.

However, I liked the world. It is a fact that I was here first in this world. The people of my same skin throughout the world who inhabit the reaches of the earth along with me, all these people I am not leaving out. These many people I am now observing and as they, along with me, suffer, this fact our instructions have, this white brother in it, the one who will stand up for us and so I am speaking to this boy, who will work on this thing for me and how he will, if any, hear an answer. So you hear my story.

I know my instructions well. I know how things will come out to the front. It is because I know these well that I have not been lured to the new ways of the government. I have not erred. I know much. That is why I shall let you know now.

Those of you across the seas, those of you across the seas, those of you who live on the continents and lands, I look to you. But it is you who are in the centre, who, in our instructions, are called the 'red one', whom we came to know as Russia, and also the one who has the Sun for a symbol, whom I do not know the name for, the short people who have the same head and appearance as we, and also this swastika-like symbol (*moeha*), which never ceases to exist on this earth, this cross which the Hopi call *moeha*, which has a useful purpose on this earth, so that the earth may be encouraged on, so that the Hopi shall always go by his faith. This is how it is, this is why I am telling you. And so, if you get my message, you, who are in the centre, the one called 'red', will be called upon to work for us. That is why I call on you specifically and so, if you get this message, gather yourself and think it over and see if I am not speaking correctly or similar to your own instructions. I am willing because it is said you would be waiting. This is in our instructions. I am willing because it is said you would be waiting. This is in our instructions. That is why I am not scared while I am telling you this.

We have suffered much because of this way of the government and so now I tell you this. However, this will not get too far. Those of us who have suffered, remember this brother of ours, who shall come to our aid. This is what we are waiting for, all of us, people, throughout. That is why I ask you this. So gather together and think about this — if there is one thing similar to yours. It does not have to be exactly the same and all to your instructions for they will all come out true. Then, when you gather there and think it over, and if you feel that I who know all these things, should go over there in person and should tell you — if you want this, then I shall do it. There shall be this person who shall be my tongue and ears and the one also who has been waiting for these things, shall go with me. Then the one, who has suffered and who is willing, shall be my ear. Then there, I shall tell this which I have suffered, how we separated, I shall tell completely throughout. I am just asking now. That is why I am not telling the whole story. This much with which I am to find my awaited brother. That is what I say.

However, we have gone through scary ways, that which is made up and which will destroy us. This is why I hasten and I suffered confinement. Now I find myself in old age. It is with this prolonged confinement that I find my hair white but I have gone this far. I have been waiting to tell this to someone. But nobody is living without cause. It is a fact that we will not doubt the instructions from someone. This is what we know, those of us throughout the world. So think about it. I have not doubted these instructions and I have gone this far. So I tell without fear. If I had erred somewhere, I would not be telling this now. I have gone to everything.

However, it is only this, the Sun, my guide, which guides and helps at all times, to be strong, shall be with me, with us. Then this 'red one', whose lifepath is made, then the one to the front, this 'red one' in the front of the bow, which is our blood, which we prepare for a child who is not yet corrupt or baptised. Then this rattle, I also prepare this for the child, in the centre of which there is this 'swastika' — so-called by the younger generation. Then this girl, the conceiver — for her, this rattle is green in the centre. It represents the young shoots of the grass. This *homina*, which is eaten during the winter and which is pretty. It represents us. Then this bow, whose front represents two things — *powaka* (devil, witch, 'two-hearts',) *nupkana* [Voth translates this as 'dangerous' — 1905:12] and *kenitionikat* (meaning unclear). That is why it has red ends. But if we reach it without giving up, we shall be cleansed. The devil's head will be taken off. Then everlasting life shall prevail, happiness will prevail and then we shall all be brothers for we are of one kind by the same maker and so we finally get together as brothers. There we shall all help each other and that which will be of benefit to us all will be available. This is in our instructions and this is what I tell you.

And so this shall be enough for this time, so think about it and if you should call me, I shall go. I shall go from my village. With whom I shall go, with what I shall go and how to shrink the world and how I shall accomplish all this, shall be taken care of. I have not erred anywhere. I want to fulfil my instructions. That is why I am letting you know. This should be about all.

However, when you receive this, when you have read my message, be happy among yourselves. Let us be happy toward ourselves. Then let us look towards this happy day of happiness among ourselves, among everyone, the purification day of everlasting life. With that, we shall brace ourselves. Then from there on, life will not be destroyed. This is called everlasting life and this is what I want. This will be all for this time.

NOTES

1   Based on a paper presented to the staff seminar of the Department of Anthropology, University of Toronto, in January 1968. Grateful acknowledgement is made to S.B. Philpott, whose detailed comments upon the original paper were most helpful.

2   For chieftainship of Hotevilla, see Titiev (1944:211). Dan is spoken of by the Hotevilla people as a 'religious leader', 'adviser', and 'chief' (*Mongwi*) but never as a village chief (*kikwimongwi*). His photograph appears in Yamada (1957:38).

3   The Hopi names, including *Thomas*, are spelt according to how they appeared in various publications. There is no standardised way of spelling Hopi names, including in the government census. I follow Voegelin and Voegelin (1957) with some modification in transcribing Hopi words. *Ng* is thus pronounced as *ng* in *bring*, while *oe* is an *umlaut* of *o* in *German* and an apostrophe is for a glottal stop.

4   Some of these publications are mentioned in references under *AIRE* (1961) and Yamada (1957).

5   I could not find any reference to the 'Red Ants' and the 'Thin Eyed Ones' in the published accounts of Hopi prophecy I collected. The closest reference to these is in *The Hopi Message*, edited by Thomas Banyacya, and in the following context: '310. It is known that our *true white brother* when he comes will be all powerful and he will wear *red cap or red cloak* ... 311. With him there will be *two great ones* ... one of which will have a symbol or sign of *swastika* ... 313. The Third One or the Second One of the two helpers to our true White Brother will have a sign of a symbol of *sun* ... 314. When the time of Purification Day is near those with these signs, Swastika and Sun, will shake the earth first for a short period of time in preparation for the final day of Purification ... 315. If these *three* failed to fulfill their mission then the *one* from the *west* will come like a big storm. He will be many, many people, and unmerciful One. When he comes he will cover the land like ants' (Banyacya, 1961:32-3). Incidentally, the text from which the above excerpt is drawn is entitled: *Letter from Thomas Banyacya, Oraibi Village, to Germany*, 12 January 1961.

6   Hopi farmers do not use fertilisers in their farming and are very fastidious about keeping their farms clean.

BIBLIOGRAPHY

Aire 1961: 'American Indian Restoration Enterprises'. Bulletin No. 2 September 2, place of publication unknown.

Arizona Republic 1941: May 25, Phoenix.

Banyacya, Thomas 1961: 'The Hopi Message' (mimeographed). Oraibi.

Clemmer, Richard O. 1972: 'Resistance and the Revitalisation of Anthropologists; A New Perspective on Cultural Change and Resistance', *In* Dell H. Hymes (ed.) *Reinventing Anthropology*. New York.

Dobyns, Henry F. and Euler, Robert C. 1967: *The Ghost Dance of 1889 among the Pai Indians of North-western Arizona*. Prescott, Arizona.

Ellis, Florence Hawley 1951: 'Patterns of Aggression and the War Cult in South-western Pueblos, *Southwestern Journal of Anthropology*, 7:177-201.

Fallers, L.A. 1961: 'Ideology and Culture in Uganda Nationalism', *American Anthropologist*, 63:677-86.

Festinger 1956: *When Prophecy Fails*. University of Minnesota Press.

Geertz, Clifford 1964: 'Ideology as a Cultural System', *in* D. Apter (ed.), *Ideology of Discontent*. New York.

Gerth, H.H. and Wright Mills, C. 1958: *From Max Weber*. Oxford University Press.

Goldfrank, Esther S. 1948: 'The Impact of Situation and Personality on Four Hopi Emergence Myth', *Southwestern Journal of Anthropology*, 4:241-62.

Hopi Hearings 1955: Hopi Hearings, conducted by a team appointed by Commissioner of Indian Affairs, BIA Phoenix Area Office. Phoenix, Arizona.

Horton, Robin, 1960: 'A Definition of Religion, and its Uses', *Journal of the Royal Anthropological Institute*, 90:201-26.

Little, James A. 1909: *Jacob Hamblin* (*Narrated Autobiography of Jacob Hamblin*). Salt Lake City.

Mair, Lucy P. 1959: 'Independent Religious Movements in Three Continents', *Comparative Studies in Society and History*, 1:113-36.

Mayer, Adrian G. 1966: 'The Significance of Quasi-Groups in the Study of Complex Societies', Michael Banton (ed.), *The Social Anthropology of Complex Societies*, ASA Monograph No. 4, London.

Nagata, Shuichi 1968: 'Accomodative Context of Moenkopi Factionalism', unpublished ms.

Prescott, William H. 1936: *History of the Conquest of Mexico and Peru*. New York.

Talayesva, Don C. 1942: *Sun Chief: the autobiography of a Hopi Indian* (ed. Leo. W. Simmons). New Haven.

Titiev, Mischa 1944: 'Old Oraibi', *Papers of the Peabody Museum of American Archaeology and Ethnology*, 22,1-277.

Voegelin, Carl F. and Voegelin, Florence M. 1957: 'Hopi Domains'. *Memoirs of the International Journal of American Linguistics*. Indiana University Publications in Anthropology and Linguistics.

Voth, H.R. 1905: 'The Traditions of the Hopi'. *Field Columbian Museum Publication*, 96 (*Anthropological Series, Vol.8*).

Waters, Frank 1963: *Book of the Hopi*. New York.

Weber, Max 1958: *The Protestant Ethic and the Spirit of Capitalism*. New York.

Worsley, Peter 1957a: *The Trumpet Shall Sound: A Study of 'Cargo' Cults in Melanesia*. London.

———— 1957b: 'Millenarian Movements in Melanesia', *The Rhodes-Livingstone Journal*, 21,18-31.

Yamada, George (ed.) 1957: *The Great Resistance: A Hopi Anthology*. New York.

Divinations and Decisions: *multiple explanations for Algonkian scapulimancy*

ADRIAN TANNER

Cognitive, Ecological and Sociological Theorizing

The use of divination rites during hunting by various Indian groups in the Canadian sub-arctic is well known, due initially to the distributional studies of Cooper (1928, 1936), and to the detailed ethnographic work of Speck (1935). The principal technique described by Speck is called scapulimancy, in which a flat bone of an animal, usually the shoulder blade, is burnt and the resulting marks interpreted to provide information, most often about the location of game or the outcome of a future hunt. Speck's description is given without any theoretical conclusions in a chapter which includes information on several other forms of divination, although none in such thorough detail. But it would be misleading to say that Speck provides no analysis of divination. Everything Speck says about the various techniques of divination is presented so as to confirm the overall analysis of the religion of the Montagnais-Naskapi, an analysis which is to be found elsewhere in the monograph.

Speck's data have since been used in two further studies of scapulimancy, neither of which challenged Speck's approach, but both of which provided quite different interpretations. O.K. Moore tried to show that scapulimancy was functionally adaptive, on ecological grounds, to Montagnais-Naskapi hunting (Moore, 1957). G.K. Park placed the same data within the framework of a general theory of divination, one in which group structure and leadership are the dominant explanatory factors (Park, 1963). Both of these articles are explicit contributions to branches of theory which remain important today, cultural ecology in the case of Moore, and sociological functionalism in the case of Park. Both articles have beenwidely reprinted, and have no doubt been influential. Speck's monograph, although it is an extraordinary piece of work, has not been influential as theory, but it can be shown to embody something of the approach, if not the methodology, of what is now called 'cognitive anthropology'.

In this article I will examine these three approaches to the use of divination by hunters, and offer some new material on the subject. I began field research into the use of ritual by hunters of the Mistassini and Nichicun bands in northern Quebec with the working assumption that the constraints of an ecosystem and the constraints of human modes of understanding must be seen as existing in some kind of interrelationship. However, the tendency in the field was to think out each problem twice: once to consider the significance of behaviour in terms of the material

89

circumstances, and a second time in order to work out the significance in terms of native categories of thought and native symbolism. I was unable to see how all of the cognitive significance could be generated out of the material conditions, or how the ecological adaptiveness could be derived from the belief system alone. My present view of this difficulty is that it derives from the fact the attempt was made to incorporate two developed systems. It is more fruitful to see the integration of material and cognitive factors within a culture at the much more basic level of specific elements. For this reason my examination of the previous analyses of Algonkian divination is undertaken not merely to reject arguments that appear unsound, but also to break down, as it were, those parts of the arguments that remain, in order that they may be incorporated into a more powerful analysis.

The aim, then, is to uncover a rationality which incorporates the material exigencies of survival and group life at the same time as it generates the essential features of the way the group explains events to itself. This is not to say that the magical view of the way the world operates does not directly contradict the view of the world as an ecosystem. However, the gap between these two views can be lessened if we begin by using the categories which the group itself uses to conceptualize material conditions. This folk classification can be shown to relate closely to the way the group regularly interacts with the environment, that is with its system of production. At the same time, the system of folk classification can be seen as imposing an outline within which the folk system of explanation is formulated. We may take as the underlying characteristic of this system that it is ideological, meaning that it makes leaps of logic in order to connect facts so as to reach conclusions beyond a simple summation of the ideas which it takes account of, and that these conclusions have implications for further human action. The disparity between objective conditions and subjective beliefs is in part a result of an ethnocentric illusion of objectivity, and can also in part be accounted for by a general tendency to remake the world in a more satisfactory way.

The foregoing outline of the direction of study goes far beyond any possible conclusions that might be arrived at in the present work. It stands as an explanation of why it now seems important to discuss together what have previously appeared as a number of incompatible approaches to the understanding of divination.

A Religion of Divination

We have already mentioned that Speck presents the scapulimancy data in the context of a whole series of divinatory practices, most of which refer specifically to the outcome of hunting activities. The others include scrying (that is, divination by gazing into a pool of water, a mirror or a bright or decorated object) and a number of rites which, like scapulimancy, involve the manipulation of animal bones as oracles, e.g. the tibia and the innominate of the beaver, a bear's patella, the mandible or clavicle of certain fish, the skull of a muskrat and the paws of an otter. He also mentions divination by dreaming, by drumming and singing (activities which are also forms of offerings to spirits), and by the playing of various games. This list might be extended by reference to other published material on Algonkian magic, and to my own field notes. Speck considered this material so central that he said, 'Theirs is almost wholly a religion of divination' (1935:127).

In Speck's view, Montagnais-Naskapi religion is essentially an intellectual activity of the individual hunter, and is a direct extension of the hunger's ideas about his subsistence. 'Obtaining subsistence solely by the chase, they have worked out a spiritualist system as complete and as artificial for gaining control over animal spirits as their hunting devices and weapons are effective in accomplishing the physical slaughter of game' (ibid: 15). The system is not learned from elders, has no standardized formulas, but is, according to Speck, discovered 'by a process of individual experience interpreted out of the background of suggestion levelled upon the mind of the native by the tribally-inherited pattern'. (ibid:18). Speck noted a lack of communal religious belief and performance, which he attributed to the lack of large and sedentary communities (ibid:20).

Individuality is central to Montagnais-Naskapi religion for Speck in the additional sense that all religious activities are seen as dominated by the independent 'soul spirit' of each individual person. The hunter caters to the needs of this personal spiritual being, and is rewarded by him, for instance by receiving information useful in his hunting activities. A person's wishes and will power are thought of as emanating from the soul spirit, and are in themselves sources of power. Speck says that 'autistic thought and behaviour become dominant factors of life' (ibid:44).

According to Speck, scapulimancy derives from a system of beliefs about a process of interaction which takes place between two kinds of spirits: the soul spirit of the individual hunter, and a number of spiritual beings, particularly the 'animal masters', which control the various game animals. This intellectual process of interaction parallels the physical one which takes place between the hunger and his prey. It is as if the hunt takes place twice. The first takes place at the spiritual level, when the soul spirit gains information about the location of the game and passes it on to the receptive hunter, by means of a dream or a vision. The hunter then undertakes a divination, which clarifies for him the details of the game and its location. In other words, the essential details of the hunt are believed to be found expressed symbolically in the oracle. Following this the second, physical enactment of the hunt plays out at the mundane level what has already been revealed spiritually.

While Speck is known in other publications for his work on the social organization of Algonkian hunters, he treats the religion, including divination, as a phenomenon which is played out at the level of the individual. The fact that there are no large permanent groups does not mean that there is no social life for hunters, or no group rites. Hunting divination, for example, takes place publicly and involves the whole residential group of at least four to twelve adults. Speck, moreover, fails to include in his account of divination a rite which is especially public in nature when conducted for the purpose of hunting prediction, one which has often been reported as occurring during summer gatherings. This is the 'shaking tent' ceremony, which Savard has called 'le rituel le plus spectaculaire de cette religion de chasseurs' (1971:8, fn. 3), and which well illustrates the parallel already referred to between the prior interaction of spirits followed by the mundane actions of men in hunting. Speck did not include the shaking tent as part of the religion because he considered it to be 'professional conjuring' as opposed to 'unprofessional, or individual conjuring — the minor individual rites' (1935:48). Here we see that his assumptions about individuality lead him to neglect a form of divination which in many ways completes the picture given by his other material.

In the shaking tent ceremony, a shaman[2] enters a small cylindrical tent at night, around which the rest of the group is seated. In most parts of the Quebec-Labrador region with which Speck was concerned the host spirit of the tent, whom the shaman uses as an intermediary to contact initially and to communicate with, is called *mista:pew*. This is the same term which Speck uses for the soul spirit of the individual, and which he translates as 'Great Man'. Although there is a considerable variety in the other spirits which appear in the tent, and the different divinations and tricks which are performed, according to the various accounts of the ceremony, one very common feature is a fight which takes place between *mista:pew* and one of the spirits which is the master of a class of animals, usually the bears. The victory of *mista:pew* is said to be the indication that in the future men will be able to kill bears. Here again we see the idea expressed of the hunt played twice: once at the level of an interaction between two spirits in the context of divination, one spirit representing the hunter and the other representing the animal; and a second time, at the level of the physical encounter between the hunter and the game.

Speck describes *mista:pew* unambiguously as the soul spirit of the individual hunter, but other ethnographic sources from this region suggest that the concept is more complicated (Flannery 1939, Preston 1971, Vincent 1973). Apart from the individual soul spirit, and the shaking tent host, the term is used to refer to a spiritual being who resides in the forest and who assists hunters seeking his help, and to any of a variety of spiritual beings appearing in the shaking tent who may either help or harm men. While the concept does not have a standardized single reference throughout the area, it appears that Speck's fascination with the individualistic nature of Montagnais-Naskapi religion again allowed him to overlook important social aspects of the beliefs underlying divination.

This emphasis on individuality does correctly reflect the ideological thrust of the folk explanations of religious behaviour which are often heard from informants. Each hunter by himself is theoretically capable of exercising power through direct contact with spirits, just as every adult man is capable of killing all game animals. Such an ideological position is held even though in fact men always hunt cooperatively, and at times collectively. Collective hunting is almost always used in the case of those animals for which divination is employed. Men differ in the extent to which they seek powers and communicate with spirits; there can also be observed differential rates of success as between individuals, both in material productivity and gift giving, and in the use of spiritual power. Such differences may be the source of tensions within the group, and such matters are usually glossed over.

Speck's approach to Montagnais-Naskapi religion may be seen as cognitive, in the sense that his analysis is founded on native beliefs. However, the beliefs which he has taken to be fundamental must unfortunately be seen as ideological conclusions.

The Conquest of Judgement

Like Speck, Moore looks at scapulimancy as the essentially individual act of a hunter trying to find out ahead of time the location of the animals he wishes to kill. The answer which is provided by the oracle, Moore argues, is a randomly selected direction. The following of such a direction, rather than the choosing of a location according to his judgement as to where game is most likely to be found, could improve the hunter's chance of success. Moore sees a problem with choices based on judgement: 'like all people, ... [the Montagnais-Naskapi] can be victimized by their own habits; in particular, habitual success in hunting certain areas may lead to depletion of the game supply — it may lead, that is, to success-induced failure' (1957:72). By turning instead to the decision of the oracle they can bypass the effect of their judgement and preferences, and follow instead a pattern of hunting in random directions.

Moore's theory assumes that divination is used to decide hunting locale when and only when other methods of finding the location of game have failed. 'When the Naskapi do have information about the location of game, they tend to act on it. Ordinarily, it is when they are uncertain and food supplies get low that they turn to the oracle for guidance' (ibid:71). This assumption is not entirely warranted, however.

The timing of hunting divination is an important question, for which few empirical data are available. Speck says that he was told by Seven Islands Indians that they consult the shoulder blade oracle frequently when there is a shortage of food (1935:151). Henriksen, who worked with the Naskapi after the time when they had abandoned the practice of scapulimancy, says that it was used only in times of extreme uncertainty. This presumably was what he was told by informants (1973:30). Hunters of the Mistassini and Nichicun bands told me that using scapulimancy too often was frowned upon, as this was considered to be making fun of the rite. We do not have enough data to indicate that scapulimancy is only used at times when hunters do not have any information about the location of game, and have a great need for food. Speck's account gives the impression that scapulimancy was used fairly often. Comeau's description of a scapulimancy, one apparently not put on simply for his benefit, indicates that use was made of the shoulder blade of a caribou of which the carcass was butchered the same day, indicating that a shortage of meat was not a necessary condition (quoted in Speck 1935:148-9). My observations of approximately twenty scapulimancies used in hunting groups of the Nichicun and Mistassini bands indicate that the rite need not be, and was never in my experience, held under conditions of a shortage of food and a lack of information about where animals were likely to be found. Divination is not used before every hunt, but is used at intervals, usually to coincide with a change in activity or location by the group.

Moore makes two other challengable assumptions, that hunters using their judgement tend to return to the location of an earlier kill, and that game animals tend to avoid such places. These assumptions seem far too sweeping to cover even the few species hunted by the Montagnais-Naskapi. It would seem to be appropriate, therefore, to place this in the context of an overview of the key ecological features of the region, as they relate to hunting techniques and to the practice of divination. In particular, there is a major ecological contrast which marks two quite different forms of hunting adaptation.

Speck shows that in Quebec-Labrador the practice of scapulimancy is found in two variant forms. Moreover, the distribution of these forms conforms in the most part to the major ecological contrast. Among what Speck calls 'the bands to the south and west' (i.e. the eastern Cree, and the western Montagnais) the oracle is the bone of any of a number of small or large game animals, according to the preferences of the person performing the rite, and its prediction may refer to any of various future events, not only the outcome of hunting. There is, furthermore, a belief that only men with special power are able successfully to use the bones of the moose or caribou. Finally, in this region no prompting dream prior to the divination is obligatory (1935:140, 146, 150). With the 'bands to the north and east' (i.e. the Naskapi and the eastern Montagnais) the oracle refers exclusively to hunting, and tends to be an entirely pictographic indication of the location of the game. It is performed by practically all hunters, who tend to use caribou scapulars exclusively. A prompting dream prior to the divination is obligatory (ibid:147-8, 150).

The ecological contrast is reflected in two subsistence patterns. Beaver, fish and solitary big game animals (i.e. moose and/or woodland caribou) are the major food sources in the southwest part, while barren ground caribou in large herds and fish are the dominant sources in the northwest (cf. Rogers 1967). The distinction is roughly co-terminous with that between closed-crown boreal forest, as opposed to lichen forest and barren ground. An exception to this is in the region of the eastern Montagnais, north of the Gulf of St Lawrence, which lies for the most part within closed-crown forest. However, hunters from these bands are dependant on hunting herds of barren ground caribou in the northern margins of their territory, and they seldom hunt solitary big game, since moose do not occur in quantity east of Seven Islands.

This contrast results in two kinds of hunting productivity, small groups scattered throughout the area in the southwest, as opposed to more nomadic groups which came together at places of caribou concentration at various times during the year in the northeast. The question of whether hunters return to the places of earlier kills has a different significance in each of the two regions. In the southwest a pattern of rotation of hunting locations from year to year is used, both within the general area to which a group tends to return annually, and between such areas, through an exchange of hunting privileges with other hunters (Tanner 1973). In the whole of Quebec-Labrador, as Moore himself points out, the movement of hunting camps is a frequent occurrence (1957:464-5). However, in the case of migratory game which are found in large groups, like the barren ground caribou or waterfowl such as geese, hunting at favoured locations rather than on a random pattern is essential.

Like Moore's theory, the Montagnais-Naskapi are concerned over the idea of not being able to locate game. Starvation in the past is known to have been caused by this. One recent ecological analysis suggests that starvation or shortage may have happened on a regular basis of once every several generations (Feit 1969). The ecological differential I have been discussing would impose different strategies on the groups of different subsistence areas, in the event of such failures. The groups to the southwest have various small game and fish which they rely on until signs of larger game are sighted. If these fail also, the tactic seems to be to locate a nearby group who might have food. Among the Naskapi the non-appearance of caribou at a gathering place or regular migration route necessitates the decision of whether to remain in the area, or to undertake a journey to another location of possible caribou concentration or to where some other resource is available, such as fish or porcupines.

The concern over starvation and hunger is influential not only at the time of such shortages. At other times the concern is not with practical tactics, but with the explanation of such situations and the assurance that techniques are available to deal with a recurrence. For this reason the native account of scapulimancy emphasizes its use in times of hunger.

While it is doubtful if randomizing has any utility in hunting, given the conditions of hunting production, it is clear that there is a demonstrable relationship between the mode of production, reflecting ecological conditions, and the practice of divination.

The Externalization of Authority

We now turn to Park's approach to scapulimancy. He begins by making the assumption that divination, in whatever culture it is found, is employed when a particular kind of decision has to be made, a decision which is both difficult to make and of great concern to everyone in a social group. The decisions are particularly problematic because whatever choice is made there is a necessity that it be accepted by everyone in the group. Divination, according to this view, gives to a decision an apparently external and compelling legitimation. The reason why Montagnais-Naskapi decisions about where to go hunting are crucial, argues Park, is that the hunting group is without a permanent structure, so that without a unified decision the group might break up.

Park does not presume that the oracle need be employed in an entirely objective way, since it is unlikely that hunters would go off in an obviously wrong direction as the result of an odd crack in the bone. It may not therefore be a randomly selected direction, but once the interpretation is made it has the appearance of objectivity. The belief in the basis of scapulimancy, that is, its religious significance, give the outcome an authority which is its necessary attribute.

As in the case of Moore's theory, Park suggests a possible function scapulimancy might have when hunters have failed in their normal hunting methods. The group has no plan of action, only a set of equally intelligent possibilities, and an anxiety since there is no rational means of choosing between them. Divination takes the choice out of their hands (1967:199). This suggestion must be viewed in the context of the systems of decision-making and authority which are used under normal conditions. In this regard, there are significant differences between the two subsistence areas that we have already mentioned.

In the case of the southwest bands, the hunting groups are made up of commensal families, each of which is able if necessary to function as a productive unit independently of the others, and which maintains a strong ideology of independence. At the same time exchanges of food and equipment between families ties the group together, while there is a leader, who often has title to the land the group uses, around whom the group is unified. Communal labour is necessary for hunting large mammals, for moving camp, and for transporting meat to camp. Groups of less than two commensal families are extremely rare, because of the need for coopera- tion, and the danger to a single family alone if someone should fall ill. The group is not a kinship unit, although recruitment most often follows kinship lines. The fact that the group has no simple recruitment rules, and may change its composition from year to year, does not mean that it is in danger of falling apart; I came across only one group that broke up during the winter due to an internal dispute at Mistassini, and was told that it would be considered very improper for a household to break away from the group in mid-season without some prior arrangement.

The leader's authority is not openly asserted among the Mistassini, but it is decisive in matters such as the moving of the main camp, where individual members should hunt, and the timing of communal hunts. The leader must exercise his authority within an etiquette which does not permit him to issue direct orders, but his power is recognized for the season. Splits within the group are handled by a change in group composition the following year.

Among the Naskapi, as reported by Henriksen, food sharing within the hunting group is also very important. However, the situation with regard to the way leadership is practiced is quite different from the Mistassini pattern. The Naskapi openly acknowledge the authority of the leader; they say they cannot be without one (1973). The leader is followed without question. There is also a continual competition for leadership within the group, competition which actually can cause the group to break in two if another man openly competes with the leader for followers. Henriksen considers the competition for leadership to be status-seeking, in terms of Naskapi values of manliness. The leader exemplifies these qualities through his ability to find and to kill game, and to give away meat to others in the group. The Naskapi leader is expected both to find and kill game for his followers; he is also in charge of the equal distribution of all meat killed.

Given the Naskapi concern with authority, and the way it is tied directly to the ability to find game, Park's suggestion that scapulimancy is a technique of leadership has a certain attraction. This assumes, however, that the oracle is actually employed as a decision-making device, in the sense that it provides an unambiguous result that everyone must agree upon. This is open to doubt. Speck noted that the same charred bone was interpreted differently by different people (1935:148). We do not have information on this point for the Naskapi specifically. In the Mistassini hunting groups the bone usually received a variety of interpretations. After the burning it was carried around the camp to each of the households and everyone was invited to give a meaning. The person who did the burning had no special reputation for accuracy, and neither had the hunting group leader in all cases. Among the Mistassini, at least, scapulimancy is not used to unify group action or to support the authority of the leader.

The Ideology of Hunting

Our examination of Moore and Park's work has indicated an armchair acceptance by these scholars of the notion that scapulimancy is a device that is used more or less objectively to make decisions in hunting. This apparently arises because Speck failed to distinguish clearly between what his informants believed and how they behaved, so that it is necessary to show how it is that the Montagnais-Naskapi can both believe that the oracle foretells the truth, and continue to employ their own judgement in finding animals.

As we have said, Montagnais-Naskapi hunting magic consist of divinatory techniques, charms, taboos and offerings, all of which are directed towards spirits which are thought to control the animals. The killing of an animal is seen as one point in a cycle of communications between men and spirits. Although the cycle is continuous, it can be thought of as beginning before the hunt and continuing through until the disposal of the inedible remains. It is not necessary for a hunter to be aware of all of the details of this interaction; for the most part it takes place as long as he follows a number of rules. However, the killing of certain animals are marked events: in general, animal classified as 'big kills' (for the Mistassini these include Bear, Caribou, Moose and Beaver, the first and the last of these being the most important) are accompanied by special rites, and this is particularly the case for the first of such animals killed after a long period. The use of divination is the sign that a spiritually important hunting event is imminent. Divination, whether it is scapulimancy or the shaking tent, provides the group with a theatrical representation of what is normally a hidden aspect of the killing of animals. It reaffirms the relationship with the spirits, and acts as a starting mechanism in the cycle of exchange.

The practice of divination among the Mistassini does not depend on shortages and failures, even though it is believed to prevent them. It does mark the return to hunting a species of game after a period when the animal was not hunted. Throughout the winter season the hunters attention is centred mainly on beaver. The hunting group will maintain a main camp for a few months, from which the hunters leave each day alone in search of new beaver houses, or to check traps already set. After several weeks the hunters have, between them, covered an extensive territory. Careful note is taken of all signs of wildlife, and if fine fur tracks are found a trap is usually set. In the case of signs of larger animals or of porcupine, the evidence is carefully examined, but only if the game appears to be close by and needed by the camp at the time is the routine of trapping broken spontaneously, and a hunt undertaken. Evidence of game is discussed with the other hunters each evening, and a systematic knowledge of the wildlife and the habitats is built up. In addition, members of the group usually have knowledge of the general area from previous years, from having flown over the area if they traveled to the area by bush plane, or they may have spoken to another hunter who had hunted nearby in the previous winter. The decision to break the trapping routine of individuals and to begin hunting big game as a group in a particular area is normally carefully planned. In some cases, for instance when woodland caribou signs are seen, it may be necessary to organize a hunt in a hurry. However, at particular times of the year and in particular habitats hunters expect to find caribou and are prepared to be surprised.

Throughout the winter season the group moves its camp many times, and this again entails the suspension of the trapping routine. The moves are carefully planned and timed, based again on general environmental knowledge gathered from various sources. If insufficient knowledge exists about a new area an expedition of several men may conduct trapping there in order to investigate its suitability.

In my experience it is when changes like the above are under consideration that divination occurs. However, I do not know if such a pattern exists with the Naskapi, who have quite a different set of material circumstances, and I do not know what happens in situations of prolonged hunting failure. The pattern of divination, in its broadest sense, does not consist only of rites undertaken for the purpose of discovering the outcome of hunting. Most of the features which have significance to the pattern of divination either 'arrive' involuntarily, or are games which are only performed for fun. The involuntary signs include dreams, and various peculiarly shaped natural objects. A porcupine may be found with a small appendage to part of its intestine. This is called 'his elbow'; it is made into a miniature replica of a container for fat, and filled with fat rendered from the porcupine's intestines. This sac always has a bend in it, and it is the shape of this bend which provides the group with an indication of the kind of game which is about to be killed. A sharp angle (i.e. one looking like a caribou's 'elbow') indicates a caribou, a rounded one indicates either a bear or an otter, and an intermediate one indicates a moose. Another sign is a lump found on the clavicle bone of a pike. This is called 'he is full'. The size of the lump indicates the importance of a kill which will take place, and the relative position of the lump on the bone indicates how far in the future this event will occur. Other signs include a particular noise made by the fire, certain bird calls which are not often heard, the appearance of a particular kind of moth, and the discovery of a rare kind of dermoid cyst on a game animal that is killed (Banfield 1958). These involuntary signs are passed around and commented on by the group.

A variety of games are also played by the group, usually in the evening. These are not undertaken as serious attempts to discover future hunting, but they all express the idea, usually directly, but sometimes symbolically, that the player's productivity is being foretold. Although the games may center around the children, adults partake in them, and often initiate them.

We have seen that divination takes place even when the group has knowledge with which to make tactical decisions about hunting. Instead, it appears that divination marks the preparation for an alteration in the group's activity, in particular the preparation for coordinated group activity. These same characteristics can be seen in what must be a newly-developed use for scapulimancy, the prediction of the arrival of an aircraft.

The prediction of the arrival of strangers at the hunting camp has frequently been noted as one of the uses made of divination by the Montagnais-Naskapi, including the use of scapulimancy (Speck 1935:142-3, Rousseau 1953:138). For about fifteen years all of the hunting groups which trade at Mistassini Post, except those who hunt close to a road, have been visited twice each winter by the manager of the Hudson's Bay Company, using ski-equipped light aircraft. An arrangement for the time and location of each visit is made well in advance with the hunting group leader, but the date which the group must be at the agreed place is the earliest possible time that the visit might be made, so that there is almost always a wait of an unknown number of days. In the case I observed, thirteen scapulimancies, using the scapulars of hares which had been saved for the purpose, were performed over a period of five days, with at least one performance each morning and evening, and with a maximum of six performances in one day. A negative prediction had no implication for action; although the group did not enjoy the enforced idleness, everyone remained in camp until the arrival of the aircraft. Yet, as we have said, the Mistassini explicitly deny that scapulimancy can be used merely for fun.

From the native point of view, the explanation of why scapulimancy does not actually make decisions is that they are no longer able to interpret it clearly. The bone continues to provide the truth, but it is not always possible for a person to see what it is. A person who wishes to correct this situation can do only one thing; he must begin with the conviction that the charred bone contains the truth, and each time it is burned he attempts to see what that truth is. He is given various hints by others, such as the fact that the time it takes for a prediction to occur depends on the species of the animal whose bone is used. Thus a porcupine, as a slow animal, provides a forecast which takes a long time to come about, while a hare scapulimancy refers to the immediate future. But the cultural emphasis is placed on discovering the ability alone, by inspiration and by experiencing what transpires in order to confirm or correct the first attempt. This may be the reason that bones used in scapulimancy are kept for some time before being discarded. As we pointed out, the bone is passed around for everyone to make an attempt, so that there is an element of competition between different individuals, including the women, played within the bounds of an etiquette which forbids its open expression. While any particular interpetation is unlikely to be used as an authoritative basis for action by the whole group, there are numerous stories told of cases in which men or women with particular talent were able to do just that. Nevertheless, the oracle is believed always to show the group what they need to know, for while the hunt is underway, and after it is over, the events and the outcome are seen in the light of what is assumed in advance to be true, as expressed however dimly on the surface of the bone, whatever immediate difficulties are experienced in making out the details of that truth.

In summary, then, the most immediate relevance of divination for the Mistassini under normal circumstances is as a means of thinking about their hunting activities. There is no reason to suppose that this way of thinking sets aside their own conception of the sociological and ecological conditions of this mode of production. At the same time it appears doubtful if the practice can be seen as a response to a single one of these conditions, as earlier approaches have attempted. In more general terms, divinations use magical thought to reach ideological conclusions about the meaning of everyday activities, and mark the transition from one productive activity to another. Because of the common association of other rites with such states of transition, it might suggest that a new examination be made of the category 'divination' to discover if it is a useful and significant category of rites for theoretical analysis, beyond its ethnographic descriptiveness. For if divination has an ecological or sociological function under particular limited conditions, in a crisis situation, we must also take into account its use under more normal ethnographic circumstances.

NOTES

1 An earlier version of this article was given in the form of a paper delivered at the Annual Meeting of the Northeast Anthropological Association April 1973. If the later version is an improvement, it is in no small measure due to conversations with, or comments from, Georg Henriksen, Marguerite MacKenzie and George Park.

2 The term 'shaman' is slightly misleading. There is a category of specialists who are able to perform the shaking tent, but almost all adult hunters, and some women, can claim some kind of shamanistic skill.

BIBLIOGRAPHY

Banfield, A.W.F. 1958: 'Dermoid cysts a basis of Indian legend', *J. of Mammology*, 39:451-2.

Cooper, J.M. 1928: 'Northern Algonkian Scrying and Scapulimancy', Koppers, W. (ed.), *Festschrift P.W. Schmidt.*

―――― 1936: 'Scapulimancy' Lowie, R.H. (ed.), *Essays in Anthropology presented to A.L. Kroeber.*

Feit, H. 1969: 'Mistassini hunters of the boreal forest; ecosystem dynamics and multiple subsistence patterns', unpublished M.A. thesis, Department of Anthropology, McGill University.

―――― 1973: 'The Ethno-ecology of the Waswanipi Cree: or, How Hunters can manage their Resources' in Cox, B. (ed.), *Cultural Ecology: Readings on the Canadian Indians and Eskimos.*

Flannery, R. 1939: 'The Shaking-tent rite among the Montagnais Indians of James Bay', *Primitive Man*, 12,11-16.

Henriksen, G. 1973: *Hunters in the Barrens: the Naskapi on the edge of the White Man's world.* Institute of Social and Economic Research, St. John's, Newfoundland.

Moore, O.K. 1957: 'Divination — a New Perspective', *American Anthropologist*, 59,69-74.

Park, G.K. 1963: 'Divination and its Social Contexts'. *J. of the Royal Anthropological Institute*, 93,195-209.

Preston, R.J. 1971: 'Cree narration: an expression of the personal meaning of events'. Ph.D. thesis, Department of Anthropology, University of North Carolina.

Rogers, E.S. 1967: 'Subsistence areas of the Cree-Ojibwa of the Eastern Subarctic: a preliminary study', *National Museum of Canada, Contributions to Ethnology*, V,59-90.

Rousseau, J.J. 1953: 'Rites paiens de la forêt québécoise: la tente tremblante et la suerie', *Les Cahiers des Dix*, 18:128-55.

Savard, R. 1971: *Carcajou et le Sens du Monde.* Québec, Bibliothèque Nationale.

Speck, F.G. 1935: *Naskapi: The Savage Hunters of the Labrador Peninsula.* Norman University of Oklahoma Press.

Tanner, A. 1973: 'The significance of hunting territories today', in Cox, B. (ed.), *Cultural Ecology*, op. cit.

Vincent, S. 1973: 'Structure du rituel: la tente tremblante et le concept de *mista pew*', *Recherches Amérindiennes au Québec*, 3(1-2), 69-83.

Part II
AFTER STRUCTURALISM

Some Outstanding Problems in the Analysis of Events

EDWIN ARDENER

Recent theoretical developments in social anthropology have moved so fast that it will perhaps at least be helpful to clarify or develop some of my own usages, scattered in various places (1970, 1971a, 1971b, 1971c, 1972a, 1972b, 1973).[1] I regard most of them as mere stepping-stones to understanding. I shall inevitably be touching on the place of the linguistic in the social, but the time has come when social anthropology must reject some criticisms couched merely in terms of the data of other subject-matters. I have exercised almost total self-restraint in citing parallels from other disciplines or from other anthropological writers whose views I have considered to have had priority, or to have matched mine in some respects. Nowadays, so many authorities recant or revise their views (with an admirable provisionality), that instead of referring to them, I shall present my argument from anthropological scratch, and relatively unadorned. I have cited numerous references elsewhere. On this occasion, I shall begin from the point reached in 'The New Anthropology and. its Critics' (Ardener 1971c), and take some of the implications of post-structuralist theory for our view of the social as a manifold of both 'thought' and 'behaviour'. In this paper I try to lighten the heavy load that specific terms lay across analysis.

Events as Output

The image of a stream of events which the social anthropologist's initial task was to meter was never far from the minds of early field workers. The journalist's idea of a 'newspaper of record', the old historian's conception of a 'chronicle' or 'annals', and the whole modern development of methods of 'documentation', suffice to show that the image of the notionally complete registration of events has a respectable genealogy — respectable enough for its implications to have the invisibility of either the self-evident or the unexamined. Everybody now knows and acknowledges that the 'events' that are registered are inseparably related to the mode of registration. Yet, as commonsense beings, we are used to identifying an event determined by one mode with an event determined by another, as by sight and by sound; or (at another level) by radio, press and television, or by a document and by an oral communication; or (at another level still) by a theory of economics and a theory of psychology. Still, we come at once to an intractability about events; they have to be 'recognised', 'detected' or 'picked up', by modes of registration. We must know as much as possible about these modes.

Let us suppose that the stream of events is there, 'as advertised'. A simple output model would suffice. The 'events' pass the social anthropologist as on a conveyor belt. He describes them according to selected criteria. He defines the events, as it might be carburettors. From records of stretches of output he sets out relations, redefinitions, and the like. On a real conveyor belt a sequence from 'carburettors' to 'dynamos' is a more significant one than that from one carburettor to another. In our output of events, however, we pass figuratively from carburettor to dynamo without guidance. The first dynamos are described as aberrant carburettors, or a new term is invented to subsume both types. Given 'enough output', classifications may fit more and more closely to the new units. But it will be seen at once that the view of our subject matter as an output of events leaves us gravely handicapped — because of the retrospective nature of our interpretations, and our inability to return to check our original specifications, save through our record of them. Nevertheless even this simple picture enables us to grasp the nature of one use of 'significant' as applied to events.

If the output model is now strengthened by the addition of a programmatic component, we see that a discontinuity as between carburettors and dynamos would be discoverable in the programme (cf. 1971c:452). On a conveyor belt it is a laborious waste of time to observe the output in order to determine the nature of the units in it, for the programme is available — not only laying down the significant units: carburettors or dynamos, but specifying, perhaps, that 10 carburettors will be followed by 50 dynamos. But even this superior combination, 'output and programme', is only of a crude and elementary assistance to us — a temporary crutch — for two reasons: 1. Our definition of units in the output, 'the events', depends upon the modes of registration available to us. 2. The programme for the stream of events does not 'exist' in a separate box or office from the output — at least not as far as we are concerned.

This must be the end of that image therefore. Nevertheless, it throws light on some dilemmas. If you wish to continue to separate the anthropologist observer from the object of his study, as heretofore, you must visualise that the programme is located in the output, and generated simultaneously with it. Or if you like, each event is differentially 'marked' for programmatic content — some are nearly all 'output'; others are nearly all 'programme'; others in between. Even the anthropologist as observer is thus required to see himself as a being with a mode of registration somewhat more sophisticated than that of a camera. As the 'programmatic' content is not crudely observable we shall need a definition of 'event' which includes the supposedly inobservable. Since the so-called 'observer' can himself only register his apprehensions of those events through his own mesh of social and psychological categories, we see that a satisfactory number of current anthropological concerns are before us. Before we leave the conveyor belt, therefore, it is worth noting that social anthropologists even in their most empiricist garb have rarely assumed they were only checking off output. Even when counting stocks of yams they were also charting myths. Thus the 'observed' events always included (for example) linguistic events, even when those events were inadequately delineated.

Structures

The structures which social anthropologists have hypothesized out of the foregoing are:

1 structures homologous with those of the programme;
2 structures homologous with those of the output; and (for the observer)
3 the modes of registration he has: systems of interpretation;
   technical and cultural categories of his own; aware and unaware.

Only 1 and 2 will occupy us for the moment. These I have termed elsewhere 'paradigmatic' and 'syntagmatic'. It is unfortunate that the term 'paradigm' has achieved common conversational currency as often little more than a vogue synonym of 'pattern', sometimes only of 'tabulation'. It is already far gone on the road taken already by 'model' and 'syndrome'. In addition, those of us who have used the paradigmatic/syntagmatic terminology have had to cope with the different levels at which this relation can be applied. The relation is an abstract one of great power and importance. Yet it has become data-laden in different ways through its applications, quite legitimate in themselves, to the material of varied disciplines.

I want here to demonstrate that social anthropologists do not need to turn to any material but their own to express this abstract relation. We shall consider anthropological usages. In so doing we shall discover that we are dealing with matters that are not parasitical on the terminology of other disciplines. We are concerned with certain structural universals which cannot help appearing in all fields concerned with human beings. It is with reluctance then, that I here cut the painter linking our terms with those of other disciplines for the moment. Let no one turn to a dictionary, or to Saussure or Jakobson or Roland Barthes or Kuhn or even to Lévi-Strauss to elucidate or to 'correct' the following remarks. Erase all images of 'paradigms' from the mind.

Ethnographic

The necessity for a distinction between 'levels' in structural analysis has been a commonplace. In considering the case of the Bakweri *nyongo* phenomenon, a distinction emerged in this way. Certain kinds of zombie-manifestations were correlated with low economic performance. Yet that which correlated on each occasion was not the symbolic content of the behaviour. This was separately 'assembled' at the different periods of manifestation, or so I hypothesized, through new symbols, or newly arranged old symbols. The content was not continuous over time, but something else was; a repetitive, distinctive, structuring tendency which I called then the 'template' (1970:155).

On another occasion, the Bakweri (who live on a long-quiescent volcano) blamed a serious eruption upon Posts and Telegraphs engineers who had scraped the mountain's back to build a rough, rock-strewn road to a VHF station. A new rite of exorcism and appeasement was devised by elders for performance on the road, which upon Bakweri representation was barred to vehicles for the time being (1959). The content of the new rite was congruent (we see by hindsight) with other rites, but the new one did not derive from any other. It could not simply be generated from all previously extant rites. Merely to verbalise this distinction requires us to propose at least two structuring processes: one that shapes, and a second that builds. In this case, a 'well-formed rite' for a Bakweri is recognized in terms quite different from one devised by Sicilians for an eruption on Mt. Etna. The Bakweri would be able to produce a rite, even in the absence of traditional props, and with the use of foreign or modern symbolic elements, that was still 'well-formed'. The building process may be likened to the *bricolage* of Lévi-Strauss.

To take a further example: the Bakweri mermaid (mammy-water) or *liengu* rites for women, are built up from elements common to the peoples of the whole Bight of Biafra. The 'template' in this case was peculiar to the Bakweri, with elements derived from the ambiguity in self-classification between men and women as expressed through a characteristic contradiction in the Bakweri view of the 'wild' (1972a).

Again, certain peoples like the Ibo show a remarkable lability in their symbolic forms. 'New customs', modifications and 'modernizations' follow each other rapidly. It seemed here that the *bricolage* facility was exaggerated, 'overdetermined'. The new shapes were 'Ibo' despite their frequent transformations of content. The 'novelties' were not relevant to a definition of what was Ibo. This feature seems to be characteristic of highly adaptive, 'strong' but 'modernizing' cultures of which the Japanese may be a supreme example.

In all these cases the need for a distinction between two kinds of structures is strengthened by a practical difference in the methods available for their analysis. The former are in one terminology 'template structures' and the latter are 'structures of realizations'. The latter present no problems. All observational and recording devices provide data. In addition, linguistic and textual analyses of many kinds are possible and in order. That point must be stressed, since some 'structuralists' are concerned with these structures in their own data quite as often as most 'functionalists', although with characteristic difference. The *s*-structures then, as we may now call them, appear in the normal flux of experience. They are studiable in the 'stream of events' itself.

The *p*-structures, as we may call the others, are a different class, set up as unknowns, posited before identified. As far as social anthropology is concerned, they are its pions or muons. But we can say something about them. We apprehend (or construct) them out of the same world as the *s*-structure, but we can document them only by their reflections, or their 'reflexes'.

S-Structures

In studying witchcraft (to take that example) it is a commonplace to examine the 'personnel' involved. There may perhaps be an analysis of the sex, age, and socio-economic status of the accused. It is no surprise that a category labelled 'marginality' or 'deviance' may frequently seem appropriate to cover the human constellations revealed. Prof. I.M. Lewis has expressed essentially the synchronic form of such an approach, Mr. K.V. Thomas the diachronic. Explanations of phenomena in terms of the observable characteristics of the participants, their demography, their relative positions in 'social systems', and the like, are all explanations based upon *s*-structures. In the Bakweri case of the zombie witchcraft it would be possible to plot *s*-structures of these kinds.

The problem presented by *s*-structures lies in their contingent quality. That may appear strange, for such structures, or more precisely terms whose only embodiment lies in such structures, form the common basis for conventional sociological analysis, and the 'social structure' itself is simply its most inclusive example. The problem becomes acute where *s*-structures are considered over time. If the phenomenon that an *s*-structure is to explain 'disappears', as for example, witchcraft in late eighteenth century England, we may be forced to propose that the *s*-structure itself has no longer any validity: the formerly marginal categories no longer exist, let us say, or at least, that this kind of marginality is no longer 'significant'. It is obvious that we are soon in difficulties. Few students of witchcraft can nowadays bring themselves to argue that the *s*-structures *are* witchcraft, in some way. They nowadays admit that they are handed the term 'witchcraft' 'in advance' as part of a system of ideas — even as a word among words. The question of *whose* system of ideas, a word in *whose* language, is quite commonly discussed, but more perhaps by social anthropologists than by historians.

A *p*-structure

It must follow from the argument so far that *p*-structures cannot appear to the analyst by the methods which will generate *s*-structures. It is quite wrong to be asked to be 'shown' a *p*-structure. *P*-structures are unknowns', almost by definition. On the other hand, it has been stated that such structures, if they have any existence, must be revealed in the stream of events. If so, linguistic problems loom very large in their consideration. The normal terminological and onomastic process ascribes labels to *s*-structures with ease, for most of our categories in social studies are of *s*-type. We can sense what a *p*-structure should have in it, but the terms available to us are either over-specific or under-specific, the result of using an educated discourse brought up on *s*-structures.

For example, one *p*-structure which we require for the specification of a witchcraft system has in it some component for relating persons to misfortune through other persons. In the Bakweri zombie-witchcraft case, we can begin to shade in the elements of the *p*-structure with preliminary hints like this:

individual self-betterment ←——→ *public misfortune*

You will recall that when boom agricultural conditions occurred, the threshold of 'activation' of the *p*-structure rose: no zombie manifestations. In slumps the threshold fell: zombie manifestations appeared. Bakweri talked of *inona* (envy) as being generated by *nyanga* (pride, ambitious achievement). Self-betterment resulted from the killing of fellow Bakweri (particularly one's own children) and using the dead bodies to work as zombies. All these elements present a complicated problem for description by the anthropologist, since what is describable is realized in *s*-structures. String these emotive words together (Diagram I):

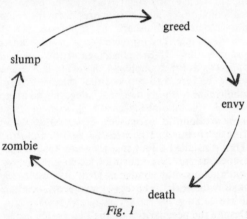

Fig. 1

We have an impression of the *p*-structure when activated: the hollow shape of its shadow in language. Nevertheless, this one is rooted in concepts of 'property', and in economic behaviour, as well as in 'affective', even adrenal matters. For the moment we may just note that this structure may be difficult to express but may be easier to 'locate'. I fear that even this example will have over-concretized the anthropological view of such a structure. Critics should remember then that for the moment we are concerned entirely with generating such structures from purely anthropological data.

The Calibration of P-Structures and S-Structures

P-structures and *s*-structures cause difficulties because their calibrations do not directly match. To make them fit we must propose something between them, a black box, as it were, in which all calibration problems are solved. I will call it a 'mode of specification'.

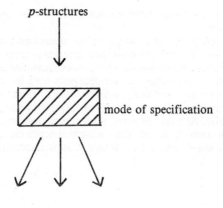

Fig. 2

Mode of Specification

The black box in Figure 2 specifies the particular realization of the elements of the *p*-structures. The mode of specification for the Bakweri zombie witchcraft included a very practical one: 'owners of metal-roofed houses are zombie masters'. Another was: 'all sudden deaths, especially of young persons, are caused by zombie masters'. We can list a whole string. When we talk of 'witchcraft' as having elements of universality it is easy to see that we are talking of certain similarities essentially between *p*-structures. Despite the peculiarities of the observable aspects of Bakweri zombie manifestations compared with English witchcraft, the difference between the *p*-structures is much less great. We can hypothesize (the language shadow of) a *p*-structure so: *misfortune* ←————→ *personal cause*. We require a 'mode of specification' of the kinds of events which qualify as misfortunes and where to find the personal causes. Very similar *p*-structures may have very different modes of specification, thus generating very different *s*-structures. Statements like 'deprived, marginal persons' belong now in the mode of specification, through which the *s*-structures are generated.

When we look at this phenomenon that we have chosen to call 'witchcraft', we see at once that changes may occur in the *p*-structures, in the 'mode of specification', and in the *s*-structures. If the *p*-structure changes to: *misfortune* ←————→ *impersonal cause*, the mode of specification and the generated *s*-structures automatically change. 'Witchcraft' vanishes. If the mode of specification changes, but the *p*-structures do not, we see different types of grounds for witchcraft emerging, or changes in the kinds of person accused. Again the *s*-structures inevitably change.

Why should not the *s*-structures change independently? This would occur (let us say) when there are no actual events that fit the specifications — no people of the sort heretofore specifiable as witches.

The introduction of the black box, the 'mode of specification', is merely another mechanical crutch and we shall eventually dispense with it. It has been necessary because of the confused way in which we apprehend *s*-structures. The contingencies or accidents of reality set up chains of events. The observing social anthropologist may set up *s*-structures that are not 'imperative', that is: not generated by the society concerned. As if the contingencies of reality had produced, for example, a set of temporary correlations in the Bakweri case between ownership of metal-roofed houses and blood-group O. Some such correlations might be 'well-founded', in the sense that they might be derived from the sorting-out effect of the mode of specification. But even such well-founded structures may be rendered inoperative by a change in the mode of specification. Consequently, certain *s*-structures of 'observers' may seem to have 'explanatory' value, for a time, and then to cease to do so. It was precisely the interest of this question that led us to hypothesize *p*-structures in the first place, in order to help with the conceptualization of what is essential, continuous and 'imperative' in the structuring of society, and to separate it from the merely contingent and from the realization processes themselves.

The resolution of simultaneities into linear chains is a mode of exposition with many practical advantages. It is important, however, to grasp that the

$$p \longrightarrow \text{▨} \longrightarrow s$$

levels are present together in our experience. Questions that leap to the lips like 'Is not the black box (the mode of specification) part of the *p*-structure', should strictly speaking be immediately stifled. The black box does not exist; it merely diagrammatizes the relationship.

We have already gained something in clarity by this stretching out of a simultaneity. It is helpful, for example, to see in passing that the term 'paradigm' is used by various authors for quite disparate parts of the sequence. The key to their differences lies in the placing of the black box. For some scholars *s*-structures plus their modes of specification are commonly called the 'paradigms' (they fail to register *p*-structures at all). Many structuralists, on the other hand, collapse *p*-structures and mode of specification together as 'paradigms'. It is an irony that the processes in the black box, which was only a temporary hypothesis, should loom so disproportionately large in analysis. It is as if the zone of calibration between *p*-structures and *s*-structures were disproportionately magnified, were specially enlarged because of its critical importance.

A Simultaneity

It is a strain upon our language to express the nature of a simultaneity in practical anthropology, such that the *p*-structural, the specificatory and the *s*-structural elements can be all shown to be present at a stroboscopic instant. Examine this sequence:

A crowd howl at an old man hiding under a bed. Dismantled sheets of rusty corrugated iron lie in the vicinity.

That is already part of a record masquerading as a real instant. Suppose it to represent an instant in the wave of detections of zombie-masters. Everything in that scene can be set up into *so*-structures by behaviourist-empiricist methods, hence the latter's power. Yet the participants 'know' the significance 'at a glance'. Only the iron sheets can be assigned to the mode of specification, by which the old man was also specified. Thus they are also a link with the *p*-structure. The 'corrugated iron' then in this tiny, inadequate stretch of time, is mysteriously lit up. It is a 'marked' element. It is simultaneously (for that snapshot instant), part of the evidence for the *p*-structure, a part of the mode of specification, and an element marking the *s*-structure so specified — the group of builders of metal-roofed houses: the zombie-masters.

We seem to be gaining some fleeting reflected insight into 'symbol', 'association', 'metaphor', 'metonymy' and the rest. Once more we have only a language-shadow, this time of the articulation of *p*- and *s*-structures.

Dead Stretches

Most of our analyses are done upon dead stretches of experience; upon data as recorded. The problem that was alluded to at the beginning of this paper, of the intervention of the recorder into the process, now emerges more clearly. We do not possess those successive instants, only our records of some of them, and from instant to instant we select aspects only. These are our 'events'. With the naive and unreflectingly ethnocentric observer, the General G. Custer or H.M. Stanley, events he records or registers are totally structured by specifications from the *p*-structures of his own society (1973). There can in such a case be no records of the other society that would yield material for the reconstruction of any *p*-structures save his own.

The step from experiencing society to analysing a record of the experience is thus a crucial one. Unlike the historian the social anthropologist does both the living and the recording. The ethnography is a kind of slaughter of the experience and a dissection of the corpse. That increasing modern preoccupation with attempts to understand the generative elements of a living society which is now becoming apparent requires some appreciation of the exact point at which the opportunity for such an understanding both exists and vanishes — the exact moment of the slaughter, as it were. That moment was exactly when we wrote (e.g.):

A crowd howl at an old man hiding under a bed, etc.

The opportunity existed of a record which would separate the programmatic from the accidental, read the marking on the signs, determine the signs, and note the dispositions they reveal for particular subsequent events to occur. The opportunity vanished because the language for that record has been beyond our normal powers. The language of the record quoted is merely blocked together (*bricolé* it might be said) out of the categories of English. The resulting petrification of the Bakweri experience that is given us has a different kind of weight in a normal English experience. For example, those sheets of corrugated iron strike a banal note — surely no drama could rest on them? A tinge of the ridiculous creeps in.

The good ethnographic observer must therefore use categories and labels in an ambiguous manner, or use some that have a degree of ambiguity already in his own language, and hope that by applying enough of them, he will enable the reader to create from their elements new combinations which will be closer to the 'native experience' being recorded. I call this the method of language-shadows.

The 'Mode of Registration'

The condensation of concepts to illustrate the instant at which the anthropologist apprehends his 'event', has enabled us to answer questions that were raised in dispensing with the 'conveyor belt' or output model. We left over from the discussion of structures the problem of the 'structures of the observer': the 'modes of registration' with which we began. We now see that the reference to the definition of events according to the 'mode of registration' of the observer is to set up another black box. Indeed, it is not a new black box but a different aspect of the 'mode of specification' of a $p \longrightarrow s$ sequence. The registration of the simultaneity that has just been discussed is the matching of the s-structures of the observer to the s-structures of the event. If the p-structures of the observer come from the same set as the p-structures that generate the event, then the s-structures of the observer may be 'imperative', will match. If not, the s-structures will be contingent, *not* imperative. Once more that enlarged portion of the relationship, the purported 'black box' area, is a curious complication. The highly-self-conscious observer figure is a manipulator of some p-structures and their modes of specification into s-structures, but he may still fail to match those of the participants.

We may generalise the relationship so (Diagram III):

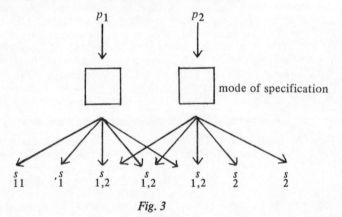

Fig. 3

Where: p_2 is a p-structure of the social anthropologist (or of his society or culture); p_1 is a p-structure of the other society; s_1 are the s-structures of events specified by p_1; s_2 are the s-structures of events specified by p_2; $s_{1,2}$ are s-structures of the observer that are 'imperative'; s_2 are s-structures of p_2 that are not imperative, are contingent, are not generated by p_1.

I have had to put it in that lengthy way in order to show that the third element in understanding the event, the modes of registration of the event by the observer, is analysed in the same way as the event itself. We have also been brought to consider that the p-structures of thinking individuals and those of the social continua in which they live will require some differentiation. (See below: *World Structures*)

So far we have progressed from the data and necessities of social anthropology itself, to the step of setting up p-structures and s-structures. We have suggested that such structures have homologies in the reality with which anthropologists work. An analytical device that the anthropologist needs to make sense of social events turns out to be a usable image of the way social events are generated. Having said that, we may like to dispense with p-structures and s-structures and tell it as it is. Dispense with the terms though we may, 'telling it as it is' requires more than ordinary skills. Most anthropologists end up by still telling it in terms of such structures, disguised as technical terms, *ad hoc* jargon, or expressive language. That is why I must now leave these mechanical formulations, and repeat (to the regret of many) that p-structures and s-structures, embedded although they are in the particular data of social anthropology, are related as the *paradigmatic* is to the *syntagmatic*, and the properties of this relation are all available to help us on from the unwieldy language of structure. The path we have followed, however, was necessary to show us that these terms, as used in linguistics, are expressed in a different reality. I want to explore some of these differences. In order to do so I must allude to some elementary linguistic matters, although many social anthropologists may wish to turn straight on to the section headed 'Why linguistics is different'.

Paradigmatic and Syntagmatic Again

We know that, in language, at each stage of a sentence the morphemes fall into place unbidden, as it were, into sequences, the structures of which are demonstrable, by examination, over the length of the sentence. Yet, simultaneously, paradigmatic relations determine the kinds of morphemes which must be selected. Where are the paradigmatic relations? No one asks that question in linguistics, any more than one asks 'Where is the ten-times-table?' Yet such questions are asked in social anthropology, as if our audiences cannot hold abstractions in their heads. Still, some linguists might try the reply that they are in a paradigmatic rule-book, a kind of Liddell and Scott, just as words are conceived of as being in a lexicon, and the syntagmata are in the book of syntax. We might say, then, that in social anthropology the p-structures exist in the appropriate section of an ethnography.

There is no doubt that the ordinary grammarian is aided in his mental imagery by the external representations of his abstractions in real volumes, indexes, and dictionaries. To such an extent does this occur that the syntagmatic chain of utterance is commonly visualized as already in its 'completed' state, as the discipline's version of 'a dead stretch': that is, as a recorded sentence, or the like. The syntagmata are seen as wholes, as if taken in at a glance on the page. But in natural speech syntagmata are generated 'live', and the same questions that social anthropologists ask can in fact be asked in the live situation. We could answer then that the paradigmatic specifications are generated in the same acoustic chain as the syntagmatic. The receiving brains sort it all out almost without noticing.

But the social anthropologist asks his question because no on as far as he knows is 'uttering' society, and he is not at all sure if there is anyone 'receiving' it. It all gets very complicated when we note that the 'utterance' of events is in three dimensions over time; and that among the behaviour uttered is linguistic utterance — nesting like a small detailed replica of the whole, and yet purporting to render acoustically an image of some of the whole. It is not surprising that to some it seems easiest to see it all as an excrescence of language in the first place. Then the syntagmatic and paradigmatic axes would be coordinates inevitably based on language, giving us artificial horizons and vertical planes for stabilizing our discourse at all levels. The clear expression of this relationship outside natural language in quite simple mathematics, makes it of greater interest than that (1971:466).

Diachronic and Synchronic

There is an occasional anthropological misconception that the paradigmatic is diachronic, and the syntagmatic is synchronic; some think the exact opposite. Both are wrong, of course. The linguistic case will be genuinely helpful here. An utterance may be analysed:

1   according to the syntactical arrangements between its parts — syntagmatically,
2   according to the kinds of parts which are required (a choice of *I, you, we*, etc. among pronouns for example) — paradigmatically,
3   diachronically — by which the utterance in all its parts is traced historically over time,
4   synchronically — by which analysis is concerned only with the utterance as a system of parts at any one time.

It will be seen that the terms 'diachronic' and 'synchronic', which to some seem simpler to grasp than 'paradigmatic' and 'syntagmatic', are really much more confusing. It has been pointed out elsewhere that both diachronic and synchronic as terms applied to systems are static in nature. This is a result of looking at our data as dead stretches. Gct the system moving (even in very slow motion) in natural time: utterances are generated lineally, specified paradigmatically, unrolling well-formed syntagmata. The synchronic is a freezing of this process. The diachronic is an examination of successive freezings of the process (1971b). Once more the tremendous weight of the conceptualization of language in terms of kinds of record lies heavy over even Saussurean linguistics. That is why we cannot always take the usually welcome advice of linguists in examining these matters. Fictions convenient on the scale of language become cumbersome andmisleading at the scale of social events.

In natural time both the paradigmatic and the syntagmatic change continuously. Consider the following sequences over three centuries (the change from an impersonal to a personal construction in the use of 'like' in English illustrates all four terms: synchronic, diachronic, syntagmatic, paradigmatic).

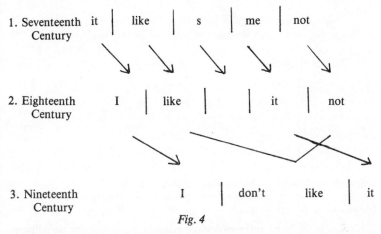

1. Seventeenth Century — it | like | s | me | not

2. Eighteenth Century — I | like | | it | not

3. Nineteenth Century — I | don't like | it

Fig. 4

In Figure 4, 1, 2 and 3 are each a sequence from a synchronic state of English (dates are only illustrative). Together they form a diachronic sequence. Each sentence is analysed from left to right syntagmatically. Each may be divided into paradigmatically selected units. The arrows show the changes in paradigmatic selection over time. The sentences are staggered to the right to suggest the element of syntagmatic change over time. Once the system is visualised in continuous operation (Saussure's 'panchronic' was groping towards this: 1971a:xli) it begins to cry out for devices like rewrite rules and transformational analysis. This is still 'a dead stretch' nevertheless. In order to visualize the process in natural time we must put in all the speaking individuals, and all the versions of the utterance. Modern linguistics moves rapidly off on its own here.

Such a moving diagram (4) for the three-dimensional grammar of even a single ritual over time would be a 'model' worth having indeed. Some research is already in hand on this. For the living grammar of the whole set of systems which is loosely labelled a 'society' we have quite a task before us. It is because the homologies between language and society are so many and so varied that it is necessary to point out that the social expressions of the common principles involved are working through much more intractable material than the linguistic.

Why Linguistics is Different

The social homologues of utterances churn themselves out very burdensomely compared with speech. Were language to be like that, the significant units would be occurring at generally long and always very irregular intervals, among contingent events, and on a time scale of the same order as the normal rate of deterioration of the system. As if the telephone wires had time to corrode away, or the vocal cords to mortify, before the speaker got it all out. The 'system' is one of permanent emergency routing. That is why there cannot be the cosy meshing of paradigmatic with syntagmatic that occurs in speech. Circumstances so change between successive 'utterances' that the actual 'mode of expression' may have radically changed in the meantime. A kind of memory of what the system is about is stored in *ad hoc* ways. These are the *p*-structures, that are so difficult to locate. Since there is no homologue of the speaker, however, the *p*-structures must have a certain unconscious, blind, or automatic quality. They are not all open to awareness. They are in some direct relationship to the 'infrastructure'. It is no surprise then that we find ethologists, ecologists, biologists and psychologists converging in separate dog sledges upon this zone, where the theologian, the philosopher and the social anthropologist already pace the ground.

The old 'template' for the zombie belief of the Bakweri was a combination of infrastructural (agricultural productivity), and biopsychological elements, and theories of causality. Looked at now as a *p*-structure, it behaves in the appropriately immanent manner: generating an *s*-structure at one time of zombies and corrugated iron roofs, and later on of Frenchmen and deep-sea wharfs (see 1970:155). If this were any language studied by linguists it would require some exaggerated form of continuous restructuring, a series of repeated and unpredictable creolizations. That is why I have related it in another paper to the logic of a programme with continuous rewrites. We are much closer to systems as diverse as the language of infants, of the insane, or of animals. We may take a cue from this, to ask ourselves whether there is lacking a 'meta-linguistic' faculty in the social system, or whether it if does exist it is of only a haphazard function. The matter is a serious one because successive realizations of a *p*-structure may be so different in their *s*-forms that the supposed 'actors' do not easily link the sets of events together. Once more I remind you that the successive 'zombie' manifestations were apperceived as separate by those that lived through them. We are rather like high-grade aphasics of the type studied by Luria.

'Storage' and 'Location'

These terms from warehousing have since moved into computer studies, but perhaps they are more literally appropriate when they are applied to society as a system of structures. It is beginning to appear as if what may be treated as abstractions in language have for society to be separately 'stored' and 'located' in the unstable series of social events. Human beings even build physical structures and rearrange the environment, and thus incorporate physical events into the system. Society is thus a 'brain' trying to be a 'language'.

When we tried to understand p-structures we found that their 'location' and their evidence for existence were linked problems. The p-structure homologues in language (the paradigmatics) are in the last analysis 'stored' no doubt somewhere in the brain — i.e. outside the acoustic chain. That is one of the great steps forward we took with language. In the 'social' the separation of media is rudimentary and unstable. Having asked about the 'metalinguistic' faculty, which is so difficult to detect in the grunting, noise-ridden, idiot-tongue of society, we may then ask whether it is separately 'stored' or 'located' (I would emphasize here that the p- structures do not provide a 'metalanguage', they are part of the 'language'.) A 'black box' for a metalanguage of the system will require a device for monitoring the whole system, reporting on it, substituting in it and modifying it. The only social phenomenon that is a serious candidate turns out to be real language — that is language properly so-called: the system of acoustic speech. If so it shows that the social is not like real language in its detailed structure. In real language the metalinguistic faculty is expressed *in* real language, not in an independent system. We have to get used to seeing different analytical levels expressed in different media. And separations between media in ways that are momentarily surprising.

Consider the social as a surface composed of receptors operating on the slow-moving scale that I have tried to depict. Real language operates like a system of comparatively instantaneous links between receptors: real language deteriorates more slowly than the surface. It is not surprising then that in this aspect real language is (or was) the only thing fast enough to provide a meta-system for the social. It can hardly be efficient: when we speak of the difficulty of 'unpacking' non-verbal semiotics into language, we are using another terminology to express the lag in awareness which the 'infrastructural' source of so much of the social 'output' (leading to unconscious, automatic features) makes difficult to overcome.

The language-like continuum of society cannot be apprehended, without recognising that real language is such a great improvement on society, in some particulars, that it cannot be a perfect mirror of society. It can usefully map much of the social, into a medium that can delineate and label structures. Thus far it stores. It is not at all bad in storing language images of s-structures. It is not good at imaging and storing p-structures. We can suggest reasons why not, but it is sufficient to note the phenomenon. To demonstrate a new p-structure through language we have to run through metaphors, analogies, and symbols of multiple reference, until we have created a 'language-shadow' of it. Those who can express the process in other than natural language — possibly mainly mathematicians — are at a great advantage, but it appears that this faculty is not widely spread in any society. Language certainly creates its own problems. Furthermore it adds some new automaton-like processes, out of its own peculiar 'wiring', even as it helps us to plot some of those due to the peculiarities of the social. The totality of action and partial awareness may be termed a 'world structure' (1973).

World Structures

A 'world structure' is a manifold of the relations we have discussed; it is also a system of people. It is like a communication system in so far as it has certain properties shared by systems which have a transmitter and a receiver. It is also like a homeostatic system, in so far as the chief receiver of its communications is itself. This duality comes from the position of individuals both as elements of the system and as communicating beings themselves. There is a high degree of automatism in the world-structure, and human beings, by investing their fates in it, sacrifice a great deal of their freedom of action. They cease to experience events, and instead they experience 'events' — where the inverted commas express the transformation of experience through the world structure. In another place, I have discussed, for example, the reduced capacity of a world structure to respond to its own demographic changes (1973).

In confronting the 'unaware' parts of the world structure we may recognize (with the strongest possible emphasis) that human beings as individuals are much more complicated than they are as parts of the structure. Those expensive and sophisticated intelligences may serve in their social aspect to signal relatively simple messages — many no doubt of on/off binary type (e.g. acquiescence/non-acquiescence). With certain conventions a small structural chain can be set up generating behaviour in a way that is 'unconsciously' constraining on each individual. Such chains are set up every day in laboratory experiments, not only with rats, but in studies of human behaviour. The structure, as such, is not stored in individual nervous systems. We can, for a game, devise a bureaucracy which will work with no single individual knowing the whole structure. We can go further and say that a mature bureaucracy may work for long periods in that way. From the useful evidence of the Watergate inquiry we note that two major 'decisions': to enter the building and to cover-up the affair, each took place in automatic sequences. Mr. Jeb Magruder said of the latter that, on the news of the Watergate arrests, the cover-up simply began. 'I do not remember any discussion that there should not be a cover-up'. The sleep-walking effect was very noticeable, when individuals were asked to examine their consciousness of the events.

We need not jib, therefore, at accepting that human beings in a world-structure will not be conscious of all of it. We may be glad just to be able to conceive that we may be in one. The Watergate case illustrates another way in which we see events as 'significant' from outside. If the Nixonian White House be taken as a convenient model of a world-structure, the two events mentioned earlier were 'significant' in the light of that world-structure's subsequent collapse. To the participants 'event' followed 'event' linked with syntagmatic logicality: while certain triggers set themselves unnoticed. Such 'triggers' belong in the p-component. (For those who still need the 'black box': they reset the mode of specification of the s-structures.)

Simple predictivity in human science is revealed as a misguided goal when we consider the discontinuity of p and s components. A p-change may release a 'trigger', leaving a disposition in the structure which does not realize itself because the precipitating conditions simply do not occur. Or, given a major social entity, over time, triggers may be released, or thresholds overridden, that are realized in the *s*-structures only a generation later. There seems no doubt that *p*-structures are labile, and may set or release triggers under the influence of infrastructural changes. We have discussed problems of 'storage' and 'location' and deterioration. We have hinted at the demographic problem as a modifier of the human content of the system (for details see 1973). The major outstanding problem in the analysis of events is to spot the triggers moving — to catch the *p*-component in events.

The world structure occupies a space which is neither 'idealist' nor 'materialist'. Looked at through language it is one; looked at through 'events' it is the other. I have always thought that 'Whorf — the fire assurance assessor who found he could not stop fires without correcting language — well understood the world-structure as a sometimes dangerous generator of reality.

What is a World-Structure like?

At various stages in this presentation we have set up 'black boxes' to help to solve problems, and we have then dispensed with them. The whole language of structure is ultimately a process of that type and the world-structure is the biggest black-box of them all. How might it work? We have suggested that it may be like a surface with particular properties. Let us compare it with a special memory surface. That surface both 'registers' and 'recognizes' events by fairly simple principles. The traces of different events reinforce each other only in the parts that overlap. Old traces die out if not reinforced. This creates a continuous movement across the surface. The configurations on the surface are stable or change shape or become 'deeper' or 'shallower' according to the degree to which they are reinforced. The newer, or the rarer, the event the less readily will it be registered. Only those aspects that reinforce existing configurations will register, indeed a deficiency of such a surface is that those configurations are thereby further strengthened.

It is unlikely on the other hand that the world-structure as a surface would work with such relatively simple excitation rules as De Bono suggests for individual perception. It is both more rudimentary and more complex, for example, the surface itself has important discontinuities caused by the irregular demographic distribution of the human elements of the surface. On an ideal memory surface, the flow across the surface is uninterrupted save by the processes of the surface itself. Still it is probable that any degree of mutual sensitivity between enough like organisms could set up some elements of a memory surface. Two bonding attractions would be enough: one into the physical world (say hunger) and one into like elements in the surface (say sex). A simple pair of *p*-structures (using our previous terms) would generate the activity of the surface. The continuity of the 'social' through animal species to man may, indeed, merely exemplify this kind of proposition. Thereby we confront once more the prospect of some automatism in our subject matter.

The rudimentary form of the surface is importantly modified by incorporating ways of scanning the surface supplementary to the operations of the surface itself. We can do this by superimposing on the surface a second surface (II) which will register events on surface I. What has been said of surface I applies *mutatis mutandis* to surface II. This time it is configurations newly established on surface I that will not register easily. The configurations on surface II would tend to overdetermine the most deeply reinforced parts of the configurations on surface I. If, furthermore, surface I now has the faculty of registering the configurations of surface II as well as physical events, we have some of the properties of a world structure. Surface II is like the scanning effect of language, and exemplifies some defective features in that scanning. The mutual registration of surfaces I and II creates a duality of configurations on surface I, some registering the 'environment', some the scanning process. The new elaborate surface thus registers 'markers' indicating some of its own states. Some of the events that are thus registered càn be said then to be 'symbolic' of states of or in the surface.

To translate this back into the terms of the social anthropological subject matter, language (that is real language) provides a map of some of the main regularities of the social. I have suggested elsewhere (1971a:xliv) that multiple 'semiotic' systems must have prepared the way, and still coexist with it. Language represents a much fuller exploitation of the human capacities of the surface, but as we saw earlier, whole regions of the automatism in the surface are only inefficiently mapped through it.

We are led to the probability that even the extraordinary complexity introduced into the surface by the rapid transmission of provisional maps of its own configurations still does not utilize more than some fraction of the complexity of the individuals composing it. That may be said, even though over recent millennia the storing of language by recording devices has accelerated the process of 'linguification' of the surface: to the degree that there is now a somewhat greater resemblance between the surface and an elaborate memory surface than there can have been in the remotest past.

We have suggested that this introduces more and more complicated 'automatisms'. The surface registers natural events, but generates a welter of 'events' of its own. There may well come a state of the surface such that most events individuals contend with in that strange 'real world' are mere automatisms of the surface. The failure of language to discriminate rapidly or even (as far as untechnical discourse is concerned) at all between its own processes and the processes of the surface becomes critical at this stage.

In this condition individuals may make the necessary discriminations, step outside the surface, as it were, but lack a common real language for their expression.

Temporary Conclusion

We have tried, in the last section, another way of visualizing how strange a world structure might look if we were not in one. Even were I to defend the attempt as a mere language-shadow, I would not claim it to be very successful. The capacious terminology of structures is more reassuring to us at the moment, and certainly more closely matches our research capacities. But we should recognize the provisional nature of even these rich theories.

The bringing of world-structures to consciousness is a bigger task than social anthropology on its own can tackle. It has got the small distance that it has because of its privileged experience of a multiplicity of such structures. The terminology of 'structure' is however itself becoming exhausted. It has had a good life in social anthropology, although in the lay world its vogue is only just beginning. 'Structure' does not always help us to visualize the multiple realizations that we are dealing with. We are, of course, not waiting for new terms for 'structures'. We are simply in a post-structuralist situation parallel to the post-functionalist situation of the 1940s and 1950s. In the post-structuralist period the capturing of the life of events as they articulate with structures will certainly be one outstanding problem requiring a new phase of specially collected data. In this place, it is not necessary to specify the methods that could be used, but they might include the detailed study of what I have called 'simultaneities'. As an alternative to the method of definition, the method of language-shadows may be used to delineate immanent structures.

We are in a *post*-structuralist position however. This means that old Durkheimian problems such as that of the 'location' of structures no longer seem to require a metaphysical solution. The problem of 'validation' — that is, of determining the 'truth' of structural analysis derives from the degree of 'match' or 'fit' — a feature I have called imperativeness. We have learnt also that the human is a world on a very grand scale indeed. A world in which a consistent and relatively simple set of structuring principles are fleshed out in the most diverse ways. It still appears to me that individual human minds are much more advanced than the structures through which a kind of sleep-walking ratiocination occurs. An awareness of structure is a first stage in stepping out of it.

NOTES

1 The main references are as follows: Ardener, Edwin, 1) 1962: *Divorce and Fertility: An African Study*, Oxford University Press; 2) 1970: 'Witchcraft Economics and the Continuity of Belief', in *Witchcraft Confessions and Accusations*, (ed.), by M. Douglas, A.S.A. Monograph 9, London: Tavistock; 3) 1971(a): Introductory Essay in E. Ardener (ed.), *Social Anthropology and Language*, (ed), A.S.A. Monograph 10, London: Tavistock; 4) 1971(b): 'The Historicity·of Historical Linguistics', in *Social Anthropology and Language*, (ed.), Ardener; 5) 1971(c): 'The New Anthropology and Its Critics', *Man* (n.s.) 6; 6) 1972(a): 'Belief and the Problem of Women', in *The Interpretation of Ritual*, ed. by J. La Fontaine, London, Tavistock; 7) 1972(b): 'Language, Ethnicity and Population', *Journal of the Anthropological Society of Oxford* (*JASO*), VIII, 3, pp.125-33; 8) 1973: 'Population and "Tribal Communities",' Wolfson lecture; Ardener, E.W., and MacRow, D.W., 1959: 'The Cameroon Mountain', *Nigeria Magazine*, 62, pp.230-45.

The Post-Structuralist Position of Social Anthropology [1]

KIRSTEN HASTRUP

What is it all about?

At various occasions in the recent past the notion of post-structuralism has emerged in discussions and seminars within our discipline. Although those occasions may still be few and involve a relatively limited number of people, it is impossible to deny the strength of the proposition that anthropology indeed finds itself in a post-structuralist position. As will become obvious in the course of the paper, there is no one single position in terms of a unitarian theory: post-structuralism is not an *-ism* by itself, but as the *post-* indicates, it is a phase of anthropology which succeeds structuralism. If nothing else, the mere irreversibility of chronological time makes the post-structuralist position almost a historical necessity. This explains why it is that the concept has started leading an independent life, independent of the actual number of 'followers', that is, and it provides us with the strongest possible inducement to analyze its implications for social anthropology.

The post-structuralist position as a concept was only born in 1973 at the ASA Decennial Conference in Oxford in the paper by Edwin Ardener entitled 'Some Outstanding Problems in the Analysis of Events' (published in the present volume). What a post-structuralist position would entail may still be a matter of opinion due to its peculiar nature, but before sketching out my own opinion I shall give further brief consideration to the concept itself. In the *Journal of the Anthropological Society of Oxford*, Malcolm Crick wrote 'Some Reflections on the A.S.A. Decennial Conference' which are worth citing at some length:

> Ardener concluded his paper on 'Some outstanding problems in the analysis of events' with the reflection that the terminology of structuralism might now impede our progress. He was, in short, trying to sketch the lineaments of a post-structural epoch. But, although some may now be thinking their way beyond Lévi-Strauss, there are dangers in suggesting that the discipline as a whole is now post-structural. After all, many anthropologists have not yet even reached the structural phase, and it is inconceivable that those who are still happy to announce themselves as unregenerate functionalists or as structural-functionalists should have any idea of what 'neo-' anthropology is without a prior and genuine encounter with structuralism. It may well be therefore, that post-structural declarations at the moment will cause events to happen at a velocity which will be tactically unwise. And in this respect the rudeness of some of the rebuttals of Lévi-Strauss in recent writings by the few most influenced by him may harmfully reinforce the prejudice of the

more conservative that they were right never to have shown any interest in his work. Neo-anthropological trends are anthropophagous; post-structuralism is obviously an anthropology which has consumed Lévi-Strauss. (1973:177)

Crick goes on to say that it is only because of Lévi-Strauss that we can now think beyond him, and this is precisely the point. Post-structuralism is not a rejection of Lévi-Strauss (unlike some of the rude rebuttals to which Crick refers): it is a contribution to the very trend of anthropology which he himself inaugurated some thirty years ago, and which I believe that he, least of all, should like to see stopped by a concern for the more conservative among us. It may be that post-structuralism has consumed Lévi-Strauss, in that it has certainly incorporated him, but I cannot see why we should or how we could renounce, or rename, our theoretical interests for the sake of those who have not yet reached the structural phase. Those who have not experienced the 'epistemological break' (cf. Ardener 1971b:450) by now are hardly likely to do so anyway — not at least on the basis of an encounter with structuralism as such, but maybe they will experience another break through an encounter with post-structuralism. As in a game of chess any particular position (i.e. post-structuralist)

> has a unique characteristic of being freed from all antecedent positions: the route used in arriving there makes absolutely no difference; one who has followed the entire match has no advantage over the curious party who comes up at a critical moment to inspect the state of the game; ... (Saussure 1916; 1974:89).

In my view it is perfectly conceivable that even present-day non-structuralists may sometime form a curious party and come up to inspect the state of the game at a critical moment. In anthropology all moments seem to be critical in this sense, and I take it that curiosity must be a distinctive feature of people who have become anthropologists. Thus I suggest that we go straight into the post-structuralist epoch (indeed, I do not think that we have much choice) and we shall probably find a good many people already there. Among others, I believe that we shall find Lévi-Strauss; at least potentially, *he* is in a genuine post-structuralist position.

This last statement leads me to certain very basic considerations, which in the first place may seem to merely illustrate the 'results' of Lévi-Strauss' structuralism, but later on we shall see how these reflections have a meaning beyond this, a meaning which reaches directly into some of the problems to which various post-structuralist trends draw our attention and even offer some means for solution.

In the forties when Lévi-Strauss began to appear on the anthropological scene, the novelty which he represented was mainly interpreted as one of *method*. This is hardly surprising given the strong methodological emphasis of Lévi-Strauss (1945). As a method structuralism presented a new way of arranging data so as to understand their organization and operation, and it was in this sense that structuralism crossed the Channel and became for some British anthropologists 'a way of looking at things' (Leach 1973:37). For many this still sums up the achievement of structuralism, especially as it relates to the realms of kinship and mythology as derived from Lévi-Strauss' *Elementary Structures of Kinship* (1949) and *Mythologiques* (I-IV, 1964-71).

However, to some anthropologists the advent of *Totemism* and *The Savage Mind* (Lévi-Strauss 1962a, b) meant that structuralism became more than just a method, it became a kind of epistemology as well,[2] since it claimed to regard the relationship between man and his being. Structuralism, therefore, gained a new and significant dimension, when it was realized that what might seem

> like methodological peculiarities of structuralist analysis stem in fact from the particular form of complexity of the systems which underlie and which generate the observed features of social and cultural life requiring explanation (Mepham 1973:107).

For those who received this message from *The Savage Mind* of Lévi-Strauss the method became only the instrumental part of structuralism, and it was most importantly realized that the epistemological dimension had already been present in the preceding works, at least implicitly. Thus, the course of historical events, expressed in the successive publication of his various works, changed our conception of the earlier of these events: the new vision of *The Savage Mind* in particular meant a change in our view of the content and meaning of *The Elementary Structures*. The latter, as a book, and Lévi-Strauss, as a person, may in a sense have remained the same: it was our understanding which changed radically.

A similar thing happened when systems theory and related theoretical trends were 'discovered' by for example Anthony Wilden (1972). When confronted with this kind of theoretical procedure, we realized that 'the systemic insight' was already presented by Lévi-Strauss. We knew, of course, that Lévi-Strauss had admitted inspiration from cybernetics and communications theory in 1953 (1967:275), but even when he refers to Troubetskoy in his 1945 article, his methodological criteria 'might have as easily come out of a work on cybernetic theory, communications theory, or general systems theory as out of a revolutionary new approach to phonology' (Wilden 1972:241). The point, of course, is that neither of the three former theories were developed in 1945, only the phonology existed.

One of the distinctive features of the new systemic approach is the rediscovery of Russell's theory of logical types (Bateson 1972:279-83; Wilden 1972:122-4 *et passim*), which is seen to fit the general idea of a system; an *open* system, that is, not to be confounded with for instance Piaget's conception of a structure as essentially a closed system (1968). Even in this particular aspect we experience a convergence between Lévi-Strauss' work and systems theory. The object of *The Savage Mind* clearly belongs to a higher logical type than either of the objects of *The Elementary Structures of Kinship* and *Mythologiques*, both of which are subsumed by the former. This explains why it is that the organizational principles of *The Savage Mind* are less complicated than are those of the other two works, a low complexity of organization being a feature of a high logical type. It also explains why the condensation of information is rather more significant in the case of *The Savage Mind* than in any other work by Lévi-Strauss.[3]

Granted, then, that the essentially mathematical modes of thought from which systems theory is derived are already presented by Lévi-Strauss, at least by their logical implications if not by declarations of faith, we may discover how it pervades all of the Lévi-Straussian phases: when he for the first time sets out to define a structure, what we are offered is a structure 'which exhibits the characteristics of a system' (1964; 1967:271). This becomes even more striking when we realize that the basic structures behind the marital exchange, as delineated in 1949 (1969:84), are but organizational necessities for a logical system. The elementary structures are bundles of logical preconditions for the social system to work, rather than descriptions of the organization of the elements within the system.[4] This point is demonstrated convincingly by Wilden (1972:239), and it is also implied by Friedman (1972:12-13, 1974:451), to both of whom we shall turn in a while.

We may translate our point into general terms and state that the present shapes our conception of the past. Naturally, the consequences of this proposition are not exclusively related to the history of structuralism, let alone to the fate of Lévi-Strauss. After all, the point was already implied by Saussure's notion of *valeur*, as illustrated by the chess-analogy, alluded to above. The respective *valeur* of the different pieces (i.e. the works of Lévi-Strauss) depends on their position on the board; any single move has repercussions on the whole system: a change that affects only one piece directly, will indirectly affect the position — and hence the *valeur* — of any one piece (cf. Ardener 1971a:xxxvii). Thus we understand the nature and status of 'rediscovery' on a general level,[5] and as particular instances we might mention how it took an Evans-Pritchard to get sense out of Lévy-Bruhl (1965), and how 'the new anthropology' (cf. Ardener 1971b) made it possible to attach a particular kind of significance to the work of Max Müller (Crick, in press), at a time when both Lévy-Bruhl and Müller had been long since expelled to a museum collection of anthropological curiosities.

We are now in a slightly better position to grasp some of the constitutive elements of the post-structuralist state of anthropology. The platform for the take-off into a new era is not simply supported on a variety of single pillars, named as schools or phases within anthropology, but on the solid base of a reorganized whole. Post-structuralism is more than the sum of what has already been labelled, it is a new kind of theoretical consciousness.

In this statement we meet the contradiction between history as a discipline and history as an experience. As a *discipline*, history is a methodological device for organizing events according to a chronological scale. Here events turn into memories. I believe that this was the implicit notion of history which made Malcolm Crick fear the concept of *post-structuralism*: his concern was that structuralism should not be turned into a memory from the past. As an *experience*, history relates the present to the past by means of a hierarchical inclusion and subsummation of 'epochs'. In these terms, history is a mode of cognition which turns events into consciousness. Obviously we need not fear progress in this sense, and almost as self-evidently we can make no retreats: to go beyond structuralism is not to forget about it by way of suppression of an unpleasant memory, rather it is to incorporate it as part of our anthropological consciousness.[6]

By comparing, or rather by separating, history as memory and history as consciousness we strike a very important theme for the 'newest' anthropology to investigate. The theme is neither located in history nor in memory and consciousness, but somewhere in the relationship between these terms, as this is manifested in the real world. Phrased the other way round the theme amounts to the question of how different realities are conceived of and remembered, and where they are located and stored. In short, we are faced with the fundamental question of what is anthropology all about? I do not pretend to be in any sense novel in putting forward this question, which presumably has occupied anthropologists ever since anthropology was born, but I shall claim that the problem as posed in a post-structuralist position will yield a radically new answer. It is through the dim outline of this answer which we are now able to perceive, that we can see the lineaments of a virtually new epoch, however this may be evaluated at a later stage, when our presently dawning consciousness of what it *is* all about turns into somebody else's memory of what *was*.

In the course of investigating what it is all about, we shall have to specify the nature of the relationship between the different kinds and levels of logical structures, towards which structuralism directed our attention, and the multiplicity of empirical variations of cultural systems, social formations and events taking place within these; next we should ask how this relationship is located in history. It is beyond the possibility of the present paper to present any final answers to these immense problems. We can hardly achieve more than a mere sketch of some of the frontiers of the post-structuralist state of anthropological knowledge. Our task is the more difficult since we have to deal with relations between relations (Evans-Pritchard 1940; Ardener 1971a:lviii) which *'cannot be talked about* in the analytic logic of lineal causality and unidimensional sequence. It is even possible that they cannot be talked about (digitalized) at all, whereas they can certainly be (and in fact always are) *communicated'* (Wilden 1972:40, our italics). That is, by using language we can do no better than to present our insight by its 'shadow' within this medium (cf. Ardener in this volume). By a direct and fearless investment of our personal, cultural and anthropological consciousness into this 'hollow shape' of the problem's representation in language, we may, nevertheless, be able to communicate something valuable.

Of the more important systems of anthropological thought which direct us towards the post-structuralist theoretical frontiers, we shall examine three in this paper, represented by three persons naming important historical events which revolutionize the anthropological game and affect the *valeur* of all pieces on the board. The authors that we are about to consider are Edwin Ardener (espec. 1973, in this volume, and 1975b), Jonathan Friedman (1972, 1974, 1975) and Anthony Wilden (1972). In spite of detailed differences between the intellectual backgrounds of these authors, I shall maintain that they all work within a genuine post-structuralist frame of reference, in the sense that their relationship to Lévi-Strauss' structuralism is one of incorporation rather than rejection.

By concentrating on a few general themes and some more particular points within the three systems of thought, we are able to see how they fit together to an astonishing extent, and it is this fit which makes me believe that what we have now, after the three moves, is in fact a new plane for taking off into the post-structuralist era in search for an adequate answer to the new *how* of social anthropology.[7]

The Analysis of Events

These new questions raise on the technical level the problem of how we can integrate our fieldwork and its results with our theories. Or phrased otherwise, it is the problem of how we may turn out field-memories into anthropological consciousness; as well as the other way round: to which extent does our anthropological consciousness shape our memories. In short, the apparently merely technical problem of how to register social reality, which did not by itself cause any uncertainty in the hey-day of Malinowskian field-methods, becomes a major theoretical problem which throws us right into the heart of post-structuralist rethinking. This constitutes the point of departure for Ardener, when he considers 'Some Outstanding Problems in the Analysis of Events' (1973, this volume). Ardener's paper is epoch-making in the literal sense of this word, since it was here that the concept of the post-structuralist position was first advocated. And certainly, the formal announcement of a new epoch is fully justified by the radicality of the content of this paper. It is radical because it challenges structuralism from within, so to speak, and outlines a whole range of analytical and theoretical problems which traditional structuralism could not deal with, neither as method nor as epistemology.

It is Ardener's point that the apparently common-sensical stream of events which anthropologists set out to 'register' in the field may be conceived of as consisting of three levels of ordering: a set of *p*-structures (template structures), appropriate modes of specification and a set of *s*-structures (realization structures). The *s*-structural level presents the immediately observable order of things on the surface of reality, with its particular historical accessories. The 'mode of specification' is the means by which this order is classified within a particular context. The classification is in part dependent upon the *p*-structural marking of the observable order. The *p*-structure is the programme behind the output, but the degree to which this output is marked by the programme varies greatly.

The *s*-structural order is studiable in the stream of events itself, and this kind of order therefore furnishes the functionalist anthropologist with what he thinks of as his main body of raw data; yet in a post-structuralist position we can hardly claim that these data are ever truly raw. Not only will they represent a selection, and thus be subject to even the most elementary discussions on the nature of objectivity, but even if we knew perfectly the grounds for our selection the mere *mode of registration* would still affect the appearance of the data. There is no pure or immaculate perception possible in cultural beings, let alone in anthropologists. This is why we should investigate our own anthropological mode of registration alongside our investigation of alien cultures, as Ardener suggests.

Before proceeding with the exposition of the problems involved in the analysis of events, we should realize that the tendency to introspection into the anthropological — and more generally, human — mode of registration is expressed by several authors each in their own way. Within the anthropological field it is most cogently illustrated by David Pocock's notion of a 'personal anthropology' (1973) and by Judith Okely's demonstration of the importance of biographies in the interpretation of field-material (1975). Within another discourse 'the new philosophy' of Althusser provides a further example (Jenkins 1975), and this striking convergence of different systems of thought points to an epistemological break which is not exclusive to our own discipline. In the terms of Ardener (1975b) the break reflects a 'parameter-collapse' appertaining to several academic fields.

Apart from this initial, and crucial, difficulty in respect to the classification of our observations we also realize that if they are eventually to become more than just a kind of memory, we have to look behind them and search for the template (p-) structures, of which the s-structures are in part realizations, built up by bricolage from whatever at hand at the particular time. And this is where a second set of difficulties starts, since we have to apprehend the p-structures 'out of the same world as the s-structure, but we can document them only by their reflections, or their "reflexes"' (Ardener 1973-4). Whereas we are able to express the s-structures in language because they belong to the same level as the normal objects for language, we cannot rely on language for a description of the p-structural relationships: as virtually unknown relations between relations the p-structures can only be 'encircled' by language. This difference in the relationship between our language and the two structural orders is owed to the fact that the s-structures rely on single medium storage, whereas the p-structures are cross-media concepts (Ardener 1975b:18).

In any event we do have, then, two kinds of structures: one which is homologous with the programme (p-) and one which is homologous with the output (s-). The former *shapes* the events, the latter *builds* them in a bricolage fashion. Some events are more marked by the p-structure than others, which are almost totally output. To specify the relationship between p- and s-structures Ardener introduces a black box between the two, in which the problem of calibration is solved. The black box is termed the *mode of specification*, and we are then presented with the following general model:

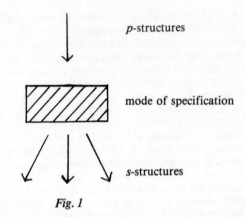

(1973:6)   *Fig. 1*

'The black box specifies the particular realization of the elements of the *p*-structures' (ibid.) and we understand how crucial this specification is, when it is stated that 'very similar *p*-structures may have different modes of specification, thus generating very different *s*-structures' (ibid.). It is the culture that specifies; as observers (whether native or not) we register the events by means of the mode of registration, which logically is a counterpart to the mode of specification. The processes of conceptualization just take different directions, as it were, within the two notions.

The apparent incompatibility of the two directions of these processes becomes immaterial when we dispense with the time factor and realize that what we do have in front of us is in fact a *simultaneity*. The process is not a process at all, the levels are not levels in reality although they do convey messages belonging to different levels *of* reality, and hence to different spaces in the anthropological model.

The problems in the analysis of events reach beyond those concerning their analysis, however. The major outstanding problem in relation to events is to account for their happening at all, and to spot the triggers moving. Why are certain *p*-structures realized at a particular time, and why are they prevented from being realized at another time? What is the social space that generates, or fails to generate, particular realizations of particular *p*-structures at particular times? These are immense questions, which we cannot yet answer satisfactorily, but Ardener takes us a good step forward by introducing the notion of *world-structure* (1973) and *definition-space* (1975b). The world-structure provides a frame for happening and being, which carries beyond the traditional dichotomy of idealism and materialism and which accounts for a certain automatism of the system. As a kind of definition-space the world-structure is continuously transformed: it is a moving frame for conception and action, indeed even for 'populations' (Ardener 1974:47) and infra-structural articulations (1975a:25).

To convey the general idea of this very powerful concept of world-structure we can do no better than to quote Ardener himself:

A World-structure is a manifold of the relations between *p*- and *s*-structures we have discussed; it is also a system of people. It is like a communication system in so far as it has certain properties shared by systems which have a transmitter and a receiver. It is also like a homeostatic system, in so far as the chief receiver of its communications is itself. This duality comes from the position of individuals both as elements of the system and as communicating beings themselves. There is a high degree of automatism in the world-structure, and human beings, by investing their fates in it, sacrifice a great deal of their freedom of action. They cease to experience events, and instead they experience 'events' — where the inverted commas express the transformation of experience through the world-structure (1973:13).

Further, we learn that the world-structure is 'the totality of action and partial awareness' (ibid), and as a kind of summary we apprehend that 'most important it is "like" a reality-generating system with its own events, its own parameters, and its own automaton-like features' (1975b:16).

As individuals, people are much more complicated than they are as elements in the world-structure.[8] As thinkers on our own we have the potential for developing a certain individual mode of registration of events; but we are very rarely on our own, in fact. Something is imperative to our conceptions, namely our positions in a world-structure of which we are only partially aware. Increasing awareness of the world-structure is a necessary means to transcend its constraints; and built in into Ardener's model is the possibility to step out of the world-structure, so to speak. This is especially the power of 'prophets', indeed it is a distinctive feature, since the 'prophetic condition' is pre-eminently structurally defined (Ardener 1975b). Essentially a prophet is a person who stands out from the world-structural definition-space and redefines himself, but only at certain periods, under specific structural conditions are the prophets registered, at other times they 'may exist but they are not registered: their category is collapsed with that of irrelevant deviants' (ibid.:19). The structural condition required is essentially one of 'parameter-collapse', that is a major transformation of the world-structure.

We shall return to the world-structure at a later stage; at present we shall attempt just one more linguistic encircling of it by suggesting that if 'society is a "brain" trying to be a "language"' (1973:12) when seen from the world-structure, then the world-structure is a 'mind' trying to be a culture, when seen from the society. More soberly, we could say with Ardener, that the world-structure 'is "like" a mind: a system of perception (apperception is better), or of knowing' (1975:16).

The introduction of the concept of mind into the notion of world-structure should not confuse us here and tempt us to label Ardener's system of thought as idealism. The dichotomy of idealism and materialism is altogether inadequate in relation to the world-structure, at least as an ultimate either/or (cf. 1973:14).[9] When it is further realized that the *p*-structures 'are not all open to awareness' and that they 'are in some direct relationship to the "infrastructure"' (ibid:12), and in fact this relationship is so that infrastructural change may cause *p*-structures to release triggers (ibid:14), then it is obvious that Ardener's contribution to the post-structuralist position goes hand in hand with structural-marxism, towards which we shall now turn.

The Evolution of Social Formations

From a prime concern with events, we now proceed to an inquiry into the complex whole, in which the events take place, as it is envisaged by structural-marxism. As a distinct body of thought, this line of anthropology is essentially preoccupied with the evolution or this complex whole, as compared to Ardener's concern with the world-structure as a dynamic continuity. Both systems offer a 'historical' model, in terms of transformations, but where Ardener's main concern is the nature and the conceptual implications of the transformation itself (see espec. 1975b), the structural-marxist approach seems to emphasize the reason and social consequences of an ongoing process of transformations, which is part of the nature of the social system. The two methods thus suggest themselves as complementary to each other from the very outset. In what follows, I rely upon Jonathan Friedman as a representative of the structural-marxist branch of post-structuralist anthropology.[10]

In Friedman's general model of society, the most inclusive concept is that of *social formation*. This concept is derived directly from traditional Marxism, and as such it comprehends several other concepts, which are hierarchically related as in the following model:

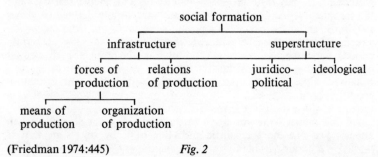

(Friedman 1974:445)   *Fig. 2*

We are told that 'a particular social formation is no more than the global structure which unifies the elements of infra- and superstructure in a historically specific way' (ibid:445-6), but although the social formation is 'no more' than this, it is not at all trivial, neither when seen by itself nor when it is depicted as the junction of infra- and superstructure. As we shall demonstrate later on, there are certain problems involved in this conjuncture because the notion of super-structure is so weakly defined. However this may be, we shall note that what is implied by the hierarchical model is 'a set of *functional distinctions*. No restrictions are made regarding the kinds of cultural elements which take on the functions nor the number of functions which can be embodied in a single element' (1974:445). This is very fundamental since it distinguishes the structural-Marxist approach from the wide variety of vulgar-materialist trends, which adhere to a hierarchy of *kinds* of elements. Within structural-Marxism it is realized that, e.g., a kinship system may function as both relations of production as as ideology. What the model represents, therefore, is a way of maintaining a truly holistic approach to the anthropological object, despite the fact that it does break social reality down into bounded spheres. These spheres are not aggregates of elements, defined by their kind, they are structures defined by an internal coherence and logic of their own, and they each possess a certain amount of autonomy.

To analyse the evolution of the social formation so far defined, we shall concentrate on the constituent structures of the infrastructure, since this is where the triggers are set moving. Friedman offers another model to meet this requirement: the model of social reproduction,

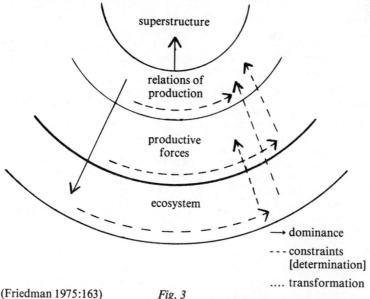

(Friedman 1975:163)   *Fig. 3*

As implied already by the model of the social formation, each of the above levels are relatively autonomous. 'This is not a question, as for some Althusserians, of partial functional independence, but rather one of the autonomy of internal structural properties (Friedman 1974). Unlike a number of materialists, we do not suppose that the different levels of a social formation emerge from one another (Harris 1968; Meillassoux 1972). On the contrary, the variation and development of the subsystems depend directly on their internal structures and their intrasystemic contradictions. But the realization of these internal tendencies depends in turn on the intersystemic relations that link the subsystems' (Friedman 1975:163). Phrased otherwise: the realizations of the infrastructural potentialities are triggered off by the intersystemic relations within the infrastructure.

The intersystemic relations are basically of two types, characterized by *determination* (in the last instance) and (structural) *dominance*. The former is represented in the model by the arrows from the ecosystem and upwards. It is a hierarchy of constraints, which does not imply anything like direct causality. Rather it is a way of selection, 'which determines the limits of functional compatibility between levels, hence their internal variation. This is essentially a negative determination, since it determines what can not occur but not what must occur' (ibid.). We shall stress this point because the concept of negative causality constitutes a distinctive feature of the structural-marxist approach as opposed to vulgar-materialism in any guise (see espec. Friedman 1974).

Working in the opposite direction is the structural dominance, and we see how the 'relations of production dominate the entire functioning of the larger system, defining the specificity of the mode of production and its developmental tendencies' (1975:164). Thus, where the ecological possibilities are determinant in the last instance, by setting the outer limits, it is the relations of production which actually determines the appearance of the system. They *shape* it, as it were.

The structure of the relations of production entails a certain organization and use of the forces of production within the limits or prior constraints, which again implies a specific use of the ecological niches available to the society. The use made of these ecological niches may result in significant changes, thereby inducing change in the nature of constraints, and we see how the system starts operating in the opposite direction again (see especially Friedman 1972b). It appears to me that we are in fact getting close to an explanation of the automatism of the system itself, seeing how change is an effect of a variety of relationships built into the system as the dynamics of its constituent structures.

More generally, evolution occurs as a result of contradictions within the system: 'There is evolution because societies come into contradiction with their "environments", a situation which is only conceivable in the framework of relative autonomy' (1974:466). When it is appreciated that infrastructural changes are more or less automatically brought about by contradictions which arise when specific structures become functionally imcompatible with one another, it is evidently the *inter*-systemic contradictions that we are primarily concerned with. Intersystemic contradictions are not original to the system, they arise in the course of the system's functioning. Another kind of contradictions are the *intra*-systemic ones, that is contradictions which are part of the internal properties of one single structure. In this crucial distinction Friedman follows Godelier (1965), also in respect to the point that it is only the intersystemic contradictions that can actually cause the system, as such, to break down.

As an illustration to the two kinds of contradictions and their significance within the model, we may invoke Friedman's own example and see how the contradiction between equality and inequality in the alliance-structure of the Kachin of Upper-Burma is a property of the structure itself. As such it was already pointed out by Lévi-Strauss (1949), but he was not able to explain the actual move between the two polar types. The structural-marxist here enters with an adequate means for solving this problem: 'The way in which this contradiction can develop depends, however, on the intersystemic relation between the social structure and the forces of production' (Friedman 1974:455). To explain the transition from *gumsa* (auto-crat) to *gumlao* (democracy), we have to study the particular combinations of the alliance- (or exchange-) structure, which constitutes the dominant relation of production, and the actual production-distribution structure; but the defining quality of each of these types (i.e. *gumsa* and *gumlao*) is inherent in the structure of the relations of production itself, in the name of the contradiction between equality and inequality.

By way of combining the model of the social formation (fig. 2) and the model of social reproduction (fig. 3), we may arrive at the following general statement: 'By determining the real relationship between forces and relations of production as well as understanding the internal structure of the latter, we can hope to go a long way towards explaining the distribution and development of social formations' (ibid:456).

It is evident that the relations of production are essential to the social system (and to the model), but contrary to 'vulgar' conceptions this does not mean that we give priority to 'economics' or to any other traditional domain of anthropology. The relations of production cut through the traditional partitions of our subject made on the basis of kinds of elements, since it is realized that kinship-systems, festive cycles, religious beliefs etc. may form important clues to the relations of production, and hence to the evolution of the system. However, we should note here that Friedman in one of his works (1975) defines the 'social relations of production' as 'the set of social (i.e. non-technical) relations which determine the internal rationality of the *economy*, the specific use to be made of the means of production and the distribution of total social labour-time and product' (p.162; italics mine), and we detect a slight incompatibility between the constituent units of Friedman's system of thought. A similar judgement applies to Godelier, who, it seems to me, is somewhat trapped between his structural-marxist intentions and a concern for 'economic anthropology' (Godelier, 1972). We shall return to this in our conclusive paragraph.

The general model of determination and dominance is not limited to the use of building a historical model of particular social forms in time. It also provides a model for analysing the distribution of social forms in space. As a spatial model it accounts for the variances of kinship structure in different environments, for instance. These two models (i.e. the historical and the spatial) are complementary in type, and their combination may result in a third kind of model, in which changing constraints are included in the operation of the historical model, whereby we are able to explain variations at all levels of organization over time. By applying the third kind of model we are, therefore, in a position to account for the *long-term* evolution of systems, as e.g. the move of Kachin-like systems towards either Naga- or Shan-systems, whereas the historical model alone can only explain the *short-term* evolution of the system under consideration, as e.g. the oscillation between *gumsa* and *gumlao*. This position is thoroughly developed and convincingly demonstrated by Friedman in (1972), and in a shorter version in (1975).

So far it appears that the structural-marxism offers both solutions and problems. We shall not deal with the former any further, after all, structural-marxists themselves are in a better position to defend (and recommend) their models than I am. As for the problems, towards which we have already given some hints, these are mainly related to the concept of superstructure and the interrelationship between this and the infra-structure, which is not satisfactorily done away with by drawing an arrow (of dominance) on the model (fig. 3). More importantly (but still related to the problem of superstructure) we are left with a feeling of something left out: the model lacks any reference to culture, which I take to name a system of meanings. This is probably quite deliberate, but it is not defendable *in terms of the model itself*.

Before developing this argument, we shall make a brief comparison of the notions of 'social formation' and 'world-structure', which will help to clarify the critique. The two notions are allied in many ways; in the first place because both of them belong to the highest systemic level of the respective models, the level where automatism takes over. Second, we note that Friedman talks about a *global* structure compared to the *world*-structure of Ardener. Although this may not be anything but linguistic coincidence, I do, nevertheless, believe that it points to a profound convergence of the two post-structuralist systems of thought. In short, it looks as if the two concepts encompass the same quantity of data; yet we cannot reduce the two notions to the same thing, since the nature of their constituent units conceivably differ. The difference is partly revealed through the choice of terms. To Friedman, it is the analyst's conception of the structures which is central: the social formation is a model *of* the social system. To Ardener the most important theme is the semantics of the system as seen from within: the world-structure is a model *for* (the conception of) the social system.

Ultimately the difference amounts to different emphases on *culture* and *society*, respectively. I take this opposition to mean something rather specific, since I conceive of the relationship between cultural and social aspects as equivalent to the relationship between the signified (meaning-content) and the signifier (the expression) of the linguistic sign.[11] In these terms, Friedman is obviously concerned with the social side, consisting in the actually sensed social manifestations, whereas Ardener is mainly pre-occupied with the cultural meanings of these manifestations. Clearly, the two points of view complement each other; only by resort to the level of the total sign produced by the combination of the social expressions and the cultural content does the anthropological investigation become complete.

To conceptually merge the social formation and the world-structure, which shall not, of course, be done for its own sake but for its wider implications to the post-structuralist position, we, too, shall take the classical step to a higher level of discourse by invoking systems-theory.

The Emergence of Ecosystems

As this heading reveals, we are now about to take a very embracing view of our subject. What emerges is the notion of an ecosystem as this is systematically envisaged by Bateson (1972) and Wilden (1972), of whom the latter may be seen as a lower logical type than the former, which means to say that they do not belong to the same order of abstraction. If Wilden does meta-theory, Bateson does meta-thinking, and this difference in logical type entails a difference in degree of complexity of organization. The higher the logical type, the lower the degree of organizational complexity.

This initial classification of two authors in relation to each other shall not be taken for more than it is: an illustration to some of the points, which they themselves make. Russell's theory of logical types looms very large in the works of both within the frame of systems-theory. In terms of this frame, a system and its sub-systems are hierarchically related and characterized by different logical types, in almost the same fashion as was implied by the model of the social formation.

At the highest systemic level conceived of by the system-theorists of our post-structuralist sample, we find an all-embracing *ecosystem*. An ecosystem is an open system of communication and as such is characterized by *reproducibility* and *adaptability*. To say that the system is reproductive means it can duplicate itself (with or without errors); the criterion of adaptability means that the system is capable of learning, which in some of our previously used terms means that the system can transform memory into consciousness. Wilden sums up the implications of adaptability in the criterion of *memory* (1972:374-5), the notion of which is, then, used in a slightly different way from mine. This is not important to the argument, however, and it suffices to note it.

The open systems (of communication) are 'characterized by emergence in two senses: 1. the emergence of new characteristics as the system follows the "program" of its instructions ..., or 2. the evolution of the system to a stage of complexity of organization not forming part of the "program" ...' (Wilden 1972:373). Both of these two kinds of emergence offer a diachronic perspective, but only the latter regards changes of the programme, since it accounts for *morphogenesis*, i.e. 'the elaboration of new structures through systemic activities' (ibid:355). Without attempting to reduce the two things to each other, I would like to point to the fact that these two kinds of emergence are firmly locked into the two kinds of evolution conceived of by Friedman: short-term and long-term evolution, respectively.

What differs in the two models is, among other things, the use made of the concept of ecosystem. To Wilden an ecosystem is any kind of open system of communication on any level of reality. On the most inclusive level, the concept embraces both nature and culture, whereas the ecosystem of Friedman's model only denotes the *natural* environment of culture.[12] This terminological discrepancy amounts to a confrontation between ecosystem conceived of as the *context* of culture and as *environment* to culture. The distinction is crucial: 'context' includes the subject under consideration and belongs necessarily to a higher and more inclusive level than the object itself. The context is a class in relation to its elements; the elements of the ecosystem are both natural and cultural. Contrary to context, 'environment' belongs to the same level as the object itself. If the object is A, then the environment is non-A, which logically belongs to the same level as A. The nature is environment to culture, but the opposite is also true: culture is environment to nature. To make Friedman's model fit this delineation, we should interchange ecosystem for natural environment, since this is what it amounts to in this specific model.

The terminological inconsistency by no means expresses a logical contradiction between the two bodies of thought, which fit smoothly together as can in fact be illustrated by the very notion of contradiction. Within the ecosystem (from now on taken in Wilden's sense) one detects a potential contradiction between nature and culture as relatively autonomous structures of the system, akin to the contradiction between the structures of relations of production and forces of production. The parallel is not only carried through in terms of shared propositions such as: *forces of production* : *relations of production* : : *nature* : *culture*, but also in terms of its being non-original to the system, being generated by the development and functioning of this. As is the case of the mode of production (i.e. a historically specific infrastructure) it is also for the ecosystem: an intersystemic contradiction may prove fatal for the system at large. Wilden expresses this insight (of the fatal contradiction), when he talks of the industrial capitalism as being in a global double bind: 'if it stops producing for the sake of producing it will destroy itself; if it goes on producing it will destroy us all' (1972:394).[13]

I do not intend this to be yet another doomsday book, and we do not have to be totally fatalistic in relation to our ecosystemic context, in spite of its apparently self-destructive (and automatic) schizophrenia. There is at least one means of intervention still, to which we shall turn in a while; but first one further note on the logical properties of the open system.

The primary reason for conceiving of any system of communication as an *eco*-sysytem is the crucial relationship of feed-back between a sub-system and its environment. No fundamental changes can be solely attributed to the behaviour of the subsystem itself, Wilden says (1972:355), they must necessarily involve the environmental relation; and any description at all of an 'organism' and its functioning is inadequate without reference to the constraints exerted on the possibilities for behaviour by the environment (ibid:356). In its explanation of change the perspective of the ecosystem thus comprises something very different from efficient causality. What is implied is some kind of *triggering-causality*, characteristic to all open systems. Even though there might be an inherent 'cause' for something within one single structure, a triggering factor — in the sense of an environmental intrusion — is necessary.

This point immediately takes us back to the previously considered theories. Ardener spoke of the problem of how to spot the triggers moving; and Friedman almost offered a solution to this in exactly the same terms as Wilden: there is no point in describing for instance the forces of production without reference to the constraints given by the natural environment (Friedman's 'ecosystem') as is directly implied by the notion of determination in the last instance. If the model of social reproduction (fig. 3) be read in the opposite direction, we could argue that there would be no point either,[14] in analysing the natural environment without reference to those ecological niches that are actually exploitable by the people in question, given the particular structure of the forces (and relations) of production. Hence the feed-back effect is implied in the notion of dominance as well.

A logical consequence of this is that we must depict the three planes of Friedman's model of social reproduction (fig. 3) as belonging to one and the same level in the systemic context (i.e. the infrastructure), as is also implied by the model of the social formation (fig. 2) though less explicitly. Each one of the three can thus be seen as environment to the remaining two. The parallel between Friedman's and Wilden's models reaches further than to the logical composition of the systemic levels, since it does also affect the changing of these, as pointed to above. There may be an inherent cause for change within a single structure — as e.g. the intrasystemic contradiction between inequality and equality within the relations of production among the Kachin — but an external trigger is compulsory for the change actually to happen — as for instance a developing inter-systemic contradiction between the forces and the relations of production determining the actual move towards either *gumsa* or *gumlao*.

A distinctive feature of Bateson's systemic model is the position of the human mind within it. The mind is part of the context in which nature and culture are elements, but it is located in neither of these. By way of warning it shall be said that the mind should not be confused with the brain as a biological entity; it is to be conceived of as a cultural relationship.[15]

By the notion of mind we leave the close parallel to the structural-marxist model (as it sees itself, anyway; if you will excuse the anthropomorphism), and align ourselves with the world-structure of Ardener, once more. This circle closed leads us to the conclusive paragraph.

The Uniqueness of Anthropology

In the preceding pages three bodies of thought were presented, and in the course of this presentation we made some reflections on their interrelationship. My mode of (re-) presentation may have transformed the works beyond (their authors') recognition despite the attempt to be loyal to the texts. This possibility is unavoidable because of that personal anthropology which shapes the present writer's mode of registration of the historical events named by Ardener, Friedman and Wilden. Methodologically this point has a significant consequence by pointing to the inherent contradiction in the structure of this essay: (purported) exegesis is rather *un*-post-structuralist, reduction even more so; and in no doubt I am found guilty in both. This needs no excuse, being an effect of a liminal phase. Once the incorporation (of the new models) has taken place, intuition will impede imitation; the 'authorities' will become sources of inspiration.

In the course of the exposition it was suggested that the social formation and the world-structure complete each other, drawing their substances from different sources which can be named as the social and the cultural, respectively. We may summarize this to the effect of saying that the world-structure represents the semantics of the social formation. Obviously, then, the world-structure is always there, which is not to deny that objective social events ever happen. Only it is so that 'the newer, or the rarer, the event the less readily will it be registered. Only those aspects that reinforçe existing configurations will register' (Ardener 1973:15). Events that support existing patterns are more likely to be 'events' than others. But some kind of change continuously occur in the surface of the world-structure, due to demographic changes etc. At this point we should bear in mind the importance of demography in the structural-marxist model, too, which once more tends to efface the opposition of the two models. The changes in the world-structure mean that a process of evolution of the modes of registration automatically takes place, whereby the requirements of new (objective) events are met. Granted then that history is subject to conceptual punctuation, we may suddenly realize that a new pattern, or a new system, has emerged. In retrospect we experience a break. By this kind of argument we are able to account for the conceptual counterparts to the short- and the long-term evolution.

If the world-structure does not present any grave problems, when seen from the social formation, the opposite is not true. There is a certain amount of logical inconsistency in the structural-marxist argument. We have hinted at the meaninglessness of the notion of super-structure; as it stands it does seem a survival from a less mature stage of marxist theory, and even more so its constituent elements. To retain any such thing as a juridico-political structure and claim it to be distinct from the ideological appears arbitrary and totally unnecessary, unless one wants to make vulgar-materialist models. Furthermore, this kind of categorization is logically of another order than the relations of production, for instance, being based on *kinds* of elements, yet they appear on the same level in the model (fig. 2). Friedman himself goes a long way to undermine the concept of superstructure by saying that kinship-systems, religious systems etc. may function as significant parts of the relations of production, and if these things are not juridico-political and ideological in *kind*, nothing would be. Thus, while he explicitly adheres to functions rather than to kinds of a variety of elements, which to me appears basically sound, Friedman retains the significance of kinds in his model without being able to account for this. If the super-structure is to be taken at face-value, I suggest that we might as well dispense with it altogether, since it is by necessity encompassed by the infra-structure.

As a social category devoid of meaning the superstructure is' worth nothing, but we need not throw it away since it could prove useful, as a term, if its content was altered to embrace meaning, which would make ideology equivalent to cultural representations. But the problem of meaning goes deeper than this. You will recall the slight feeling of uneasiness, when Friedman suddenly let the notion of economy peep in and we all know the paradoxes to which Godelier's analysis of economic anthropology leads, as e.g. 'everything becomes economic in principle while nothing remains economic in fact' (1972:255).[16] By the mere fact of admitting the paradoxes, Godelier seems closer to a 'semantic anthropology' than Friedman does, but even on the basis of Friedman's model alone, we must emphasize the significance of meaning as such, even though the model purportedly deals only with objective social phenomena.

The very designation of the relations of production as the dominant structure should warn us that Friedman (and other structural-marxists) largely transcend the limitations of their model. *Relations exist nowhere except in people's minds,*. Hence they *are* cultural representations, they *have* to do with meaning despite Friedman's whole-sale dismissal of semantics (1974).

Of course, relations have to be accompanied by material manifestations to continue to 'exist' (Mauss 1925; Lévi-Strauss 1949), and it is from these material manifestations that we infer the relations. This illustrates one of the points made by Ardener: we have to apprehend the *p*-structures — of which the relations of production are examples in that they *shape* the social order — through their reflections in the actual ('economic' or 'political') events within the material order of the *s*-structures. Through the material events, the pattern of the relations of production is reinforced, and this pattern definitely has to do with meaning.[17]

It must be difficult for structural-marxist anthropologists to evade the significance of meaning in the future if they still give logical priority to the *relations* of production (as I think they should). And the problem is not overcome by saying that *'social relations are material relations if they dominate the process of material production and reproduction and that they owe their origin not to that which they dominate but to the social properties of the previous system of reproduction as a whole'* (Friedman 1975a:164 italics original). The relations remain relations, despite the attempt to materialize them.

If the structural-marxists insist, for ideological reasons, to deny the importance of ideology (as the system of cultural representations) within the infrastructure, and hence in relation to the evolution of social formations at large, they do not only mislead themselves (and others), but more seriously they challenge the specificity of anthropology by making it equivalent to 'social science' with all its lack of specificity and internal coherence. Only by insisting on the uniqueness of anthropology can we transcend the limitations of our detailed subjects and contribute anything original to the understanding of humanity. By neglecting the semantic dimension, one has answered the question of whether anthropology has a future with a definitive *no*.

For analytical purposes we separated the social from the cultural, and with a jump into the terminology of Godelier (1972) we could argue that the *social rationality* (i.e. the historical necessity) of a system under consideration is located in the social formation. Obviously some kind of *cultural* rationality (i.e. the historical necessity of the system of meanings) must coexist with the social rationality, and I suggest that we look for it in the world-structure. Since the social formations are living-spaces for real people, there must be such an 'entity' as a cultural rationality: a definition-space, where the calibration of meanings occurs. The world-structure is such a definition-space (Ardener, especially 1975b).

Whatever the intentions of the structural-marxist model, it has to cope with the uninvited guest: meaning. By continuously trying to close the door to this guest, the marxist model-makers may well end up in getting their own fingers jammed in the attempt.

At a conference in 1951, Lévi-Strauss referred to another uninvited guest: the human mind (1952; 1967:70). It is here again now, in fact it can never really have been absent. In the Batesonian ecosystem the mind is omni-present; there can be no communication in the system without it. However, it is more potent than just being part of the definition of a system of communication, since it is upon our mind that we shall have to rely, lest the present inter-systemic contradiction between nature and culture shall make our eco-system collapse. The mind is our means for intervention in the evolution of our system, though not at its own liberty, since it is defined as a (cultural) relationship, and thus very much dependent on features external to individuals.

Along with this goes Ardener's concept of world-structure, which is likened to a communications-system, and through this parallel we compre-hend that even the workings of the mind are governed by some degree of automatism (cf. 'The Savage Mind'), but as far as Ardener's suggestions take us, we may step out of the world-structure and increase our awareness. This is the privilege of 'prophets', as referred to earlier. And the power; because it is a precondition for initiating successful changes in the system's course of development.[18]

Turning back to one of the initial questions of this paper, we are now in a position to conclude that an all-embracing History might be understood as an emergence of successive ecosystems. As for the kind of history that can be described as a sequence of memories, we shall seek it in the evolution of social formations. In respect to history as experience, i.e. the cumulative change in consciousness in the course of events, it belongs to the category of the world-structure. The pertinent post-structuralist theme, which was outlined in the introduction as the relationship between history, memory and consciousness may, I think, be successfully analysed within this frame.

More important, the theme may be synthetisized within this frame, since the concepts of ecosystem, social formation and world-structure, which were shown to fit each other in terms of their implications, will have to register as a simultaneity in the post-structuralist reality.

The models converge, yet we may retain parts of the particular terminolo-gies as supplements to each other. When at some time a new ecosystem is perceived to have emerged, it is due to the objective *process* (phases) of evolution, i.e. the sequence of memories, as well as to the subjective *state* of consciousness, born by conceptual punctuation of the temporal context of the world-structure. The (historical) reality of the system depends on memories as well as consciousness.

Within this inclusive post-structuralist frame, the problems of whether structures are descriptive or prescriptive, whether synchronic or diachronic etc. are ultimately solved. It is not an either/or, it is evidently a both/and in each case (as always implied by Lévi-Strauss, by the way!).

So far for the relation of concepts. As for the relationship between the three authors as systems of thought (not as persons) we can easily conceive of this within the frame offered by themselves. They all constitute elements in the post-structuralist position of anthropology, which provides the shared systemic context. Within this context they are environments to each other. Whatever their actual main emphases (and these may be depicted in the 'old' terms of nature, culture and society),[19] the punctuation of the total anthropological system is arbitrary. Environmental relationships never cease to be important. In fact, the mutual environmental intrusion of the three parts into each other is so conspicuous as to have suggested this essay initially, and then to have provided evidence to the demonstration of their internal fit.

The uniqueness of the post-structuralist anthropology lies in the fact that we can now overview the integrated system of a variety of 'independently' developed models. Within this system there is a certain degree of semiotic freedom, but as it is the case of the world-structure of real people, the system imposes some constraints on the freedom of action. To some extent a kind of automatism of the anthropological system of discourse rules the behaviour of its elements. Whether we like it or not, post-structuralism has come to stay by historical necessity. It contains the present anthropological rationality.

The uniqueness of anthropology must be maintained through a new and careful inquiry into the possible answers to the post-structuralist how, without any fear of investing our persons in the course. As persons each of us carries greater potential than we do as elements in the anthropological world-structure with all its constraints upon semiotic freedom.

NOTES

1   An earlier version of this paper was read at a seminar chaired by Edwin Ardener at Oxford University, January 1975. I am grateful to members of the seminar, and most emphatically to its chairman, for valuable comments and suggestions. My interpretation of Ardener's work in this essay is, however, solely my own responsibility; there is not necessarily a one-to-one correspondence with Ardener's intention. Further, I want to thank University of Copenhagen for liberally allowing me to spend a Research Fellowship in Oxford.

2   I use the concept of epistemology as covering both the aspects of ontology and epistemology as suggested by Bateson (1972:313-15), since these aspects are not easily separated when it comes to anthropology. Attempts to describe how

things really are (which would be ontology) cannot claim separate existence from attempts to explain the relationship between the things and the people.

3   The remarks on the relative level and complexity of logical types are by their content important to the discussion of the semantic impoverishment of metaphor (Campbell 1973; Ovesen 1974) and related debates surrounding the work of Lévi-Strauss. I shall not, however, go into this except for making a point on the poverty of translation in relation to metaphors. *La Pensée Sauvage* has a whole lot of metaphorical meanings and messages for the prepared reader, which at one stroke reveals the genuine insight of Lévi-Strauss and gives the first 'proof' that his ideas are sound: being the name of the wild step-mother flower, it not only emphasizes the wild-ness of the subject, more importantly it also designates a *species* which is genetically defined, as is ultimately the savage mind. The species has an extraordinary potential in relation to conception, as can be inferred from the case of totemism; hence *La Pensée Sauvage* conveys a message about conceptualization as such, that is about the epistemological dimension of structuralism. As savage mind La Pensée Sauvage is both universal and belonging exclusively to Lévi-Strauss. Through the name of step-mother flower it is also a metaphor for that part of the structuralist method which seeks binary oppositions, since the mere notion of step-mother contains an opposition between wife and daughter. And this is where the flower becomes a metaphor of the universal marriage exchange, in the opposition between consanguinous and affinal relatives. Roughly, we could say that *La Pensée Sauvage* simultaneously is a metaphor for a mode of cognition, a philosophy, a method and its results, and a man (Lévi-Strauss). This generous offer, made available already by the title, is spilled on the earth by the translation alone.

I am not trying to reduce the present fate of Lévi-Strauss within British Anthropology to problems of translation alone, but these problems are serious, and damaging.

4   I believe this to be a clue to the continuous confrontation between Needham and Lévi-Strauss in matters of elementary structures of kinship.

5   Leach's article on Frazer and Malinowski (1966) and the related C.A. debate on the founding fathers provide a fine example of the nature of rediscovery.

6   The opposition between consciousness and memory may appear naive, since I do not attempt to relate it to a philosophical discourse of any kind. I may also do some injustice to history as a discipline by equating it to an objective device for ordering a sequence of memories. Keeping our focus distinct, however, means that we by way of the chess-analogy can depict the memories as the succession of moves, while the state of consciousness is akin to the state of the game.

7   Roughly speaking, I myself take off from the terminal point of a previous work (Hastrup *et al.* 1975), and in this connection it should be noted that especially the exegetic pinpointing of Ardener's position was inspired by the fact that his 'Events-paper' (1973, now included in this volume) was not readily available before.

Before the actual exposition of the three systems of anthropological theories it is essential to state that although we compare them at *particular* points, and are able to demonstrate a certain terminological complementarity as well as a more general convergence through this particular method, we should keep in mind that all of the three theoretical systems are 'totalitarian' in the sense that they are all-embracing. It is possible to demonstrate the convergence of whole systems only through a selective comparison of particular points, however.

Further, despite the exegetic nature of the present paper we should not forget that what is at issue is a 'new', 'totalitarian' vision, which is intended to sub-sume all of the three theoretical positions presented here (*cf.* note 19).

8 Note here the parallel to Lévi-Strauss's conception of the position of women within the exchange structure.

9 The dichotomy was already inadequate in relation to Lévi-Strauss's structura-lism, which was, nevertheless, turned down for reasons of idealism alone by some vulgar materialists of the sixties. Marvin Harris, who declares himself a cultural materialist, is a rather haunting example of this facile labeling and conjunctive dismissal of what was not easily understood (Harris 1968).

10 The notion of representative should not be taken as an indication of Friedman's representing anybody else, let alone a whole school in anthropology. In fact, in a post-structuralist position hardly anybody can represent more than himself.

11 This model was originally suggested by Dr Niels Fock, Copenhagen. It should be emphasized that at this point the model is introduced as a temporary analyti-cal device. Granted the totalitarian nature of both of the concepts of the world-structure and the social formation (*cf.* note 7) we shall eventually have to dispense with the dichotomy of culture and society (*cf.* note 19).

12 Obviously, culture means something different when opposed to nature from what it means when opposed to society. In opposition to nature it includes society. Again we should note that the use of these terms is essentially retros-pective. The oppositions entailed are presently fading away.

13 There is a striking parallel to this in Ardener's article on Social anthropology and population, where he states: 'If a crisis is sufficiently unprecedented, the social forms all too often grind themselves to destruction, because individuals simply do not 'see', that is, grasp or perceive, the nature of the crisis' (1974:47).

14 No *anthropological* point, that is. There might well be a botanic or a geological or some other point in doing so.

15 I prefer defining mind as a cultural relationship in contradistinction to Wilden's designation of mind as a social category (1972:243). As pure relation it can be no category, and as 'an ecosystemic relationship of communication' (*ibid.*) it must embrace meaning, and hence it cannot be purely social, in my terms.

16 It may well be that this statement is basically a critique of somebody else's economic anthropology, but to me it does sum up his own position, as it is expressed in e.g. his definition of economic (1972:257).

17 *Meaning* is used in (approximately) Ullman's sense. Within a linguistic dis-course he defines meaning as a reciprocal and reversible relationship between name and sense (1972:57). For anthropology the content of this definition must necessarily change somewhat, but we should retain the notions of reciprocity and reversability, and define meaning as a reciprocal and reversible relationship between conception and perception. This relationship is clearly obtaining between the (conception of) relations of production and the (perception of their) material manifestations.

18 That we are, in fact, able to do something about the possibly disastrous development of the present (Western) social system is also reflected by Prattis, when he says that 'by knowing, we are not necessarily caught in the trap of our own history, man still has the option of total change. Whether or not he takes the option *is* the final acid test' (1973:39).

19 We could tentatively represent this statement in a diagram, which in spite of the triangular shape is logically distinct from the traditional structuralist variety. It is to be taken as a historical model, showing the development from the inner triangle to the outer (post-structuralist) axes, which will (eventually) form a new coherent picture:

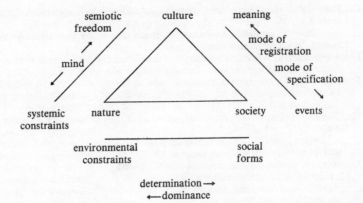

The three models under consideration operate (by emphasis, at least) along the three different axes. Ardener analyzes the relationship between social events and cultural meaning, and the key to this relationship is found in the modes of registration and specification. Friedman explores the relationship between nature and society in terms of the environmental constraints, which determine the social forms in the last instance, and those social relations, which are structurally dominant. Wilden operates along the third axis, defining the relationship between the logical constraints, which are naturally imposed by the system, and the degree of semiotic freedom; a key-notion in this connection is that of mind, which sums up an ecosystemic relationship of communication.

We should note here how the concepts of nature, culture and society change their meaning-content whenever we turn round a corner. Also, it should be understood that whichever the axis of special emphasis, the third angle is always seated in as the uninvited guest. This is especially pertinent when the new lines (of thought) are considered, which is evidence to the point that the old oppositions must give way to a new and more integrated, 'totalitarian', approach to our subject.

BIBLIOGRAPHY

Ardener, E. 1971a: Introductory Essay in E. Ardener (ed.), *Social Anthropology and Language*, A.S.A. Monograph 10 London: Tavistock.
_____ 1971b: The New Anthropology and its Critics. *Man* (n.s.) 6,3:449-67.
_____ 1973: 'Some Outstanding Problems in the Analysis of Events', paper read at A.S.A. Decennial Conference, Oxford. In this volume.
_____ 1974: 'Social anthropology and population' in H.B. Parry (ed.), *Population and its problems: a plain man's guide*. Oxford: Clarendon Press.
_____ 1975a: 'The "Problem" Revisited' in Shirley Ardener (ed.), *Perceiving Women*. London: Malaby Press.
_____ 1975b: 'The Voice of Prophecy: Further Problems in the Analysis of events', *the Munro Lecture*, Edinburgh, 24 April 1975.
Bateson, G. 1972: *Steps to an Ecology of Mind*. N.Y. 1972: Ballantine.
Campbell, A. 1973: 'Tristes Tropes: Lévi-Strauss and the Impoverishment of Metaphor', *JASO*, 4,2:100-13.

Crick, M. 1973: 'Some Reflections on the A.S.A. Decennial Conference', *JASO*, 4,3:176-9.

———, *Towards a Semantic Anthropology: Explorations in Language and Meaning*. London: Malaby Press (in press).

Evans-Pritchard, E.E. 1940: *The Nuer*. Oxford: Clarendon Press.

——— 1965: *Theories of Primitive Religion*. Oxford: Clarendon Press.

Friedman, J. 1972: '*System, Structure and Contradiction in the Evolution of "Asiatic" Social Formations'*, unpublished Ph.D. thesis, Columbia University, 1972.

——— 1974: 'Marxism, Structuralism and Vulgar Materialism', *Man* (n.s.), 9,3: 444-69.

——— 1975: 'Tribes, States and Transformations', in M. Block (ed.), *Marxist Analysis and Social Anthropology*. A.S.A. Studies, 2. London: Malaby Press.

Godelier, M. 1965: 'System, Structure and Contradiction in the "Capital",' in M. Lane (ed.), *Introduction to Structuralism*. New York, Basic Books, 1970.

——— 1972: *Rationality and Irrationality in Economics*. London: New Left Books.

Harris, M. 1968: *The Rise of Anthropological Theory*. London: Routledge and Kegan Paul.

Hastrup, K. *et al.* 1975: *Den Ny Antropologi*. Copenhagen: Borgen/Basis.

Jenkins, T. 1975: 'Althusser's Philosophy', *JASO*, 6,1:1-17.

Leach, E. 1966: Frazer and Malinowski. (A.C.A. Discussion) *Current Anthropology*, vol. 7,5:560-76.

——— 1973: 'Structuralism in Social Anthropology' in D. Robey (ed.), *Structuralism: an Introduction*. Oxford: Clarendon Press.

Lévi-Strauss, C. 1945: 'Structural Analysis in Linguistics and in Anthropology' in *Structural Anthropology*. New York, Anchor, 1967.

——— 1949: *The Elementary Structures of Kinship*, R. Needham (ed.), London, Eyre and Spottiswood, 1969.

——— 1952: 'Linguistics and Anthropology' in *Structural Anthropology*, op. cit.

——— 1953: 'Social Structure', in *Structural Anthropology*, op. cit.

——— 1962a: *Le Totémisme aujourd'hui*. Paris, Presses Universitaires de France.

——— 1962b: *La Pensée Sauvage*. Paris, Plon.

——— 1964-71: *Mythologiques*. I-IV. Paris, Plon.

Mauss, M. 1925: *The Gift*. London, Cohen and West, 1969.

Meillasoux, C. 1972: 'From Reproduction to Production', *Economy and Society*, 1,1:93-105.

Mepham, J. 1973: 'The Structuralist Sciences and Philosophy' in D. Robey, (ed.), *Structuralism: an Introduction,* op. cit.

Okely, J. 1975: 'Autobiography and Objectivity in Field-work', to appear in *JASO*.

Ovesen, J. 1974: 'The Metaphor/Metonym Distinction: A Comment on Campbell', *JASO*, 5,3:151-4.

Pieget, J. 1968: *Structuralism*. London, Routledge and Kegan Paul, 1971.

Pocock, D. 1973: 'The Idea of a Personal Anthropology', paper read at A.S.A. Decennial Conference, Oxford 1973.

Prattis, J.I. 1973: 'Metaphor and Entrophy: a Consideration of Man's Evolutionary Endpoint', *Journal of Symbolic Anthropology*, 1, July 1973; 35-42.

Saussure, F. de. 1916: *Course in General Linguistics*. London, Fontana, 1974.

Ullman, S. 1972: *Semantics*. Oxford, Basil Blackwell.

Wilden, A. 1972: *System and Structure*. London, Tavistock.

Definition and its Problems in Social Anthropology [1]

MARTIN SOUTHWOLD

Are definitions in social anthropology useful? Are they indeed necessary? Are they futile? Are they indeed impossible? It may seem odd that these questions are rarely posed or discussed, when a notable part of our effort is devoted to producing and assessing definitions. If definitions are in fact futile, then these efforts have been wasted and should be discontinued; and some of the most celebrated and cited essays in our discipline should be consigned to garbage. If, on the contrary, definitions are useful, and also necessary, then these efforts should be redoubled. And what if they are both necessary and futile — as I shall suggest they appear to be?

This paper is concerned with such questions. I am not directly concerned with the specific problems which affect the definition of this particular term or that, but rather with problems basic and common to all these: with the general problems of definition itself. These problems are philosophical, both in the sense that they are basic and general, and in the sense that they are discussed mainly by philosophers. But they are no less our concern for that. To be sure, the problems are not specific to anthropology, nor resolvable by anthropological techniques. They are potentially relevant to all scientific endeavours, including the social sciences; but in social science they are peculiarly difficult and acute. Among the social sciences, they may be especially acute for social anthropology, but also a little easier to resolve. I take up these questions partly because they are directly important: We ought to know whether we should augment or cease our considerable efforts at definition. I take them up also because they raise and bring into focus still more important methodological issues.

We cannot decide whether something is likely to be useful, still more necessary, except in relation to the purpose for which it is to be used, to the aims of the activity to which it might be an adjunct. What then are the aims of social anthropology? I shall say that they are scientific. I do not mean by that to open up the old controversy whether social anthropology is or is not a science: in the sense I intend, anthropology is uncontroversially a science. I have in mind E.H. Carr's discussion (1961, ch.3) of the related question of whether history is a science, and his observation that the question is mainly terminological — we might say, one of definition. If we understand the word 'science' in what might be called its European sense, corresponding near enough to the meaning of German *Wissenschaft*, there can be no doubt that history is a science; and hence, even by Evans-Pritchard's criteria, social anthropology too is a science. This is not to say that social anthropology is a science in the peculiarly British sense intended by Radcliffe-Brown, nor indeed that it is not; we may for the moment put that issue aside.

Lest this appear a mere empty debating trick, let me spell out more explicitly what I mean. For the present purpose I define a science as: a body of knowledge — that is, of true and well-founded statements — about related matters of a somewhat distinctive kind; and also, the collective, disciplined activity of producing it. On this definition I believe we should all agree that social anthropology is a science. This might therefore seem to be claiming little; but it claims enough to make the necessity of definitions apparent. If our terms are too ill-defined — that is, ambiguous, vague, or inexact — we shall not be able to communicate with one another well enough to engage in a collective disciplined intellectual labour; and we shall not be able to test our statements sufficiently decisively to establish them as true and well-founded.

It follows also from this, and from other facts about social anthropology, that we shall not find the task of making definitions easy. To speak of 'a body of knowledge', of 'related matters', of 'collective activity', implies that we shall not be satisfied with empirically particular statements, but will seek to combine or abstract them into more general statements. Indeed we cannot but generalise across cultures, simply because we describe the social behaviour and institutions of one people not in their own language, but in another which is shaped by a different social and cultural system. Whether we will it or not, our use of the English language continually involves a comparison of their social facts with ours. And of course, for all of us who consider our task as not confined to ethnographic description, but as fertilised by comparison, explicit or implicit, of one society with others known to us, ours is yet more a comparative and generalising science. Since comparison and generalisation require the use of terms which are interculturally applicable, we cannot rightly dodge problems of definition by mere ostension,[2] nor by claiming to use only the actors' own definitions of terms.[3]

To say that social anthropology is a science in the above broad sense is sufficient to show that definitions are likely to be needed. This is not to say that they can be got. In this paper I shall argue that definitions, at least of the kind we most want, can be got *only* if anthropology is a science in the narrower and stronger British sense: that is, a science which *accounts for* (explains) phenomena by subsuming them under established general statements, of a lawlike kind, articulated into a theory or theories. I do not say that social anthropology actually is, or could become, an explanatory or nomothetic science of this kind. On the contrary, I doubt it. It becomes increasingly borne in upon me that the supposition that there could be such a science of human behaviour rests upon a simultaneous over-estimation of the powers of the scientist's mind and under-estimation of the powers of the actor's mind: a failure to recognise that science, being but a part of human behaviour, can never encompass it. Rather, I am expanding on my suggestion above that attempts at definition may be simultaneously necessary and futile. If this is true, as in large measure it appears to be, it has large consequences for our conception of what social anthropology is about. One might even say that the chief harm done by our persistent futile attempts to define our terms is not that they waste time and effort, but that they obscure this conclusion.

Although we all, or nearly all, traffic in definitions, more or less explicitly and extensively, the fact that we very rarely consider or discuss the basic questions about definition itself might import that we consider them trivial or irrelevant — as indeed some colleagues have indicated to me. Clearly, I do not agree. On the contrary, I find the problems of definition as important as they are immensely intricate and difficult. Many confusions need to be sorted out if we are to get a clear view of that which we call 'definition'; beyond this, in sorting them out we cannot avoid involvement in several of the most basic, intractable, and contentious issues in philosophy. I cannot attempt to treat this issues fully or conclusively in a single paper; hence my arguments will appear, as indeed they are, unduly cursory. Realistically, I can attempt little more than a sketch, of the major questions and their articulation, of the ways these might be answered, and of the conclusions to which the answers point.

I begin by remarking that much of our terminology — the terms we use in description, analysis, and theorising, and have to use for want of any better — is seriously defective. That is, our terms are ambiguous, vague or inexact, to an extent that impedes understanding, and even promotes misunderstanding. In this sense one might say that our terms are gravely ill-defined.

Although this proposition is important to my argument, I can do little to prove that it is true. Strictly speaking, a term cannot be categorised as ill-defined, or well-defined, absolutely, but only in relation to a purpose or purposes. I recognise that many of our terms are well enough defined for many purposes; but I add that they are ill-defined for other purposes needed for the growth of our science. This will be clear to those who have tried to use the data of other workers to test general hypotheses,[4] who have tried to determine exactly what is asserted by general or theoretical or definitional propositions, or who have tried to diagnose just what is wrong with analyses which purport to establish that which is not so;[5] whereas it may be quite opaque to those who have long since decided to content themselves with simple ethnographic description.

I can, however, point out that I am far from alone in considering that our terminology is excessively ill-defined. From time to time other anthropologists express a similar judgment. For example, writing in 1940, Radcliffe-Brown declared:

> I am aware, of course, that the term 'social structure' is used in a number of senses, some of them veiy vague. This is unfortunately true of many other terms commonly used by anthropologists. The choice of terms and their definitions is a matter of scientific convenience, but one of the characteristics of a science as soon as it has passed the first formative period is the existence of technical terms which are used in the same precise meaning by all the students of that science. By this test, I regret to say, social anthropology reveals itself as not yet a formed science (1052:191).

Quarter of a century later — after the most vigorous and productive period in the history of the science — Professor Spiro could see no radical improvement in this situation:

Anthropology, like other immature sciences — and especially those whose basic vocabulary is derived from natural languages — continues to be plagued by problems of definition. Key terms in our lexicon — 'culture', 'social system', 'needs', 'marriage', 'function', and the like — continue to evoke wide differences in meaning and to instigate heated controversy among scholars (1966:85).

More often, criticism is piecemeal, focussed on the inadequacy of some particular term, be it 'kinship',[6] 'descent',[7] 'marriage',[8] 'witchcraft', [9] 'religion',[10] 'law', [11] 'the political',[12] 'caste',[13] 'tribe',[14] and so forth. Moreover, everyone who offers a definition, whether of his own making or adopted from another, implies that he thinks the term stands in need of definition. I suggest that such definitions are offered more often that we usually suppose. It is easy enough to call to mind papers, and sections of books, primarily directed to the definition of this term or that; but definitions subsidiary to an author's main purpose are so common as to be commonplace, and therefore easily overlooked. In my own experience, after I became concerned about and therefore sensitive to definition, I was surprised to find how much of what I read involved definitions.

Hence two conclusions: there is widespread concern about the ill-defined terms we use, and a considerable investment of effort in trying to remedy the situation by making definitions.

Two rather obvious facts should serve to indicate that our definitions are less than adequate. In the first place, where an author takes much time over proposing a definition, he is usually urging that his colleagues adopt it. In fact, very few of such definitions are widely adopted; and many of those that are adopted have been, or can be, rather easily shown to be inadequate.[15] In the second place, if the considerable effort devoted to definition had really been efficacious, our terminology would not now be as inadequate as it is.

Thus I drew two further conclusions. First, that the effort devoted to definition has been largely wasted: which is surely a serious matter. And second, that underlying the particular difficulties of defining this term or that, there were probably more basic and general difficulties of definition itself, which had better be investigated.

So I read some of the literature on definition, most of it by philosophers. Although I have severe reservations about this literature, one lesson is obvious and unmistakable: definition is a matter so intricate and confused that no one could be expected to have much success in defining unless he first sorts out the basic issues. So it became, as it is here, my purpose to sort out these issues, so that we may understand why we so often fail in defining, and may cease to waste time and effort in those ways, and so that we may see how we might succeed.

There are many different kinds of definitions.[16] Lest this imply that there is, after all, one genus called 'definition', I would rather say that there are many different things which happen to be called 'definition'; but for the save of brevity I shall speak of 'kinds of definition'. Unless one recognises this, and is able to distinguish the various kinds, one is likely to be unsuccessful in performing definition, and certain to be incoherent in thinking about it. It is possible, though tedious, to show that many particular attempts at definition have failed either because the definer was not clear what he was about, or because he did not make it sufficiently clear to his readers. I shall shortly distinguish the major kinds of definition — I lack the space to attempt an exhaustive classification.

Now it will be found — and this is my major conclusion — that once the various kinds of definition have been distinguished and understood, they can be sorted into just two pragmatically relevant categories: first those the objective of which can be achieved; but its achievement contributes rather little to our purposes. These are possible, but they do not yield the advances which many people hope for from definition. Secondly, those the objective of which promises to be of great value, but it cannot in fact be achieved by definition. These are impossible, and therefore contribute nothing. On the contrary, because they seem most beguiling, they tempt us to waste our time, and they divert us from more fruitful activities.

In order to see that all definitions fall into one or other of these two unpromising categories, it is necessary first to distinguish clearly the various kinds of definition. Most people fail to do this, and many are therefore tempted into one or another of two false simplifications. They may suppose that the beguiling sort are possible because the other sort clearly are; and then they are distressed or baffled at the actual unsuccess of instances of the beguiling sort. Or they may suppose that all definitions are impossible, and all attempts at definition a waste of time. If they act on this supposition they forego the real, if restricted, advantages of definitions of the possible sort. If they proclaim it, as Popper virtually did in *The Open Society and Its Enemies*,[17] they render their argument implausible, and thus fail to convince people that the impossible sort is impossible. A third resource is to dodge the whole conundrum by stolidly maintaining that our terminology is perfectly all right as it is.

So the first, the most elementary, error which may arise from being naive about definition is not to realise that there are various kinds of definition which must be clearly distinguished. Unfortunately, those who do realise this are not much better off, for they find it so fiendishly difficult to make the distinctions in a manageable way that either they work with an inadequate and misleading classification, or else they abandon the whole issue in baffled despair. The blame for this must be laid at the door of the philosophers who have written on definition: not only have most of them failed to resolve the problems, but also it has to be said, most of the confusion in the matter has been introduced and sustained by philosophers. I know of only two works that do more good than harm: Richard Robinson's excellent book *Definition* (1950), and the sections on definition in Popper's *The Open Society and its Enemies* (1966). If these two works are read critically and in conjunction, using each to supplement the deficiencies of the other, one may attain a very adequate understanding.

So the second, and much more formidable, hurdle to be cleared is that of seeing how the necessary distinctions are to be made. I shall not take time to resolve all the puzzles which hinder one's doing so. I shall speak only of the major difficulty which must have confronted everyone who has got so far as to see that he had better read up on definition.

Almost all the literature asserts that the fundamental distinction is that between *nominal* definition and *real* definition. I would suggest that very few people are clear what the terms mean, or are properly confident that they have grasped the distinction. I doubt if it can be grasped.

The first reason for this is that there is no one distinction. As Richard Robinson (ibid. 19-20) points out, the terminological distinction between 'nominal' and 'real' definition is employed to signify at least four different conceptual distinctions: which is to say that the pair of terms has at least four different senses. Anthropologists are most unlikely to encounter one of Robinson's four senses, so we may ignore this; but we certainly do encounter the other senses, and are in grave peril of confusing them.

The most important distinction (which does not exactly correspond to those remarked by Robinson) is that between what I shall label the 'Classical' and the 'Modern' senses of the terms. The Classical sense seems to be the original sense in which the terms were used, and is still the most common; it is found it both the Oxford and Webster's dictionaries, and in most textbooks of traditional logic. It is adopted, provisionally, by Robinson, and I shall also employ it, with reservations. In this sense, nominal definitions are all those which seek to inform us about the meaning of a word (or other linguistic expression), whereas real definitions are those which purport to inform us about the nature of a thing (a non-linguistic reality). I spell this out more fully below (p.156).

The Modern sense restricts the category of nominal definitions more narrowly — and thus extends that of real definitions. In most versions, nominal definitions are those which assert that two linguistic expressions are synonymous, and thus that one may be substituted for the other. Such substitutions may be useful in the symbolic manipulations in which logicians engage; which is doubtless why logicians writing on definition tend to adopt this Modern sense. Empirical scientists, on the other hand, have more use for definitions which define linguistic expressions by correlating them to items of empirical reality. Such definitions are *not* nominal in the Modern sense — and hence are classed as 'real' — whereas they *are* nominal in the Classical sense. C.G. Hempel, whose work *Fundamentals of Concept Formation in Empirical Science* (1952) is sometimes cited by social scientists, restricts the category of nominal definitions still more narrowly. For him, only those assertions of synonymy which introduce a 'new' expression — new at least to the domain of discourse — are counted as 'nominal' definitions; hence even those which assert the synonymy of two familiar expressions become 'real' (1952:9).

A major drawback of the Modern sense is that it places virtually all the varieties of definition which are of concern to empirical scientists into the one category of 'real definition', where they are liable to become confused with one another; worse, it bridges over the rather important distinction which the Classical sense was concerned to register, a distinction which is close to that between useful and pernicious varieties of definition. Because it thus obfuscates analysis, I shall not take space to discuss it further. My immediate point, however, concerns not the weaknesses of the Modern distinction, but its difference from the Classical distinction. Because these divide the phenomena in different places, several varieties of definition — including most of those which concern empirical scientists — are nominal in the Classical sense, but real in the Modern sense.

It should be obvious that if one sometimes encounters the distinction between nominal and real definition in the Classical sense, and sometimes in the Modern sense, without realising that these are different, one is sure to be confused. Alternatively, one may be led into errors of Equivocation, as seems to have happened in Spiro's essay on the definition of Religion.[18]

Now if most of the authorities on some topic agree that a certain distinction is fundamental, but cannot agree what that distinction is, one may reasonably suspect a basic error in their analysis. And so it is here. Obviously it is useless to discuss the distinction between nominal and real definition without first specifying *which* distinction is in question. But even when this is done, the distinction will be found unsatisfactory. In the Modern sense, as we have seen, the distinction fails to differentiate between most of the varieties which chiefly concern us. In the Classical sense, the distinction breaks down: one will find that some of the most interesting kinds of definition cannot be unequivocally placed in one class or the other, since they belong to both, or neither. I shall show that the most interesting kind of nominal definition must fail unless it can be rooted in a real definition, so that attempts at this kind of nominal definition commonly mutate into real definitions. I shall also maintain that real definitions which are not wholly chimerical are either nominal definitions misconceived, or else represent an impossible attempt to combine nominal definition with scientific concept-formation.

I am arguing, therefore, that the philosophers confuse matters radically when they propose as fundamental a distinction which is unworkable and unsound. This may seem a bold claim to make; so perhaps I should cite in support Robinson (op. cit: 190-1), who concludes that we ought to cease speaking of real definition: which of course would abolish the distinction. I can also explain what is the root of the error. In order successfully to distinguish varieties of phenomena — in this case, definition — it is necessary to classify the phenomena. But every scheme of classification rests upon some theory, or view, of the phenomena. The distinction between nominal and real definition is founded upon a grossly unsound theory of meaning — which is to say, a grossly unsound theory of the relations between language, thought and reality.[19] Ultimately, it is because the foundations are rotten that the structure built upon them is unserviceable.

You might therefore ask me how else I should propose classifying the varieties of the definition. The short answer is that I shouldn't. In my view the use of the word 'definition' leads us to confuse together things which are very different, and to attribute validity to operations which, correctly perceived, are clearly futile. As Robinson suggests, though I go further than he, it would be salutary to stop using the word 'definition', and to rename those of its referents which are not invalid by terms less liable to misinterpretation.

But our present purpose is rather different: it is to explain why we are unsuccessful at definition by exposing how we are confused about it. The simplest way to do this is to start with the accepted classification, and to show the weakness of each of the major varieties it presents us with. If I start by assuming what I actually reject, I do not more than follow the precedent of arguments which refute by *reductio ad absurdum* — though my argument is not strictly such a reduction.

I shall therefore proceed by distinguishing each of the *major* kinds of definition, asking of each two questions:

1 Is this possible? and
2 If it is, can it do much to realise our objective, which is to produce a sufficiently well-defined terminology?

I shall seek to show that in no case can we confidently answer Yes to both questions.

Since, then, I am working within an orthodox classification, I had better begin by explaining what the supposedly fundamental distinction between nominal and real definition is. I shall set out only the distinction in the Classical sense; as it happens, little more than verbal revision would be necessary to show how the conclusions of my analysis also apply if one started from the Modern sense.

That which is defined by a *nominal* definition is a word, or phrase, or other such signifier: for brevity, let us say 'a word' to cover all three variants. Let us introduce the technical term *'definiendum'*, which means 'that which is defined by a definition'. Then, the *definiendum* of a nominal definition is a word.

The definition states or declares what is the signification or meaning of the word: i.e., what the word means. Hence, a nominal definition is called for when there is ignorance or doubt as to what a word means. Its proper purpose is to ensure, as far as may be, that our words effectively signify what we have to say. This is important, since if something is worth saying it will be lost if it is not effectively signified. *But*, even perfect efficiency in signifying cannot make what is signified any more worth saying. Nominal definition can repair and clear the channels of communication, but it cannot improve the quality of what is put into those channels. It can help us to avoid loss of understanding of the real world through verbal error; but it cannot directly increase our understanding of the real world.

Real definition purportedly can, since, as the name implies, it is not merely about words but about 'things', elements of reality. The *definiendum* of a real definition is, purportedly, a *thing*, and the definition claims to give us important information about that thing. In the usual formulation, a real definition seeks to tell us the 'essential nature' of the thing defined. This idiom is unfortunate, since it is rooted in the mysticism of Plato and Aristotle, and to some philosophers[20] renders the whole notion inconsiderable. But the notion can be presented in a less obviously questionable manner by saying that a real definition purports to tell us what are the most important characteristics or attributes of the thing.

Now if the author of a real definition is to tell his readers about a thing, he needs to draw their attention to that thing: and this must normally be done by using the word which designates that thing. Hence one may sometimes be uncertain whether the *definiendum* is that word — so that we have a nominal definition — or the thing designated by the word, in which case we have a real definition.

We may apply a simple rule of thumb, which I may illustrate by supposing someone has claimed he is going to define religion.

1 Does the definition focus our attention *on the word* 'religion', and work on the assumption that its signification is problematical? If so, we have a nominal definition.

2 Does the definition focus our attention *through the word* 'religion' to the reality which it designates? Is the signification of the word treated as unproblematical — as it must be if the word is to lead each of us to attend to the same thing? If so, we have a real definition.

Of course, this test does not always yield a certain decision since, as I have argued, the most interesting kinds of definition tend to be both nominal and real.

I have said that a nominal definition states what a word means. That, of course, is ambiguous: we should say that a nominal definition states what a word *does* mean, or *shall* mean, or *should* mean. On this basis we can distinguish major varieties of nominal definition.[21]

A definition which tells us what a word does mean reports, or describes, the meaning of the word in the established usage of members of a specific linguistic community — a meaning which may include a number of distinct senses. I call these 'descriptive definitions'.

Such definitions are certainly possible. Any dictionary is replete with them — although dictionary definitions usually serve more than a descriptive purpose. Even purely descriptive definitions may serve a useful purpose. Only, not our purpose. For, if we find a term ill-defined, we are dissatisfied with its meaning in established use. Merely describing that meaning does nothing to alter it. Hence descriptive definitions are possible, but not to our chief purpose.

In the second kind of nominal definition, the definer assigns a specific meaning to a word, saying 'By this word I shall mean such-and-such' — or more formally, 'I stipulate that I shall mean ...'. These are therefore called 'stipulative definitions'.[22] At the beginning of this paper I produced two examples of this kind, relating to the word 'science'.

It should be noted that the content of a stipulative definition is normally somewhat different from the content of a descriptive definition of the same word. If the assigned meaning were no different, there would hardly be need to stipulate it; if it were wholly different, there would be no basis for using the word. Hence the meaning stipulated normally modifies the meaning the word bears in established usage. Very often the modification is intended to remove ambiguity, singling out one among several established senses of the word; it may also be intended to remove vagueness or inexactness.

I would also stress that in what I am calling stipulative definition, the modified meaning is assigned only for the author's own usage. If there is any claim that other people do or should use the word with just this meaning, then to that extent we are dealing with a significantly different phenomenon.

I have said that stipulative definitions are intended to remove ambiguity and/or vagueness and/or inexactness. There can be no doubt that they commonly succeed in this, to a sufficient extent. Hence they are both possible and relevant to our chief purpose. They are of genuine value — but unfortunately this value is severely restricted.

For while stipulative definitions are useful, they have rapidly diminishing marginal utility. Since a stipulative definition gives a word a modified meaning for the author's own usage only, what meaning he chooses is largely his private concern and prerogative. This gives him the measure of freedom which enables him to assign a meaning sufficiently unambiguous, unvague, and exact. But a freedom which is available to any man is available to every man. If this freedom is taken up, it can easily happen that one person stipulatively defines a word in one sense; a second person stipulatively defines the word in another sense; a third defines it in yet another sense and so on. Though each sense may be satisfactory, and may help to make each author's account clear, considered singly, the total effect is to make it hard to decide how far every author is speaking of the same phenomena, and what distinct and common meaning the word may have. Stipulative definition tends to create a sort of Tower of Babel.

Suppose, for example that three anthropologists, who have different theoretical positions and who have done fieldwork in different societies, each decide to write an account of religion in the society he has studied. Each may use his liberty to define by stipulation the word 'religion' in a sense appropriate to his interests and to the ethnographic reality he is dealing with. It may well be that each produces an admirable definition for his purpose, and with its help an admirable account of the phenomena. But it is possible, and indeed likely, given that each is analysing different phenomena and from a different theoretical standpoint, that each will have given the word 'religion' a rather different sense. This must make it difficult for anyone to work with their accounts comparatively, in order to draw out any kind of generalisation. He will find it hard to formulate just what the facts are; and harder still to decide what words to use, and in what senses, in order to refer to all their several accounts generally. Since anthropology cannot but be a comparative science, and to that extent at least a generalising science, this would clearly be unfortunate.

The trouble is that while any one stipulative definition may render a word unambiguous in the author's individual usage, a series of stipulative definitions by different authors will usually render the word polysemous, and hence potentially ambiguous, in the common or collective domain. And since science is necessarily a collective enterprise, this must be harmful. Stipulative definition tends to produce a series of improved semi-private languages, at the expense of weakening the public language.

Let us be clear: a word cannot be really well-defined for scientific purposes unless its meaning is not only sufficiently unambiguous, unvague and exact, but also *standard*[23] in the usage of practitioners of that science. When this is realized, as it often is in some degree, the person who would improve the meaning of a word goes beyond mere stipulative definition. Instead of declaring only '*I shall* use this word in this sense', he proposes '*We should* use this word in this sense'. I call such definitions 'prescriptive', to contrast with 'descriptive'; but I do not imply that the 'prescription' need be any stronger than a proposal or suggestion.

We have seen how stipulative definition naturally leads to prescriptive definition; and it is easy to suppose that no great difference is involved. If it is quite easy for *me* to improve *my* terminology by definition, should it not also be easy for *us* to improve *our* terminology by definition? Unfortunately this inference, so smooth that it often escapes notice, is quite fallacious. There is a vast difference between what it is possible to do with a private, or semi-private, language, and what it is possible to do with a public language. It is vast enough to encompass the fact that while stipulative definitions are possible, and even quite easy, prescriptive definitions are virtually impossible, at least to our chief purpose. Let me explain why.

Normally, prescriptive definitions are issued when various practitioners of the science are using the word in various senses. Occasionally, it may happen that the word is used in a standard sense, but the definer seeks to introduce a new and better sense. In either case, after the definition has been issued the word has *at least two* different senses between which a choice must be made. And this is the rub: any proposal that we adopt one standard sense for a word *ipso facto* requires that some of us cease using that word in the sense or senses that we have hitherto favoured. Since a person presumably has some reason for using a word in his favourite sense, and is likely to be attached if not addicted to it, such a proposal is likely to succeed only if we are given very powerful reasons for changing our usage. No doubt we should all think it desirable that a word have a standard sense: what we need to be persuaded is that *this* one sense, rather than some other, be adopted as standard. How could it be shown, to the satisfaction of all of us, that a given sense is decisively better than any competitor?

It is sometimes argued that the meaning we should adopt as standard is the meaning the word bears in established usage, as registered in, say, the Oxford English Dictionary. Other things being equal, we should indeed conform to established usage; but other things are rarely equal. It is rather unlikely that this meaning will be satisfactory for scientific usage, since it is the product of lay or colloquial usage; indeed if it were entirely satisfactory, it is hard to see why practitioners of the science should have chosen to use the word with other meanings. Prescriptive definitions of this kind, which I call 'conformative', might conceivably lead us to standardise one meaning for a word; but it is most unlikely that that meaning would be sufficiently well-defined for scientific purposes.

If the prescriptive definition is not 'conformative' it must be 'reformative': it must propose a sense rather different from the established, the dictionary, meaning, just as a stipulative definition does. Since such a proposal cannot appeal to the authority of established convention, on what other grounds could it be successfully urged?

One sense of a word can be shown to be *decisively* better than any other only if that sense is a concept so clearly advantageous that we must all wish to employ it. The only really valid way to demonstrate such advantage is to show that the concept is a necessary element in a theory which explains the phenomena adequately, and decisively better than any competitor. Since we have no such theories, and can barely imagine what they would be like or where and how they might be sought, such demonstration is presently impossible. Without it, there is no valid and reliable way of producing standard well-defined terms by prescriptive definition.

A major reason why this fact is so often overlooked is that real definition appears to offer us an alternative, and available, way to show that some concept, and hence some sense of a word, is decisively preferable to its competitors. Suppose that we actually could, by real definition, determine the essential nature, or the most important characteristics, of a thing. Would it not then be clear that this essential nature is just the concept we should all wish to signify by the word which designates that thing? Suppose, for example, that Durkheim had convinced us that concern with the sacred is the essential nature of religion, could we disagree that the word 'religion' should be used to mean that class of phenomena distinguished by such concern? A successful real definition could, and indeed must, entail a successful prescriptive definition; and in the absence of any other available recourse, it would be the only way to get there. This is why attempts at prescriptive (nominal) definition so often shift into attempts at real definition.

It remains, therefore, to show that no attempt at real definition can be successful, at least to the purpose. This is difficult simply because the whole notion of real definition is so thoroughly confused[24] that to disentangle it can be extremely tedious; and, shirking the tedium, we fail to get thoroughly convinced that real definition is indeed futile. I shall try to circumvent the tedium by presenting a somewhat abstract analysis which may also prove trying in its own way.

A real definition, as we have seen, purports to tell us the most important characteristics of the *thing* designated by a word. Just what could this *thing* be?

The word which designates it is nearly always a noun — and a common noun, not a proper name. Typically, such a noun may refer to, or denote, objects — or at any rate, empirical phenomena of an epistemologically objective kind. These we may call its 'referents'.[25]

Almost invariably the noun has a plurality of referents; since *the thing* is plainly singular, it cannot be a referent. Yet it certainly bears on the referents; to be singular it must be collective, in some sense the *set* of all the referents.

But we are to be told the most important characteristics or attributes of the thing. Examination would show that these assuredly are not character-istics attributable to the set only as a whole or aggregate — as some characteristics are attributable to a population but not to any of its members. On the contrary, these are characteristics of the members of the set, the referents, each and every one of them. Now we cannot usefully seek the most important characteristics of every member of the set unless we can be confident that there is *at least one* characteristic common to each and every member. Which is to say that the set is necessarily a class, in the strict logical sense.[26]

But now recall that the set was originally specified to us as the set of referents of a given word. Can we be confident that such a set will always constitute a class, in the required sense? Indeed we cannot: as is well known, the referents of a word often constitute but a mere family (in the sense of Wittgenstein).[27] A family is a set of elements linked by relations of similarity where there is no nontrivial[28] attribute common to each and every member.

Now to seek for the most important common attributes of the members of a Wittgensteinian Family, which have no important common attributes at all, is plainly futile. All those many real definitions which are attempting this can thus be dismissed out of hand: they are seeking to inform us about a Thing, i.e. a class, which is wholly chimerical.

Let us now attend to those which escape this doom: those which are about sets of referents all or most of which do constitute a class. We are to be given the most important characteristics of these referents: it is time to ask, important for what? There seem to be two alternative answers which deserve to be taken seriously.[29]

Plato, in his real definitions, imagined that he was uncovering the mystical forms or Ideas behind empirical phenomena. He would find few takers for this today. But several philosophers[30] have pointed out that his analyses actually achieve something more solid and useful. By way of example, let us consider his analysis of justice in his *Republic* — and assume that his analysis be as objective as he pretends, and not tendentious as it actually is.[31] He analyses the way we use the word 'justice' in order to get clear what characteristics a phenomenon must have if the word 'justice' is to be used correctly and confidently: the characteristics which are most important for determining the application of the word. In this way he makes explicit what is implicit in our usage of the word, just as a grammarian makes explicit the implicit structure of our syntactical usage. This is worth doing: it helps us to perceive and apprehend our linguistic behaviour, and the conceptualisations which underlie it. The exercise may be termed 'meaning analysis',[32] and it rather clearly belongs with nominal defini-tion of the descriptive kind. As such, as we remarked summarily above, it can contribute nothing to improving our terminology. To be sure, meaning-analysis goes rather beyond strictly nominal definition: it involves some ethno-science, some analysis of the concepts of lay-folk. But this won't help us either: if the concepts of lay-folk were adequate for scientific purposes, the words which express them would also be adequate. But we are agreed that to give our words a better sense we must use them to signify better concepts.

Moreover, real definition purports to give us understanding of real phenomena and we are entranced by it because we hope that that might be a scientific understanding. But how can exploring the way that lay-folk talk about and think about phenomena be expected to yield scientific understanding of those phenomena: when scientific understanding has hitherto normally required the setting aside of lay notions and replacing them by special scientific concepts?[33] There is just one circumstance in which such an expectation can seem even half-way plausible: where the habits of speech and thought of lay-folk are a constituent of the phenomena we are concerned with. And this condition is satisfied not only with regard to justice but also with regard to all the phenomena for which *social* scientists provide real definitions. This is surely a major reason why social scientists remain in thrall to real definition when natural scientists have long since outgrown it.[34]

I need not now discuss whether the truth that lay-notions enter into the facts we study requires that we give them priority as concepts by which we analyse those facts.[35] There is a special reason to justify the use of real definition, as meaning-analysis, by anthropologists. When social scientists engage in such real definition, the words they analyse tend to be English words. But normally English words are not used by the people anthropologists study: hence the usage of English words does not enter into the facts we study. We are therefore privileged above other social scientists in being able to exercise the enchantment of this kind of real definition.

There is another sense in which we might interpret the expression 'the most important characteristics'; and this is surely what most anthropologists have in mind when they attempt real definition. They are seeking those characteristics which are most important for providing scientific understanding of the phenomena. If we can show that the members of a class of phenomena have a characteristic, or attribute, which is handled by some scientific theory, then we connect the phenomena to that theory and bring them within its explanatory scope. And if that theory provides an adequate explanation for the phenomena and the most adequate available, then we can indeed consider that characteristic the most important for scientific purposes. But first we must have the theory; if we have not, then to claim that some characteristic of the phenomena is their most important is gratuitous, and is unlikely to carry conviction. Most authors of real definitions overlook this rather obvious fact; and so, implicitly, or explicitly like Spiro (1966:91) in his attempt to define religion, have lamely to fall back upon an appeal to intuition.

Here, as in several other respects, Durkheim's (1915) real definition of religion, for all its faults, was at least basically on the right lines. He singled out the dichotomy between sacred and profane as the essential characteristic of religion because, as he supposed, he thereby brought the phenomena within the scope of his theory. For the sacred/profane dichotomy could be identified with the dichotomy between the social and the individual: thus religion and the sacred could be identified with the social. We may not think much of this theory; but at least Durkheim tried to rest his definition in a theory, which is more than can be said for many of those who have offered alternative definitions of religion.[36]

Durkheim's example serves also to bring out the basic flaw in this kind of approach to real definition. A characteristic can be treated as most important only if it connects the phenomena to a powerful theory. Such theories are exceedingly scarce. The only possible way to work is to start with the powerful theories and to take up whatever characteristics they can handle, and not to choose characteristics on some other basis, hoping they will attach to some powerful theory.

Now from the moment we single out a specific attribute, we have automatically determined the class, and the set, of entities which have that attribute. We have no more degrees of freedom in establishing the boundary of the class, which inexorably runs its course between those entities which do and those which do not possess that attribute. And it is exceptionally unlikely that the extension of a class determined by an attribute chosen on scientific grounds will correspond to the extension of a class designated by an everyday word. For where the referents of an everyday word do constitute a class, it is one distinguished by a common attribute evident to lay-persons and significant in relation to lay-purposes. There is no valid reason for assuming that the distribution of such an attribute will correspond to the distribution of an attribute which yields scientific explanation: most scientific experience shows that such distributions do not correspond (Toulmin, loc. cit.). Although Durkheim stoutly maintains the contrary (1938:42-3; 1915:4-5), as he must if his procedure is to appear plausible, his contention is mere bluster.

It is nearly certain that everyone who follows through this kind of real definition will, if he does distinguish a scientifically useful attribute, face a dilemma. He will have two classes notably different in their extensions. On the one hand the class of phenomena having the attribute which founds scientific explanation, which is not as a whole designated by any familiar word; on the other hand, the class of phenomena designated by a familiar word, which do not have any common scientifically fruitful attribute. If he concentrates on the former class, what he is doing does not look like definition, and is not usefully thought of as such. If he concentrates on the latter, he can claim to offer a definition but not one which has sufficient merit to command general acceptance.

Durkheim's example illustrates both the dilemma and our reluctance to find a satisfactory resolution. As we all know, the class of phenomena exhibiting the heterogeneity of sacred and profane does not correspond to the set of phenomena we call religion: much of the latter must be excluded from it. If he had employed labels less 'question-begging' than those of 'sacred' and 'profane' it is even likely that some non-religious phenomena would have to be included within his class (cf. Goody 1961:49). He would have been wise to have concentrated on the class of phenomena distinguished by application of his theory, and to have abandoned any pretence to define religion. That he tried to have it both ways, and thus fell between two stools, is doubtless due to the fact that his explanatory theory just isn't strong enough to stand on its own merits. It requires the additional, though actually chimerical, bolstering of the old notion of real definition.

But we must also remark that nearly all social scientists, confronted with the choice between reconceptualising, and inevitably relabelling, phenomena for scientific purposes, or trying to define the terms we already have, settle for the latter, sterile, alternative. Thus even Leach, who is not the least intelligent among us, can solemnly propound the quite absurd question. 'What should we mean by "caste"?' (Leach, 1960). This general tendency, as my argument has been designed to show, is largely attributable to muddle-headedness. But there is surely a special reason why we social scientists are most notably muddle-headed in this regard than our brethren.

As Andreski clearly remarks in his *Elements of Comparative Sociology* (1964:85), social phenomena are so enormously complex as to be almost beyond the power of the human mind to grasp. Yet, as Durkheim points out in the second chapter of his *Rules* (1938) — which says many admirable things regarding definition — we, as laymen, as social beings, confront these phenomena, and have to act within them and upon them, and this without delay. To do this we have to represent the phenomena in our minds by crude, reach-me-down, categories which facilitate action. These categories facilitate social action partly because, for all their crudity, they do bear some resemblance to the actual shape of the phenomena, and partly because those with whom we interact also act on the basis of these categories. It is these categories, centrally, which are designated by words referring to social phenomena.

Each of us, from the beginnings of his awareness, has apprehended social reality through these categories. Through long habituation these have become for us the very shape of social reality, which indeed we have but fleetingly glimpsed in any other mode. And since these categories are not merely private but collective misrepresentations, they constitute the framework within which social interaction is consciously conducted. They constitute a social world of myth which overlies the true social reality so thickly that irruptions from below are perceived by us imperfectly, and apprehended hardly at all.

Anyone who would break up this crust of collective representations, expressed by our familiar words for social phenomena, and would set aside the reach-me-down categories in order to see the phenomena anew, would find himself desocialized, without the framework for interaction with his fellows. Thus a scientist, in his ivory tower, might be prepared to contemplate. But there is a still more daunting price to be paid for laying aside these categories: we should then be confronted with the overwhelming, baffling, strident complexity of social phenomena, without any familiar means for categorizing or speaking of them. Like Arjuna in the Gita brought face to face with God in his naked splendour and horror, we might find reality unveiled too dazzling to be borne.

In my analysis I have shown that descriptive definitions are possible, and I acknowledge that they may serve a useful, if modest, purpose. Stipulative definitions are possible, and can serve to make an author's discourse clear and intelligible. Perhaps I should go further and state that, in the present state of our subject, they are necessary for any serious scientific account.

On the other hand, they perhaps do as much to hamper as to help the development of an adequate scientific terminology. Dictionary definitions — which are both descriptive and conformative prescriptive — may on rare occasions contribute to the production of a standard terminology.

But, in the present state of our science, definitions which attempt to provide us with a proper scientific terminology — that is, reformative prescriptive definitions — must be expected to fail, as indeed they regularly do. For they could succeed only if founded on successful real definitions: and real definitions can succeed only if they take a direction which offers nothing to the purpose, or if they take a form which can no longer be regarded as definition.

Thus we conclude that definitions from which much is expected cannot succeed: attempts to provide them are a sheer waste of time and effort, and ought to be abandoned forthwith. This is quite an important conclusion. But does it entail, as some appear to assume, that we should abandon our concern that our terminology is inadequate? Assuredly not; an adequate terminology can perhaps be produced, only not by definition.

Belief in the importance of definition rests on the supposition that where our terms are ill-defined and we are unable to understand and talk good sense about the world, the former condition is the cause of the latter. Actually, for the most part, it is the other way about: it is because we cannot talk good sense about the subject-matter of our science that our terms are ill-defined. If we give sufficient attention to the facts, and to the ideas which serve us in understanding them, we shall in time evolve concepts which, being rooted in the facts, are both clear and useful for scientific purposes. Then, when we wish to express and communicate these concepts, we shall label them with words which, because they are employed to signify clear and definite concepts, are *ipso facto* well-defined. A well-defined term is a union of a word with a clear and definite concept. Such concepts are scarce, and formed only by much labour, whereas words are abundant and easily made. Hence to form the union, we must start by getting the scarce partner, whereafter the word will readily be found. Definition prefers rather to start with what is freely to hand, hoping to conjure up the scarce partner by mere talk. In empirical science it cannot be done.

What is less clear to me is whether the alternative, more rational procedure, of building from facts and concepts to terms, can be carried through sufficiently in social science. The facts that we are concerned with are enmeshed in words, constituted by the conceptualisations carried by these words: and these words and conceptualisations have not been formed by scientific procedures or for scientific ends. Can we free ourselves from these pre-scientific words and notions enough to see the facts as they really are, or do the facts themselves dissolve with the words that carry them?

I do not see how this question can be decided except by making the attempt: the attempt to do science with social facts considered inter-culturally, with terms that must be ill-defined initially, because they can be well-defined only eventually. If we succeed, the need for well-defined terms will be met without attention to the beguiling kinds of definition. If we do

not, we shall have failed with or without attention to definition. In neither
case will definition have helped us much toward our goal.

NOTES

1 This is a revised version of a paper which I read at seminars in the Institute of
Social Anthropology at Oxford, and the Department of Social Anthropology
at Manchester. I am grateful to participants in these seminars for their
criticisms and suggestions, which have helped me considerably in reworking
the paper.

2 As Spiro (1966) would appear to suggest: compare pp.91 and 87 in his paper.

3 As Richard Gombrich (1971:9) is largely content to do. Actually his claim
that Sinhalese Buddhists do call Buddhism a religion depends on his equating
their word '*agama*' with our 'religion', his justification of which (*ibid.*:58) is
far from adequate. On the contrary, his citation of such remarks as 'The
Buddhist religion is not a religion' (*ibid.*:62) or 'belief in gods is not a matter
of religion' (*ibid.*:151,176), shows that the matter is highly problematic.

4 For example, Gluckman's divorce hypothesis (Gluckman 1950 and 1971).
Part of the difficulty here derives from the imprecision of the statements by
other authors (1971:233-4), and part from the notorious imprecision of
Gluckman's formulation of the hypothesis (e.g. Needham 1971:xvi).

5 Such as Radcliffe-Brown's analyses of wide-range 'kinship' systems (1952:
51*ff*;1950). I have drawn attention in Southwold 1971 to some of the equivo-
cations which infest such discussions of 'kinship'.

6 For example, Beattie 1964; Schneider 1972; Needham 1971; Southwold 1971.

7 For example, Needham 1971; Scheffler 1967.

8 For example, Leach 1955; Gough 1959; Goody, E. 1962; Rivière 1971;
Needham 1971.

9 For example, various papers in Douglas 1970.

10 For example, Durkheim 1915; Horton 1960; Goody 1961; Spiro 1966.

11 For example, Gluckman 1955:226-31;1962.

12 For example, Radcliffe-Brown 1940; Middleton and Tait 1958:1; Easton 1959;
Swartz, Turner and Tuden 1966:4-7.

13 Notably Leach 1960.

14 Notably the contributors to Helm (ed.) 1968.

15 See, for example, Easton's criticism (1959:213-8) of Radcliffe-Brown 1940;
or Evans-Pritchard's criticism (1965:64-5) of Durkheim 1915.

16 This is made very clear in Robinson 1950. How many kinds one reckons
depends largely on how one classifies, and is thus arbitrary; but it is clear that
the word 'definition' is used in dozens, if not hundreds, of different senses,
many of which must be distinguished.

17 Popper (1966, I:31-3, and notes, and II,9-21, and notes.) Although Popper
does allow the possibility and use of one kind of definition (II:14), he is so
grudging about this, and so swingeing in his condemnation of all other kinds,
that it is natural to understand him as dismissing definition altogether. This
is in fact how Richard Gombrich (*op. cit.*:8) read him: we remarked above
(note 3) on some of the difficulties which resulted.

18 Although Spiro (1966) cites Hempel's (1952) distinction between nominal and
real definition, he seems to use the term 'nominal definition' in a wider sense.
This makes it hard to get clear just what he understands by an 'ostensive'
definition, and how such definitions relate to 'nominal' and 'real' definitions
(compare 1966:91 with *ibid*:87). The trouble is that all ostensive definitions are

nominal definitions in the Classical sense (cf. Robinson 1950:117-26), whereas none can be in Hempel's sense (1952:2-6).

19   In the original, the Classical, sense, nominal definitions are definitions of words, regarded as names (*nomina*). Underlying this terminology is the assumption that the semantics of common nouns are to be analysed on the model of those of proper nouns (names): a proper noun is the name of a person (etc.), so a common noun must be the name of a thing. But the analogy is inexact. A proper noun, e.g. 'Aristotle', names that objective entity which it refers to, *viz.* the famous philosopher; but a common noun normally refers to any of an extensive set of objective entities, no one of which it can truly be said to *name* (thus 'dog' may be used to refer to this dog or that dog, but it is not the *name* of any dog). Hence if anything is named by a common noun, it must be an entity of a different order. In fact such an entity must be a concept, and is commonly taken to be a class. But this analysis, especially if it is left implicit, introduces two grievous errors. In the first place, the objective entities referred to by a common noun often do not constitute a class, in any strict sense. In the second place, to treat a class (which is a concept) as a 'thing' (normally understood as an 'object') leads to the reification of classes, which is the source of several of the most damaging errors in philosophy.

More generally, the use of the name-relation as the basis for semantic analysis leads to such difficulties as to suggest that this is an erroneous procedure (see Carnap 1956:Ch.III).

More generally still, the attempt to deal with the semantics of common nouns on the basis of naming is a particular variety of the class of semantic theories which would treat the relation between language and reality as dyadic, in contrast to those which treat it as triadic, introducing some notion of 'thought' as a third and intervening term. Although neither kind of theory requires the matching of *elements* of the two or three domains one to another, their difference can be illustrated by considering the semantic analysis which might be given to words, as elements of language. In a triadic theory a word may be treated as representing a thought or idea, which in turn may represent objects (elements of objective reality); whereas dyadic theories repudiate speaking of thought or ideas (commonly dismissing this as 'mentalism') and seek to give an account of a more direct relation between words and objects. Despite numerous and voluminous efforts, no one has yet succeeded in producing a dyadic theory of meaning which is as adequate as even a simple triadic theory; and it is now widely recognized that the dogmatic repudiation of 'mentalism' was uncalled for. (On this see, for example, Ullmann 1962: Ch.3, csp.pp.57-8). I do not mean to suggest that any simple, or even complex, triadic theory is adequate to the facts; only that dyadic theories are too parsimonious.

20   E.g. Popper, *op. cit.*, I:31-2.

21   So far as I know, the classification I propose here is original. It is developed from distinctions made by Robinson (*op. cit.*:19, etc.) and Hempel (1966: 85-6); but my categories do not exactly correspond to theirs. My most important innovation is to divide what they, and other writers, call 'stipulative definition' into my two categories of 'stipulative' and 'prescriptive' definition. This is made clear in the text; the reader may find it necessary to remember that I give the term 'stipulative definition' a narrower sense than usual.

It should also be remarked that my categories are for the most part analytical rather than empirical; thus a particular instance of definition may sometimes have a place in more than one category. Indeed I have distinguished the empirical category of 'dictionary definitions', the members of which all have both descriptive and prescriptive functions. I have done this in order to forestall a predictable source of perplexity. Most people, when asked to consider definitions, tend to think of dictionary definitions as the most familiar kind of example; but these, so far from illustrating, rather confound the important distinction between descriptive and prescriptive definition. The fact that the most familiar kind of definition is both descriptive and prescriptive by no means invalidates this distinction; it is merely an instance of the fact that wherever the authority behind a norm is custom or convention, an assertion of the norm has factual (descriptive) as well as normative (prescriptive) content (*cf.* von Wright 1963:8-9).

22　As remarked in the previous note, I give the term 'stipulative definition' a narrower sense than is usual.

23　As Radcliffe-Brown recognized in the passage quoted above.

24　As is clearly shown by Robinson in his admirable discussion of real definition (*op. cit.*: Chap. VI). See also Popper (*op. cit., passim*, esp. II,9).

25　Following Ogden and Richards (1936:11); the term will do, although it was not altogether well-chosen.

26　A class is the set of all elements each of which has some certain property (or attribute). Since, if any two elements have a common attribute they are similar to one another with regard to having that attribute, every member of a class is similar to every other member with regard to the attribute common to all.

27　Among anthropologists this notion has been put to use by Needham (1971: 29-31, 1972:111-14). It is presented by Wittgenstein in 1958:31-2.

28　Of any set whatever it is possible truly to assert that there is some attribute common to every member, if only the attribute 'belonging to this set'; basically this is because attributes are products of our thinking and can be generated without limit. Although I cannot see how to draw a hard and fast line, there is clearly a distinction between these attributes of phenomena we would recognize as significant for understanding the phenomena, and which might lead us to think it useful to group all the phenomena having the attribute into a class, and those uninformative or fanciful attributes which might be mentioned *ex post facto* to support the claim that a set collected on other grounds could be regarded as a class. It is attributes of the latter kind that I dismiss as trivial.

29　This corresponds to Hempel's view (1952:6).

30　E.g. Polani 1958:115; Cook Wilson (1926), cited from Griffiths 1967, p.25.

31　See Robinson, *op. cit.*: 165-70; Popper *op. cit.*, I,92.

32　I borrow this term from Hempel, though he uses it also to cover what I have called 'descriptive definition' (see Hempel 1952:9; 1966:86).

33　As Durkheim insisted, rather too dogmatically, in Chap. II of his *Rules* (1938). The point is made more soundly in Toulmin 1953:50-3.

34　See Popper, *op. cit.*, I,32-3; note 30 to Ch.4; II,9.

35　This issue is briefly but clearly discussed in Hayek 1952:36-8.

36　This criticism cannot be levelled at Horton (1960), who explicitly recognizes the need to recommend his definition in terms of its scientific consequences. The hypotheses which his definition suggests could certainly form a basis for a sound scientific theory; whether the theory would be powerful enough to win general acceptance is another question. My impression is that while Horton's approach draws attention to some important features of religious phenomena, it overlooks others and must do as long as one feels obliged to stick close to common-sense notions. Once that obligation was rescinded, one could no longer claim that the conceptualisation of the phenomena was also a definition of religion.

BIBLIOGRAPHY

Andreski, S. 1964: *Elements of Comparative Sociology*. London, Weidenfeld and Nicolson.

Beattie, J.H.M. 1964: 'Kinship and Social Anthropology', *Man*, 130: 101-3.

Carnap, R. 1956: *Meaning and Necessity*. (Revised ed.). Chicago University Press.

Carr, E.H. 1961: *What is History?* London, MacMillan.

Douglas, M. (ed.) 1970: *Witchcraft Confessions and Accusations. A.S.A. Monographs, 9*. London, Tavistock.

Durkheim, E. 1915: *The Elementary Forms of the Religious Life* (transl. from the French, 1st ed. 1912). London, Allen and Unwin.

———— 1938: *The Rules of Sociological Method* (transl. from the French, 1st ed. 1895). Glencoe, I11, The Free Press.

Easton, David 1959: 'Political Anthropology', in Siegal, B.J. (ed.), *Biennial Review of Anthropology*. Stanford University Press.

Evans-Pritchard, E.E. 1965: *Theories of Primitive Religion*. Oxford, Clarendon Press.

Gluckman, M. 1950: 'Kinship and Marriage among the Lozi of Northern Rhodesia and the Zulu of Natal' in Radcliffe-Brown, A.R. and Forde, E. (eds.), *African Systems of Kinship and Marriage*. London, Oxford University Press.

———— 1955: *The Judicial Process among the Barotse*. Manchester University Press.

———— 1962: 'African Jurisprudence', presidential address to Section N of the British Association for the Advancement of Science, 1961. *The Advancement of Science*, 74.

———— 1971: Postscript to Gluckman 1950, in Goody, J.R. (ed.), *Kinship*. Harmondsworth, Penguin.

Gombrich, R. 1971: *Precept and Practice*. Oxford, Clarendon Press.

Goody, E.N. 1962: 'Conjugal Separation and Divorce among the Gonja of Northern Ghana', in Fortes, M. (ed.), *Marriage in Tribal Societies. Cambridge Papers in Social Anthropology*, 4. Cambridge University Press.

Goody, J.R. 1961: 'Religion and Ritual: the Definitional Problem'. *British Journal of Sociology*, 12,142-64.

Gough, E.K. 1959: 'The Nayars and the Definition of Marriage', *J.R.A.I.*, 89: 23-34.

Griffiths, A.P. (ed.), 1967: *Knowledge and Belief. Oxford Readings in Philosophy*. London, Oxford University Press.

Hayek, F.A. 1952: *The Counter-Revolution of Science*. Glencoe, III, The Free Press.

Helm, June (ed.), 1968: *Essays on the Problem of Tribe*. Seattle, University of Washington Press.

Hempel, C.G., 1952: *Fundamentals of Concept Formation in Empirical Science. International Encyclopaedia of Unified Science*, II,7. Chicago, Chicago University Press.

———— 1966: *Philosophy of Natural Science*. Englewood Cliffs, N.J., Prentice-Hall.

Horton, Robin 1960: 'A Definition of Religion, and its Uses', *J.R.A.I.*, 90.

Leach, E.R. 1955: 'Polyandry, Inheritance, and the Definition of Marriage', *Man*. 199.

_____ 1960: Introduction: 'What Should we Mean by Caste?' in Leach, E.R., (ed.), *Aspects of Caste in South India, Ceylon and North-West Pakistan. Cambridge Papers in Social Anthropology, 2.* Cambridge: Cambridge University Press.

Middleton, J. and Tait, D. 1958: *Tribes Without Rulers.* London, Routledge and Kegan Paul.

Needham, R. 1971: Remarks on the Analysis of Kinship and Marriage. In Needham, R. (ed.), *Rethinking Kinship and Marriage. A.S.A. Monographs,* 11. London, Tavistock.

_____ 1972: *Belief, Language, and Experience.* Oxford, Blackwell.

Ogden, C.K. and Richards, I.A. 1936: *The Meaning of Meaning* (4th ed.). London, Routledge and Kegan Paul.

Polanyi, M. 1958: *Personal Knowledge.* London, Routledge and Kegan Paul.

Potter, K.R. 1966: *The Open Society and Its Enemies, 5th ed.*, London, Routledge and Kegan Paul.

Radcliffe-Brown, A.R. 1940: Preface to Evans-Pritchard, E.E. and Fortes, M. (eds.), *African Political Systems.* London, Oxford University Press.

_____ 1950: Introduction to Radcliffe-Brown, A.R. and Forde, D. (eds.), *African Systems of Kinship and Marriage.* London, Oxford University Press.

_____ 1952: *Structure and Function in Primitive Society.* London, Cohen and West.

Rivière, P.G. 1971: 'Marriage: a Reassessment' in Needham, R. (ed.), *Rethinking Kinship and Marriage.* A.S.A. Monographs 11. London, Tavistock.

Robinson, R. 1950: *Definition.* Oxford, Clarendon Press.

Scheffler, H.W. 1967: 'On Concepts of Descent and Descent Groups', *Current Anthropology,* 8,506-9.

Schneider, D.M. 1972: 'What is Kinship All About?' in Reining, P. (ed.), *Kinship Studies in the Morgan Centennial Year.* Washington D.C., The Anthropological Society of Washington.

Swartz, M.J., Turner, V.W., and Tulen, A. (eds.) 1966: *Political Anthropology,* Chicago, Aldine.

Southwold, M. 1971: 'Meanings of Kinship' in Needham, R. (ed.), *Rethinking Kinship and Marriage,* op. cit.

Spiro, M.E. 1966: 'Religion: Problems of Definition and Explanation' in Banton, M. (ed.), *Anthropological Approaches to the Study of Religion. A.S.A. Monographs,* 3. London, Tavistock.

Toulmin, S. 1953: *The Philosophy of Science.* London, Hutchinson.

Ullmann, S. 1962: *Semantics: an Introduction to the Science of Meaning.* Oxford, Blackwell.

Wilson, J.C. 1926: *Statement and Inference.* Oxford, Clarendon Press.

Wittgenstein, L. 1963: *Philosophical Investigations.* Oxford, Blackwell.

Wright, G.H. von 1963: *Norm and Action.* London, Routledge and Kegan Paul.

The Achievement of Sex:
Paradoxes in Hagen Gender-Thinking

MARILYN STRATHERN

Introduction

There are no specific words in Melpa, the language of the Mount Hagen people in the Western Highlands of Papua New Guinea, which could be translated simply as 'male' and 'female'. Men and women have their own tools, their own spheres of activity and interests; and dress-styles, ritual and religious symbols clearly demarcate differences and relationships between the sexes. To express these very definite and perceived category contrasts, Hageners talk about 'men's things'/'women's things', or 'men's way of behaviour/women's way of behaviour'; and may refer to people of either sex as acting 'like men' or 'like women'. In what follows I use male and female for those situations where categories are implied, and men and women to refer to individuals.

It is more relevant for my exposition than it is for Hageners to be able to employ the terms 'male'/'female'. For it is possible to consider Hagen gender ideas as resting on two contradictory assertions which can be represented thus

$$\begin{cases} \text{male : female : : men : women} \\ \text{male : female} \neq \text{men : women} \end{cases}$$
$$\text{where : : stands for 'correspondence'}$$

Yet depicting it this way has the virtue merely of keeping distinct certain aspects of gender which might be confused in analysis. There is no confusion in Hageners' minds. (Though I suggest later that the idea of power in relation to the sexes does give rise to some mental contortions.)

This Hagen paradox can be dismantled with two tools — one analytical, the other ethnographic. It is only worth stating insofar as it draws attention to the theoretical point that one cannot consider gender just as a set of static classifications based on association and contrasts, or analogy and equation, which are applied to the persons and activities of the sexes. Gender is very much made use of in Hagen to talk about things other than men and women, and the fact that it is so used has a feedback effect on how the sexes are perceived. Thus there is much terminological preoccupation with contrasts between what is important and what is insignificant, and what is strong and what is weak. These notions are made concrete in explicit reference to gender (e.g. 'men are important'/'women are insignificant'); so that one may call them male or female qualities. Yet the values which they sustain also demand that they be to some extent free-floating, and it can be most inapposite to think of all men as important and all women as insignificant. Contrasts between such male and female qualities are thus both attached to men and women, thereby being expressed by a powerful set of symbols, and are detached, insofar as they are also used to mark status differences within the sexes. The ethnographic point, however, is that this is neither a greater nor lesser 'paradox' than it is paradoxical for clans which look on themselves as the descendants of a common father to be in fact made up of persons recruited through a variety of ties. Hageners do not make the mistake of thinking one is talking about the same set of facts. Their own accommodation is in terms of distinctions between the ideal and the actual; and between domains of reference (ideology and recruitment), which involve an understanding of verbal relativity. As in English one might refer to a 'mannish woman', Hageners of either sex speak of women who are like men and men who are like women. The domains of reference are distrete[1] and the relationship between them are metaphoric. There is little intellectual confusion here. Hageners say quite easily the equivalent of 'Only men can be important; and some women are like men in this respect'. What is of interest is this ease itself. It arises from the fine discrimination they make between ascribed and achieved status, between innate and enacted upon qualities, between how one is born and what one does with one's life. It is a discrimination, moreover, that seems rooted in the central concerns of many men, which are to do with prestige and success and which turn above all on achievement. It is ideas about limits and potential in achievement which are being symbolised in reference to the sexes, what is innate in the make-up of men and women and what can be overcome to must be submitted to. The particular qualities Hageners choose to consider in this light, especially the capacities for public prominence, are related directly to the areas within which achievement is socially demonstrated.

Gender as Metaphor

We can take gender as the summation of those characteristics, attributes, roles and so on, which are bestowed upon men and women so as to make them appear naturally sex-linked. The picture which is built up of the 'nature' of males and females is likely to incorporate a number of symbols (e.g. 'women's flesh is soft'). Once the images have been formed, the natures of the sexes, or the relationships between them, can be further used to symbolise other things (e.g. 'Our enemies are not men — they are women!'). We could say these symbols are powerful partly from the way they confound 'natural' sexual attributes (body size, virility) with 'cultural' ones (feebleness of mind, valour). Male-female relations also provide a means of expressing oppositeness and contrast — while at the same time including the possibility of complementarity or union. In one and the same breath Hageners will point to the radical difference in men's and women's work, for men deal in valuables while women produce foodstuffs; and to the fruitful coming together of these activities, for while the man brings pigs into the household through his exchanges, the woman tends them and rears young. Now this is more than a comment on the division of labour. At the back of Hagen descriptions of what men and women do is the implicit judgement of what they are *fit for*. And since the sexes are not equal, women being capable of less important enterprises than men, phrasing certain activities in terms of male or female occupations contains an evaluation. Exchange is more important than horticulture, and can remain so even if the necessity of gardening is admitted — in the same way as in a conjugal partnership the man maintains his superiority even though for some things he is dependent on the woman.

Hagen gender is more than just that set of stereotypes which regulates actual relations between the sexes, which gives rise to and justifies certain kinds of treatment, rules, and such. Its dimensions ('Men are wild, powerful') also furnish concrete characteristics in terms of which male-female relations are used as symbols ('Our clan is a clan of men', i.e. powerful). Hageners make use of the male-female dichotomy to structure one of the most important areas of their social life — the acquisition of prestige; and part of their definition of gender turns directly upon characteristics applicable to this area of life — on attributes of worth, capability, success, achievement. They do this both through equating certain activities with men and women (making them 'male' or 'female') and by differentiating these activities from the potential inherent in an individual's sex.

Gender in our own thinking is a no less slippery concept. We use it in studies of sex identity to refer to how individuals learn to relate their own physiological make-up to the roles and stereotypes available to them; we also use it to draw attention to the categories, values and assumptions which cluster round *notions* of male-ness or female-ness. Gender as a set of ideas can be taken separately from what people make of them. The latter point of view is sociocentric, for it is argued that the logic inherent in the way such notions are set up must be understood in relation to general values in the society.

The present paper belongs to studies of this second type. Like the idea of descent, gender-thinking in my terminology covers much more than the process of recruitment to a sex group or rules for an individual's category identification. My interest is in the ideology of gender, which, in much the same way as descent constructs use some ideas of recruitment to symbolise group solidarity or inter-group relations, uses attributes of the sexes to define certain qualities of social concern. Briefly, I am dealing not with the manner in which ideas about gender relate to personal identity but with how they relate to other ideas.

As a body of statements about the qualities of and relations between the sexes, gender comprises a language in itself which furnishes idioms for referring to other qualities and relationships. It is a metaphor in Wagner's (1972) sense. In Hagen one could regard ideas about males and females and ideas about achievement (strength, importance) as having constant feed-back effect: each can stand in symbolic relationship to the other, and notions about achievement are as significant for the way the sexes are defined as vice versa. They metaphorise one another. Wagner suggests that the relationship 'among specific metaphors within a culture can be either one of complementarity (consistency) or of innovation (contradiction)' (1972:7). Hageners' use of achievement notions in relation to the sexes is an innovation of this kind. It appears to be a straight-forward extension of a fairly specific set of ideas about the capacities of the sexes, but in using apparently natural differences to describe cultural potential has to contradict the assumption that natural differences are innate.

The Place of Nature and Culture

At two places in the preceding section a contrast between nature and culture is used. Because gender is always in part about men and women as physiologically differentiated units, it has commonly been analysed as what 'culture' makes of 'nature'; and where folk systems have been described as concerned with similar problems, as to what is natural and what is cultural, gender ideas, how males and females are perceived, are often also manipulated to talk about this relationship (e.g. La Fontaine 1972). It seems 'natural' to us that cultures should have this preoccupation; it also seems natural that gender, along with cuisine, may be used to make these discriminations, because our own folk system does exactly the same (e.g. men are inventors and artists, women are 'closer to nature').

It is Goodale's critique of these assumptions which immediately raises the possibility that in those societies where gender constructs have to do with drawing boundaries between nature and culture, it is not so much because gender itself poses a 'problem' but because symbols are needed which gender can aptly provide. And since symbols are needed in this area, elements in the make-up of the sexes are identified as natural or cultural. Goodale describes a society which is interested in contrasts between nature and culture but does not use gender to give them structure (though it does use sexuality). I describe a society which has elaborate gender constructs, but does not appear to be particularly interested in the nature/culture contrast. Men in this society[2] do, however, appear to be passionately interested in buttressing a contrast between what is significant and strong and what is unimportant and weak, in a way which confirms the innate powerfulness of males.

Hagen men seem to make strenuous efforts to avoid an explicit and categorical (as opposed to an implicit and situational) equation between women and power. They do not use a nature/culture dichotomy to do this. Whatever equations are made between the sexes and nature/culture, those are open to contextual shifts and manipulations. From some points of view women are naturally powerful (they bear children); they are also naturally weak (no good in battle); they are also culturally powerful (cook the subsistence crop and many doctor it in addition) and culturally weak (do not make *moka*). Men accuse women of artifice (operating co-wife magic to get rid of a rival); women accuse men of artifice (holding rituals of fertility which involve nothing more than a load of old stones). Men accuse women of unbounded natural desires (wanting exclusive access to a husband's sexuality); women accuse men in like manner (their rites are only a pretext for gluttony, eating pork without having to share it with women). The terms 'natural' and 'cultural' in all these examples do not reflect Hagen terminology. Yet I do not think that these ideas even implicitly structure gender concepts. There is much less emphasis on making natural or cultural attributes sex-linked than there is on linking sex to strength and prestige. We can construe if we wish the nature/culture dichotomy as contributing to contrasts between the sexes, but it has little consistency.

Not only is there not much consistency, but there is, even more telling, little manipulation. If culture: nature : : man: woman, we might expect to find contrivances which made artefacts superior to natural things,[3] but this is not the case. Men do seem to contrive always to make it seem that power is on their side. If women bear children, men in their cults control the essential source of fertility; if women do most of the gardening and stock-raising work, it is men who have access to natural powers residing in wild things which will ensure they can convert produce into valuables. It is the power: powerless dichotomy which is so assiduously buttressed; not a culture: nature one. When women's natural powers threaten men, it is not because nature must be separated from culture but because (female) power is a threat to (male) power.

One cannot understand Hagen gender ideas by saying that they are simply about 'nature', that they 'cope with' problems posed by biology and the need to control the environment, or whatever. Although they have a physiological content, there is a dimension to them which relegates physical sexual endowments to second place. From this point of view male and female natures are regarded as modifiable without the intervention of specific cultural apparatus. Perhaps here we have a clue to what has also been an ethnographic puzzle in Hagen, the absence of puberty rituals there. Does lack of concern with puberty rituals have something to do with not utilising a nature/culture dichotomy as a *basic* gender marker?[4] I make some introductory comments on this lacuna, not in order to examine why some societies perform these rites and others do not, but to point to the hope that at the end of the exposition on gender-thinking good reasons will have emerged why Hageners should fail to ceremonialise the achievement of physiological adulthood, or use physiological markers to symbolise the achievement of social adulthood.

The Failure to Ritualise Puberty

Rituals of some kind or other associated with puberty (for boys or for girls or for both) are found throughout the Papua New Guinea Highlands. From this point of view two societies stand out dramatically from the eleven surveyed by Allen (1967): Hagen, and their cultural neighbours, Mendi.[5] Hageners are as concerned as other Highlanders with the physical differences between men and women, and see a relationship between their physiological natures and community health. There is without question a biological dimension to their gender classifications along recognisably Highlands lines. Nevertheless, there is no ceremonial attention of the kind which would stamp on every individual his irrevocable commitment to the life-style of a particular sex. The people of Hagen have not, and apparently have never had, rituals or ceremonies which fall into the class of puberty and initiation rites. There is no identifiable sequence of celebrations to mark the entry of boys into the ranks of adult men; no ritual fuss made of girls' first menstruation.

Andrew Strathern (1970a) has drawn attention to the difficulties there are in correlating the presence or absence of different kinds of puberty rituals with various social values and institutions: 'In whatever direction the arguments are urged, problems remain. If we consider that initiation rites are required to resolve conflicts in sex-identity, this raises the question of the extent to which such comflicts are resolved by other socialization practices [in the absence of rites]; while if we stress that initiation rites dramatize male solidarity, male opposition to females, and so on, we are faced with the problem of assessing the strength of these values in different Highlands societies.' (Strathern A.J. 1970a:378)

This was nevertheless a task to which Allen (1967) specifically addressed himself in proposing that their occurrence is related to the extent to which the sexes are rigidly differentiated, this in turn having a bearing on the solidarity of local groups. Clan exclusiveness, for example, based on a single-sex ideology (e.g., the clan is conceived of as a body of males), can give rise both to an opposition between males and females and to a desire to emphasise the unity and solidarity of the sex through which clan membership is defined. In such a context arise cults associated with the definition of masculinity. He suggests that the absence of rituals in Hagen (Mbowamb or Melpa) is a result of diminished male solidarity brought about by status stratification (and he refers to classes). Presumably he envisages that big-men would have some kind of class interests in common with other big-men which would affect their clan loyalties; and that class would be a common link between its male and female members.

He adduces a number of factors about the social status of Hagen women to support his assertion that the 'sex dichotomy' is relatively unimportant. Apart from the weakness of his argument that *women* are given religious importance because *the female principle* is recognised in some cults, one should surely differentiate between ideas about antithesis between the sexes and the frequency or kinds of actual situations through which men and women interact. Proof that Hagen women have a 'high status' (1967:43), and are able to express some of the hostility they feel towards men in secular terms (ibid:56), is no proof that Hageners do not also indulge in sexist thinking, and that men and women do not categorise each other, project stereotypes and myths onto the perceived behaviour of the opposite sex, and see them as a threat or challenge. Moreover, 'Allen does not explain in full why initiation ritual should require actual rather than ideal solidarity' (Strathern A.J. 1970:377). In other words, why notions surrounding an opposition between the sexes and the exclusiveness of single-sex associations should be tied to social organisation (evidence that clans in reality act in a soldary way) and not simply to *ideational* constructs (e.g. a belief that the clan is a united group). It seems that Allen rests his argument on a demonstration of whether men and women do or do not form common interest groups. Where a common interest group comprises members of one sex (e.g. all males) then male-female antagonism finds its most explicit expression. In a society such as Hagen 'the elaborate class structure ... cuts across and minimizes the social and ritual differences between the sexes' (Allen:44).

The weight Allen gives to class stratification in Hagen has already been criticised (cf. Strathern A.J. 1968). It is in fact doubtful whether the stratification he describes, derived from the works of Vicedom (Vicedom & Tischner 1943-8), ever had quite the salience he suggests, and it certainly cannot be used as an explanatory divide in this context. Vicedom's material can be interpreted as a recognisable variant on leadership systems operating throughout the Highlands. There were no institutionalised rules concerning inheritance and succession which could have produced status groups with an access to wealth and to the means of production that were not only exclusive but predictable. Big-men today can be seen to differentiate themselves from the common mass of their clansmen, especially in their wide-ranging exchange networks and alliances with other big-men; but this differentiation is wholly situational. It is likely to be stressed when for other political reasons rifts already exist within the clan — if the clan *wishes* to present a solidary front, then the achievements of its big-men are presented as achievements of the clan as a whole. Moreover, even though there is some tendency for big-men to seek wives from the families of other big-men, it would have to be demonstrated that these kinds of arrangements also break down barriers between the sexes. It does not follow theoretically that such transactions *between men*, albeit on a 'class' basis, are going to modify the relations of men towards women as a category. Wives are wives[6] and do women's jobs, even if the wives of rich men receive more reflected glory than do wives of the poor. Finally, as Allen notes, women do not participate in *moka* (ceremonial exchange) in the same way as men. The fact that not all men participate equally makes for inequalities among males — but inequality is not the same thing as lack of solidarity. Some men may be leaders and others followers, and still be engaged in enterprises on a sexual basis which exclude females.

In short, class ranking, or stratification in societal terms,[7] does not exist in Hagen, and even if it did, its meaning for male-female opposition and single-sex associations would not be at all clear. This is the point to spring a paradox, not a Hagen one, but as a construct of my own argument. For the fact that early observers in the Hagen area were impressed enough by Hagen ideas about status to describe the society as stratified provides another take-off point, though for a quite different destination.

Vicedom's reification of Hagen values as indicating a society divided into classes was only a step off what was undoubtedly then and still is the way Hageners formulate things. There is almost what one might call a preoccupation with the notion of success, with the opposition between *nyim* (being successful, influential, important) and *korpa* (being rubbish, worthless, of no account). Sociological analysis of Hagen is not advanced by talking in terms of classes, and it was sociological correlates for which Allen was searching in his quest. Yet Hageners do have very definite ideas about the achievement of status.

Nyim and *korpa* are labels tied in the first place to individuals. Membership of a clan which contains *nyim* men does not mean that oneself will automatically become *nyim*. It may mean that one shares in and to that extent can claim *nyim* status vis-à-vis other groups because of the contribution big-men make to clan prestige as a whole. Groups can as a block then be labelled *nyim* and *korpa*, as their status mirrors fluctuating fortunes in ceremonial exchange or warfare. But this is treating a group a though it were a person. In relation to others the clan or tribe has done well or badly. It does not mean that all members of a clan called *nyim* on a particular occasion are themselves *nyim* or that the epithet can be held permanently, let alone be passed on to one's descendants. It does mean that individuals see the status of their group as dependent on the achievements of its particular members.

Success, failure; personal and group achievement; an emphasis on wealth and access to the means of production, run as themes through Hagen life, informing the judgements people make of others, providing goals and rationales, and appearing to structure relationships in specific situations. They also have a direct bearing on male-female relations. And the equation of some women with men who are *nyim* comes into it. But this has little to do with the status demarcation of social units or the identification of interest groups; it concerns the definition of gender.

IDEAS ABOUT MALES AND FEMALES

Pollution Cults

Concern over physical relations between the sexes is as apparent in Hagen as elsewhere in the Highlands. Through their menstrual and sexual emanations, women can harm men. To some extent men's sexuality can also be dangerous (not to women as such, but to children, and to the success of various undertakings). Clear rules demarcate the conditions under which intercourse should take place, and the precautions women should adopt to protect their menfolk (cf. Strathern A.M. 1972:ch.7). Men and women are separated residentially, an arrangement which underlines a basic dichotomy in their interests (e.g. women rear pigs — stalled in their houses; men talk about pig exchanges — men's houses being the place where plans are discussed). There is a very real contrast between male and female social life. Women spend much more time on agricultural work than do men, and this is perceived to contribute to the kind of beings they are: women stay at home, are basically domestic creatures, almost akin to the pigs they care for; men hold the public arena, they are political animals, associated with the wild, the exotic, free to go where they want like the birds whose feathers they adorn themselves with.

Hageners are also concerned with growth and maturation. They discern different developmental patterns in boys and girls; girls mature earlier but are 'softer' than boys. Contrasts between the sexes refer to physical potential (men are 'strong', women are 'weak'). This has a mystical dimension: not only are men strong enough to be combattants in war, but possess the spiritual strength to approach ancestral ghosts, and the strength of mind to pursue determined sources of action. Women are too weak to undertake the really heavy (though sporadic) work in gardening, and their weakness further makes them unfit for certain ceremonies, renders them feeble of mind and of irresolute purpose. Such weakness is also contaminating, and Hageners share with other Highlanders the belief that a man can be de-masculinised by too much contact with females. Boys have to break away from the constant association with female kin which typified their childhood in order to grow into proper men.

There is preoccupation with fertility. Men hope to have many sons; women receive special recognition at food distributions if they mother many children. Clan strength is seen to rest directly, though not entirely, on its numbers. This is not simply a value derived from the days of warfare: the support of ancestral spirits is reflected in clan fertility, and on exchange occasions, groups vie with one another to produce the longest line of dancers.

Sexual pollution, attention to physical growth, an emphasis on clan fertility — the scene would appear to be set for ceremonies to mark the many cultural implications of the physiological changes which make boys and girls into men and women. Men must be separated off from women; children must grow into adults; sources of fertility must be guarded. The mental categories all seem to be there; but nothing happens.

If there is a reason for this, it does not lie in a fundamental secularism (cf. Douglas 1970). Hageners believe that ancestral ghosts oversee and influence the daily affairs and morals of their descendants. There is a minor pantheon of Spirits (Strathern A.J. 1970b). Sickness and other events are interpreted in terms of the judgement or caprice of this spirit world. Manifest enjoyment is taken in ceremony. Since pacification there has been a resurgence of public activity centering on ceremonial exchange (*moka*), and every specific stage of the sequences is marked by emphasis on display, on proper speeches, on proper dress (Stathern A.J. 1971a). There is no dearth of capacity here to manipulate symbols and metaphors in order to draw attention to facets of power or of status. Omens and objects manipulated in rituals denote the potential of personal or of clan strength and prosperity. Verbal manipulation is evident in spells which are recited to increase certain crops, ensure a quick delivery, eradicate poison, and such like (Strathern A.J. and A.M. 1968). Ornamentation explicitly demarcates achieved status or attributed emotions (Strathern A.J. and A.M. 1971.)[8]

Moreover, some of their concerns with inter-sexual pollution, with maturation and with fertility do find ritual expression. Although there are no specific purificatory rites which a woman undergoes to terminate menstrual or post-natal seclusion, the rules which circumscribe female activities at these times clearly draw attention to her status. One of Spirit Cults which Hageners perform includes among its aims the protection of men from the contaminating powers of human females. Certain ritual procedures can be undertaken to remove the effects of menstrual pollution. Spells and minor, rather informal, rites during infancy and childhood also protect the growth and health of young children. The first hair-cutting, for example, often calls for a sacrifice to ancestral spirits. The emphasis here is on the protection of the child's future growth rather than marking a particular 'stage' in the child's life. The ghosts of the dead continue to be interested in the health and vigour of children, to whose condition their attention will be drawn at subsequent sacrifices, an aspect of their wider concern for clan continuity. Spells and sacrifices help individual couples overcome apparent barrenness. The Spirit Cults also encompass fertility as a theme. Fertility may be seen as primarily within the power of men (in the Female Spirit cult) or as an attribute to sexuality (in the Male Spirit cult).

These cults are two of several which circulate through the Hagen area. Different regions specialise in particular cults or versions of them. Performance is subject to popularity, and in recent years some cults have travelled to clans which have never held them before, while others held in the past have not been revived. For many groups one can discern no definite cycling in the holding of performances nor predict any periodicity. Certain clans are held to 'own' the cult at a particular time, a temporary status. There is no concept that all the groups which have held performances of one cult have entered into some secret society. What the cults achieve for the participants is health, prosperity and strength. Participants do not form an exclusive group; it is temporary eminence they will receive, and this will be passed along to further clans as the cult is taken up by them. Boys engaging in some of the stages of the performances anticipate their adult status. But initiation would be a gross misnomer here. All the participants are, in a sense, 'initiated' into the cult under the direction of ritual experts. But for neither the boys nor the men does this carry consequences for their status (as opposed to their well-being) beyond the duration of the cult as such.

It is true that Vicedom (Vicedom and Tischner 1943-8, II; 180*ff*) describes one cult (*koi tamb*) as concerned with the 'initiation' of boys. In its seclusion of male participants, its ritual focus of flutes representing birds, and the notion that during the cult performers acquire health and strength manifested in visible physical growth, it had many formal similarities to initiation rituals practiced elsewhere in the Highlands.[9] Strauss (1962: 396*ff*) characterises it as promoting male growth. Indeed, if it emphasised growth and maturation, it falls into the class of ceremonies which include similar concerns. For example, in the past (Vicedom and Tischner 1943-8, 1;94) there might be some celebration when a boy first donned a proper wig. One may doubt very much, however, whether the *koi tamb* was an initiation cult in structural terms. Promoting growth is a very different matter from marking a stage in growth as endowing persons with a new social status. Future health is ensured; not an effective transition from one state to another as occurs in *rites de passage* and initiation into associations. There is no evidence that participation in this, or any other Hagen cult, was a necessary preparation for adulthood or for becoming a full male.

Physiology and Rôle

Hageners certainly have ceremonies, then, which promote growth. Minor rites held during infancy or childhood centre on either sex; later participation in cults or ritual is likely to concern boys only, and to this extent sexual maturation (maleness) becomes one of their themes. But these later ceremonies are not tied to an individual's life-cycle, do not change his effective social status, and do not qualify him for adulthood. There are no additional public ceremonies for either sex at adolescence; nor are there any regularly held private rites to demarcate the onset of female menstruation or the growth of male secondary sexual characteristics. There are no bachelor cults or obligatory rituals to protect spouses from another; no ordeals or dramas to inculcate attributes of gender (such as fearlessness); so that in Allen's terminology, neither are there any puberty rites to define sexual maturity as a crucial stage in the individual's life-cycle, nor are the sexes, treated as closed groups into which initiation is a necessary means of entry. Adults are distinguished from children; and males most emphatically from females. Hageners do not discount the evidence of biology. But they do not make the acquisition of physical characteristics an exclusive idiom through which to draw attention to adulthood or to gender.

Perhaps an area has been missed out of the comparisons here, for marriage ceremonies can be a *rite de passage*. But Hagen marriage rites contain few references to physiological status. As seems to be so throughout the Highlands (cf. Glasse and Meggitt 1969) the changes in status celebrated at marriage are essentially those brought about by the alliance of the now affinal groups, and the new status of the woman who from being a member of her natal clan becomes attached to another clan as a wife. Hagen bride-wealth ceremonies do not include a ritualisation of physical maturity and have no concern, for example, with the virginity of the bride;[10] they publicise the wealth of the respective parties, the establishment of alliance, the blessings union will bring. The groom is an insignificant participant; the bride is central, for her dual status as sister to one clan and wife to another symbolises the new connection, and much of the ritual surrounding bridewealth is concerned with the potential which lies in these new avenues for exchange.

We can certainly look for gender discrimination here. Radically different roles are allotted to the groom and the bride. The one raises (or has raised for him) bridewealth; the other is neither donor nor recipient of the transactions, but the person on account of whom the transactions are made. The groom listens to speeches delivered by men; the bride bears a burden of pork from one group to the other. This contrast in their roles emanates from Hagen notions of maleness and femaleness. Men take the public stage, they are transactors; women are producers, of children, of pigs, of food, and they link groups of men through their marriages. It is a contrast which emphasises different spheres of action and capacities. While the men's oratory flows, women chatter among themselves or soothe restless pigs. For the girl or boy embarking on marriage for the first time, the contrast which these ceremonies suggest is indeed one of role rather than physiology.

The Implications for Gender

My point is very simply that while Hageners are concerned both with physical growth, including sexual maturity, on the one hand, and with social status, including sexual status, on the other, these are not brought into a metaphoric relationship of the kind which seems frequently to occur in Highlands puberty or initiation rites. A ritualisation of life-crises must in a very explicit way draw attention to at least some of the characteristics of the new status, and when these rites occur around puberty or marriage one often finds a strong demarcation of sexual attributes. Entry into an association such as a bachelors' cult, which is focused on the needs and power of a particular group defined in terms of its common sex, must also comment on the perceived characteristics of the sexes.

Allen was at pains to distinguish puberty rites attached solely to events in an individual's life cycle, from initiation rites proper, where these admit the initiand into a discrete social group. His main concern is with these initiation rites (and the implications which admission into a single sex group has for male-female relations). However, if we take gender as our standpoint, it is legitimate to look at any ceremonialisation of events which emphasises sexual attributes; and the fault Allen found in other analyses ('The failure to make an adequate distinction between puberty and initiation ritual is a direct consequence of the frequency with which initiation rites are, in fact, performed at or about the age of puberty', Allen 1967:5) becomes a virtue. Our attention is drawn, after all, to the fact that the threshold of sexual maturity in the life cycle of individuals is a point at which their future gender — what it will mean to be adults of this or that sex — is frequently defined. Whether the primary end of a particular ceremony is a *rite de passage* or an initiation, growth and status are symbols of each other.

Thus the symbols on which such rituals in the Highlands draw are chiefly physiological. The process of social maturation is concretised by reference to the development of sexual characteristics, which in turn appear to give both gender and maturity a physical base. La Fontaine writes of her African material:

> Biological changes that are thus marked by symbolic focus form *rites de passage* that dramatize not only physical changes but change in status.... Where the two aspects are associated ... it is clear that there is a meaningful relation between bodily changes and changes in social status, such that the two aspects of maturity are treated as indistinguishable (La Fontaine 1972:163).

Biological change itself is also being marked. In the context of the Highlands antithesis between the (adult) natures of males and females, it is no surprise to find emphasis on the passage from the state of childhood to that of adulthood, where one must demonstrably and inevitably be fully male or female.[11] And if the acquisition of full male or female status is seen to be associated with physiology, this tells us something about concepts of gender. So should the absence of this kind of thinking.

A major factor which seems to dominate[12] Hagen gender constructs is the place given in their thinking to personal autonomy. It is almost as though notions about the amount of control a person has over his destiny extends into his or her allocation as a member of one or other sex. While nothing can alter the biological allotment of sex, much can in fact modify the extent to which someone behaves as a 'man' or a 'woman'. The general Hagen emphasis on achievement leads them to put considerable value on behavioural as well as biological markers of gender. And while the behavioural attributes are to some extent tied to physical typing ('Men are strong/women are weak'), it is also possible for individuals to cross the lines. When they cross the line it is *not* as transvestites: transvesticism as a transformation draws attention to both the assumed and prior sexual (genital) identity of the actor. It is practically non-existent in Hagen.[13] This is not what crossing the lines means. When Hagen women behave 'like men', and Hagen men behave 'like women', they do not become physically identified with the opposite sex because physical attributes are not the basis of the manipulation here. Behaviour is. A woman remains a woman (in X ways), but can also *behave* like a man (in Y ways). Types of sex-linked behaviour patterns are laid down in fairly rigid stereotypes in the contrast between what can be expected of males and what can be expected of females. Ways of behaving are, then, very definitely attached to sex. But they are attached to ideal notions of what each sex is capable of,[14] rather than to individuals as biological units and thus to the processes of sexual maturation on which rests their physical identity.

But Whose Gender?

But is Hagen gender really a unitary concept? Are women's notions of gender the same as men's? In devising the categories 'producer' and 'transactor' as a summation of female and male natures in Hagen society (Strathern A.M. 1972:ch.6), I was extrapolating from certain Hagen ideas. It is an extrapolation which probably more accurately reflects Hagen men's rather than women's categories. Ardener's chastisement of female anthropologists pursuing male myths is well taken (Ardener 1972:136). Evidence was given to show how Hagen women manipulate or resist the premises on which men build their prestige system; but I made no study of the categories on which the alternative society, if it exists, might be structured.[15] This is relevant for the definition of gender. The terms by which Hageners define males and females relate intimately to the chief concerns of men in this society (the acquisition of prestige). It might be proper to deduce from this that gender is more likely to be of male than of female manufacture.[16] Nevertheless there is evidence that women formally concur in male constructs of this kind.

For Hagen men hold their women (and the anthropologist) in a kind of double bind. While operating their concepts of gender and of prestige to demonstrate the inherent inferiority of females, they nevertheless hold out certain prizes to the second sex. Now women are treated as 'objects', things to be exchanged, like pigs; now as 'actors', like the exchange-partners themselves, involved in the success of the enterprise. For it is possible for women to participate in their prestige system and derive a certain amount of personal status from doing so. Women are in this context regarded as persons,[17] rather than sub-social beings.

As far as prestige goes, their claims to be treated as such emerges most strongly in two related contexts; when they 1. with diligence carry out their proper female tasks (gardening, pig-raising, promoting good relations between the affines) they are 2. also showing themselves to have men's interests in heart, and for serving men they receive praise. There is also a place for the unusual woman, typically someone who elects to live with an influential brother rather than a weak husband, to promote her own *moka* (ceremonial exchange) interests. Here she will be engaging in a male activity and her exchange partners will be male. There are definite limits to what she can achieve nonetheless. She will not have a wide range of partners; her contacts will be of little political significance; she will not dance or make speeches as a donor as men would; and such women are also rare. Most who are by men accorded prestige are those whose names become 'big' by virtuous contribution to their husband's renown.

Men see women as capable both of acquiring something analogous to the kind of prestige men acquire; but also of spurning these social values to 'go their own way'. Women admit to some extent the validity of men's values, but equally cherish their own interests and autonomy. The stress put on one or the other is likely to be situational. A woman who goes home to her brother may see herself as putting pressure on her husband to fulfil his exchange obligations (she is acting according to male values) but the act may be interpreted by her husband as a capricious neglect of household duties, and thus 'anti-social'. And these notions may be manipulated: a woman wanting to go her own way, perhaps anticipating a divorce which will leave her free to marry someone she likes, will return to her brother and enlist his support (according to male values) with complaints about her husband's debts. Women go along with male ideas about prestige,[18] but it may be only for so long as it suits them.

In no sense do Hagen women have a sub-culture of their own analogous to men's. In terms of ritual, ceremony, song and such like, there is very little female specialisation. The specialisation must rest in areas as yet undiscovered. On the surface, women's alternative value-system would seem to consist almost entirely of resistance, of assertions of autonomy in particular situations (e.g. the role of wife) regarded by men as non-ideal even if typical. Yet the idea of non-conformism has not been developed to the point of an ideology or tradition, though one might in behavioural terms look for a 'sub-culture' here. Assertions of autonomy are not of course restricted to females. In a way, this is another example of women making use of notions shared also by men. A 'female approach' can be discerned perhaps from the kinds of contexts in which women chose to vaunt their independence, and in some of their aims.

If we are dealing in the main with a male view of gender, it is one they have imposed on women, and to which women react and adapt themselves, in the same way as rubbish men must. A few pointers suggestive of women's attitudes, which might sketch in a different kind of sexual image, are as follows. As one might expect women put more emphasis on hard work and the degree of physical labour necessary at various stages in gardening than men perhaps do. The consistent requirement for daily work, as well as the pain undergone in childbirth, is seen to qualify them for prestige — a prestige men admit only in relative and not absolute terms. There is also some evidence that they regard food, and food distributions, as of more significance than do men, and to some extent mainpulate foodstuffs in the wy men manipulate valuables. I would suspect that they have a more role oriented view of gender than men — males are required to behave in X and Y ways because they are husbands, brothers, and such, and default comes from a failure to observe the obligations of one's role as much as from abberations typical of the sex. Perhaps because of the role conflicts often attendant on a woman's position (and which men tend to ignore), women are more attuned to interpreting things in terms of competing interests. (Possibly men, with wider social interests and obligations to many people, put a more active interpretation on the need to balance and manage their many commitments; seeing oneself in a role conflict is a more passive view.) They will tend to see issues as a matter of the advantages different persons in different positions can gain. Prestige is part of the picture, but probably does not hold quite the central place as it seems to for men. Short-term influence may be as important for women as long-term renown.

It will become clear from the following discussion that this view does not overtly clash with men's preoccupations with success and failure, with what is important and what is not; all female values which run counter to male ones are accommodated in their scheme of gender attributes. They are *prima facie* evidence that women are not men.

The Acquisition of Sex

Sex would seem to be among the most given of all givens in a person's make-up. Yet paradoxically Hagen gender-thinking appears to associate maleness and femaleness with types of behaviour in such a way as to suggest that sexual identity can also be a matter of achievement. For a basic metaphorical relationship exists between gender and achievement itself. It could be represented as —

> *wua* (man) : *amb* (woman)
> : : *nyim* (things of importance, success) :
> *korpa* (things of insignificance, failure).

Its expanded and non-paradoxical version would be:

> *wua* : *amb* : : male : female
> male : female : : *nyim : korpa*

Achievement is used here to two senses: 1. the process by which someone attains through effort a particular identity or status, whatever it is, and 2. the value put on attainment of a particular kind, here through personal endeavour of what is a socially desirable goal. When I refer to Hageners' emphasising achievement I mean the latter, and specifically in relation to gaining renown in the public sphere. When I refer to sexual identity being achieved (sense 1) I mean that men and women are judged by the extent to which through personal effort they are seen to behave and thus to 'be' typical members of their sex. There is a twist here. Men are categorised as *nyim* (important, successful), and women as *korpa* (insignificant, unsuccessful in male terms). Achievement in the second sense is thus a male prerogative. And in this sense it is no achievement for women to behave in a thoroughly female way; they are successful achievers only if they add to their female endeavours that component of excellence and concern for men's interests which *ipso facto* is a male quality.

Sex of achievement has in either case to do with people's evaluations about behaviour. It is not at all analogous to psychologists' use of sex assignment or sex of rearing, which deals with individual problems of sexual identity, and turns in part on what is perceived to be the person's anatomical status. Anatomical sex is not at issue here. Physiology and behaviour are to some extent held separate. The maleness or femaleness of one's behaviour is not a given which stems from personal identification with being a man or a woman but will show itself in due course; so in this sense either male or female gender is a state to be achieved (sense 1). But it is the quality and kind of achievement (sense 2) which becomes the basis of people's judgements here, so that one can say that to achieve at all is to be male.

I am not therefore talking about permanent sexual ascription or recruitment to the categories of 'men' and 'women'. Anatomical sexual identity is almost wholly unproblematical for Hageners. It is not a matter for much concern, and is regarded as immutable. Men are men and women are women on the basis of their anatomy; and in those pathological cases where anatomy is ambiguous, the person will be regarded as a part-man or part-woman, or a woman who has become a man, or whatever. It is in the extended use of the behavioural contrasts which Hageners make between males (men as a category) and females (women as a category) and the way they tie this to ideas about success and failure, where one finds gender concern. Physiological status is permanent; behavioural status is situational, resting on the prejudiced judgement of oneself and others. Thus as a man or woman a person always belongs to the sex group of his genital identification. But because of the way a metaphoric relationship is created between men and women and between success (being *nyim*) and failure (being *korpa*), the middle terms, what is male and what is female, become attached from simple anatomical ascription. At the same time the force of the metaphoric relationship derives in part from what is intrinsic to both terms. Maleness and femaleness have to be seen to rest *both* on what men and women are like and on what success and failure means.[19]

Thus the potential for achievement, the capacity to succeed, is given a quasi-biological base. If the discriminations used to differentiate the sexes turn on the kind of behaviour to be expected of each, the potential for these different ways of behaving is seen to rest on mental capacities, which (it is said) are determined by sex and laid down at birth. Men and women have different kinds of minds. Some men conceive of these as contrasting in shape or structure, for example, in the plurality of compartments.

Behaviour is evidence of the kind of mind a person has.

Maleness is evinced in such qualities as steadfastness, purposefulness, oratorical ability, knowledge of the political scene, planning powers and general intelligence. These are qualities which are direct adjuncts to the success a big-man aspires to, and which it is assumed all men will aim for. To attain prestige one must have a mind of a particular calibre. If one is born male one is inherently more likely to be endowed with intellect. Femaleness, on the other hand, is evinced in waywardness, shilly-shallying, short sighted obstinacy, limited general knowledge, an inability to use words cogently and general mental feebleness. These are qualities which do not stand in the way of attention to mundane matters such as gardening or pig-rearing, though they are insurmountable obstacles to prestige on the public stage. In fact men say that women who make the best job of their female tasks have to apply a degree of intelligence to them, so they are to some extent 'man-like'.

Behaviour is seen, then, to reflect certain mental structures. These capacities are sex-linked and thus innate, resting on a kind of biological (genetic) base. Vicedom refers to the belief that children whose fathers died in the early stage of their mother's pregnancy and were thus unable to help mould the foetus through constant contributions of sperm, as is held necessary up to about the fifth or sixth month, are regarded as incomplete. Further, he suggests that low status men may be seen as incapacitated as the result of their parents stopping intercourse too soon, so that they lack the proper masculine component. If a person's behaviour is markedly at odds with his physical sex, others may point out the discrepancy by wondering whether there was not a sex-shift at some pre-natal stage. That is, the mental patterns of the sex opposite to the physical one he or she was born with were already laid down in the womb. This is more a comment on the gender paradox, than a dogma which resolves it.

In reference to the discussion on puberty ceremonies, it is illuminating to point out the way Hageners link the acquisition of adulthood to mental rather than simply physiological development. It is mature behaviour which distinguishes the adult; and this can only come about when the mind has grown sufficiently. Moreover maturity has an irregular development, for a person may be grown-up in some respects ('He is ready to marry') but not others ('Oh he is still a youth and we cannot expect him to make gardens yet!'). There is really no stage in mental development which could be marked as indicating full adulthood.

Thus achievement also comes into the picture. Individuals are seen to some extent able to control, modify, rise above or fall short of their innate capacities. And physical endowment is only in term of capacity. What the individual does with that capacity is a result both of the use he makes of it and of external circumstances and his experiences. A person is not a big-man (*nyim*) or rubbish (*korpa*) from birth; rather, all males have the potential to be *nyim*, and all females if they cannot rise above their sex will be *korpa*. Actually success or failure in the pursuit of prestige, and thus an individuals' designation as *nyim* or *korpa*, can only be the result of achievement. I would argue that it is the cultural importance of the idea of achievement (sense 2) in Hagen thinking which leads people to stress how the performance of individuals varies.

That Hageners regard persons as able to control to some degree their innate characteristics is found also in relation to ideas about pollution and fertility. First, all females are periodically polluting and can do nothing about this[20] till they reach the menopause. But a Hagen woman is seen as very much in control of the *effects* of this. It is up to her to protect unwitting males; there is nothing automatic about her observation of the rules. Keeping them stems directly from her own good will towards the menfolk. Only this (men fear) prevents her from using her deadly powers to her own ends. Hagen women are not thought to operate witchcraft or exert a malevolent influence unknowingly: they poison men and, except under special circumstances, this is thought of as being done with all mental faculties awake. Second, although a direct equation is made between numerical and political strength, in fact a clan can demonstrate the blessing it has received from ancestral spirits *in spite of* small numbers. Numbers can be increased through wealth. A wealthy clan pays allies to support it, in dancing or in warfare. Indeed, in such circumstances the achievement of a small group will be vaunted in the face of its more populous rivals: 'We are only a few men — but look at the wealth we have!' It is possible for a clan to overcome what would have been a physical disability.

Now the formula male : female : : *nyim* : *korpa* is implicit rather than explicit. Certainly on occasion men will say 'Women are just rubbish/are rubbish things', and matters concerning women which interfere with men's concerns will be contemptuously dismissed as of no importance. The appellation *korpa* can be attached to almost any aspect of female nature. In contrast, men's affairs are things of significance (*nyim*). It is in reference to men's and women's preoccupations and spheres of activities that one finds the clearest demarcation. When it comes to referring to actual men and women the contrast between *nyim* and *korpa*, which looked as though it were attached to gender, no longer appears to be so.

Actual men and women, in their achievements, can cross the lines. A man of little significance becomes both *korpa* and 'like a woman'. He is depicted as covered with the ashes of household fires as women are (cf. Strathern A.J. 1971a:188). He remains a man, but in his behaviour and status, in his interests and concerns, he is also like a woman. Moreover, women can become *nyim*. They can surmount the obstacles their sex apparently puts before them, and in devoting themselves to their production tasks and in assisting their husband's exchanges (i.e. in helping to produce a *nyim* man) evince behaviour which shows a male mentality. When women dress up and decorate at festivals the effect may be described as 'man-like', though the details of their costume leave no doubt as to physical identity. An important (*nyim*) wife may be described as having the thoughts of a man though she has the body of a woman.

These designations could be called compliments or insults. But the direction they take is significant. It is an insult for a woman to be singled out as exemplifying feminine traits, as it is praise for a man to be called a man.[21] Important women by no means gain total access to the male world: the most respected (*nyim*) of them would still not get up and make speeches at a *moka*. A big-woman thus does not become a man; to say that she is man-like is an analogy which points to the fact that she evinces those same qualities of intelligence and steadfastness which are prerequisites for big-man status and which all men have the possibility of displaying. She is a woman with some male characteristics. But it would be ethnocentric to dismiss compliments of this nature as trivial.[22] The contrasts imply a process of evaluation which has meaning in relation to what men and women are considered fit for (i.e. gender ideas). One could put it this way: that the phrase 'man-like' when applied to a woman is an analogy in respect of that individual, pointing up similarities in her behaviour and typical male behaviour; but is also an identification in respect of the behaviour itself, for it is put within the class of male rather than female activity. In the next section I take up the point that this process of classification and judgement has the effect of dramatising the claims of big-men to prestige.

Thus in the not very usual case of an unequally matched pair, where the wife is the stronger partner and is seen to take a directive in their affairs, others may say that she is really the man, 'the woman has turned into a man', in relation to her husband. If he is both ineffective and not very wealthy he is the *korpa* and the 'woman' of the pair. The phrase for 'turning into' here is that used of someone who assumes the character or appearance of something else; it is also regularly used of persons who change their group affiliation and 'become' a member of another. But no one in ordinary speech would refer to her in an unqualified way as 'a man'; it is the qualities she is evincing which are being commented upon. If husband and wife are equally ambitious and the wife applies herself to their joint interests, they may both be referred to as *nyim*. Since it is the male partner who will still take the chief directive and 'holds the talk', the woman may not be singled out as 'like a man' by comparison with her husband, though her *nyim* standing makes her like a man in relation to other women.

One young man[23] explained that being *nyim* was all about two things: the wealth one held and the talk one made. He pointed to an elder brother and his wife. The wife was *nyim*, for it was she who thought and planned when it came to sending out valuables in *moka* (in private); in this sense she was like a man. But that did not mean that his brother was *korpa*, or like a woman, for he was rich — it was just that he had little to say and left decisions up to his wife. Should a woman's interests be contrary to her husband's, however, she is an *amb korpa* (a rubbish woman). The men who are *korpa* are those who have neither wealth nor good talk. 'They fall below; they turn into something like women', he said; and like the kind of woman who does not think about the morrow, but when she digs out sweet potatoes instead of pushing back the vines to grow again leaves them torn up. Such men are also in their habits likely to associate too much with the other sex, spending their time not in public places but in gardens or houses, indifferent to clan welfare.[24]

These statements point to two things clearly. Either man (*wua*) or woman (*amb*) may be referred to as *nyim* or *korpa* (thus: *amb nyim amb korpa/wua nyim, wua korpa*). For this makes a realistic assessment of what achievement is about. It is also a very stable assessment: wherever success from men's point of view is evinced it shows the person is *nyim*. But the second point is that if one examines the criteria for achievement it turns on those items which are more accessible to men than to women: on public prominence, on being able to speak to influence people, on thinking about clan interests, on having wealth in one's own name. Even the most *nyim* woman cannot behave as the natural possessor of such attributes. From this perspective one can say that *korpa* behaviour is female and *nyim* behaviour male.

PRESERVING POWER

Gender and Status

The Hagen male version of gender draws attention to what can be achieved in terms of the kind of prestige and renown which participation in public affairs, and specially in the exchange system, brings. Sex implies certain capacities, and men (potentially *nyim*) and women (potentially *korpa*) are so as to speak distinguished by their aptitude for achievement. Men may treat women in the same way as a big-man treats his inferiors, supporters on whom he depends but who may or may not be included in the general renown he claims. In fact the analogy between male : female and *nyim* (important things/people) : *korpa* (rubbish things/people) is a construct which glosses over social complexities. In the first case, the estimation of who is *nyim* and who is *korpa* among men, or among groups, is contextual, and swings with fluctuating fortunes. In the second case not all those who are not-*nyim* are really *korpa*. There are 'ordinary' men too. One's supporters may be respectable if unadventurous; one's partners more so. In effect Hagen men have two models to choose from when considering their relationships with women. They can use the simple pair contrast *nyim*:*korpa* (for in a sense all things, ventures, enterprises and the people who do them can fall into one or other class), and they can take their model from the social reality of the differences between *nyim*(big-)men and everyone else, whoever they may be.

Elsewhere I have suggested that one stance which Hagen males take towards females is that of big-men to non-big-men. Non-big-men not only include persons of no status and less property (the true *wamb korpa* 'rubbish people'), but also one's supporters,[25] and in context one's partners over whom one wishes to exert influence. Such beings have to be treated as persons, if their wealth is to be extracted or they are to be induced to follow one's lead. In trying to be big-men males can switch from one domain of reference to another in their behaviour towards females. They may regard them as worthless and propertyless, of no account; or as beings whose work is necessary to sustain the household; or as supporters who through their planting large gardens and properly looking after pigs will contribute to one's wealth; or as partners whom one will try to dominate but whose wishes have nevertheless to be taken into consideration, and whose commitments and loyalties cannot be assumed. In other words, aspects of the male-female relationships are symbolised by elements making up the relationship between big-men and the rubbish/ supportive partnering person. The associations between *nyim* and maleness, *korpa* and femaleness involve categorical contrasts. They refer to qualities. But here are relationship contrasts. The comparison is between men/women and *nyim*/non-*nyim*. Men are like big-men in relationship to women who are like those who partner or support or fall short of big-men. Both contrasts provide idioms for thinking about gender, and whether the second sex is regarded as *korpa* or as merely non-*nyim* does not affect the association of maleness with being *nyim*.

Look at this operation the other way round. The attachment of notions about success/importance and failure/insignificance to gender must in turn colour thinking about prestige. Indeed one might suggest that when big-men contemplate the realities of their ties with others, other *nyim* men and non-*nyim* men, the categorical contrast between *nyim: korpa* probably holds certain attractions. There are two kinds of contrast here: 1. between an entity and its opposite — *nyim:korpa* and male:female — and 2. an entity and its absence. Now, whereas non-male is the same as female, non-*nyim* is *not* the same as *korpa*. Is gender-thinking the operator which makes the status categories appear to be about rank? For the antithesis between *nyim* men and others is more sharply defined when it is symbolised by the male/ female dichotomy, possibly yielding the kind of absolute differentiation which aspiring big-men would like to feel exists between themselves and others. And in the same way as there are seen to be certain genetic foundations for the capacity to achieve, the eminence big-men claim also comes to be 'natural'.[26]

Crossing the Line or the Double Helix

Briefly consider another pair of values, that of strength and weakness, which contributes to notions of *nyim* and *korpa*. The strong-minded are important; the weak are insignificant. A contrast between strength and weakness can also be applied to gender. Indeed, because of its association, though not direct equation, with physical attributes it is applied more readily to men and women than the *nyim: korpa* contrast is. People say, 'Men are strong; women are weak'. In certain respects such an assertion could be true of all men as opposed to all women in the way the *nyim: korpa* attributes could not. As well as perhaps doing some of the jobs associated with women, even the *korpa* man will build fences and undertake tasks which are seen as requiring (male) strength. And however *nyim* a woman is, this does not mean that she has all the attributes of a man and can fight with men in battle, something again for which 'strength' is required.

But ideas of strength/weakness are not simply related to physique. They are extended to other capacities, so that a person can show strength or weakness in his actions and intellectual decisions. Either sex can evince strength or its lack in this sense. Moreover when thinking of female tasks as being necessary for the maintenance of life and the continuity of the clan, men will openly refer to women as 'strong things', and to an individual as a 'strong woman'. Sweet potato is strong because it is the staff of life, and in the same way women's jobs are strong. But whereas the *nyim:korpa* oppositions contains within it an unambiguous *evaluation* (the assumption being that the state of *nyim* is one towards which people strive), the concepts of strength:weakness are more ambiguous. Someone can show strength which far from being socially valued is anti-social (the headstrong (*pundoma*) man who gets people into fights; the self-willed (*kara*) woman who listens to no-one); while weakness can be threatening — a big-man fears the rubbish man who, essentially weak in other spheres, may turn to seek revenge by poison; and the weakness of females is contaminating.

The contrast between strength and weakness is in a sense more fluid than that of *nyim:korpa*. If we regard *nyim* and *korpa* as demarcating two domains, with a boundary between them but one which individual men and women may cross, we could regard the notion of weakness as spiralling round that of strength. It is noteworthy that the term for strength (*rondokl*) has no simple opposite. *Rondokl* is contrasted with many things. There is its explicit absence, as in the phrase *rondokl ti mon* ('lacking strength'), which is often applied to women. Other contrasts are in the state of being 'soft' (*wening* or *rimbrimb*), 'stupid' (*wulya*) 'mad' (*kupor*), and so on. The central pivot as it were is the notion of strength, which males would like to appropriate to themselves. The metaphor of stability fits the cultural message that men are stable (central) and women unstable (peripheral), for women's lack of strength scatters their interests and activities into many different directions.

Now this is not so meaningfully represented in terms of equations of the kind, strength:weakness: :male:female, as is: *nyim:korpa*: :male:female. To put it another way. *Nyim:korpa* refers to a much more restricted domain than strength : weakness, and is less ambiguously tied to the sexual dichotomy. It is about rank, where the other is about power. If we incorporate the various kinds of opposition which Hageners set up through a strength: weakness contrast into a framework of binary oppositions, we shall be forced to recognise that each value (e.g. both strength and its opposite) can appear *on either side of the equation*. Further in those contexts where the equation strength:weakness: :male:female holds, we find open statements in just these terms. But where the elements shift to a point where the equations should be reversed (weakness:strength: :male: female) than men make every effort to resist the formulation fo the contrast as such. They cling, as it were, to the central pole of strength;[27] and can bring in the *nyim:korpa* contrast to reassert their centrality.

Strength:weakness: :male:female, then, is but one point in spiral, for it is power relations which are at issue. Men are powerful in relation to women who are powerless. But women also have power which puts men into situations of weakness (vulnerability) against which they seek protection.[28] Power can be good or bad. If one were to call it so, this is another paradox; for although all men and all women may be characterised as strong and powerful/weak and powerless in a way that *nyim/korpa* classification is not used, this characterisation is directly contradicted by further stages in the spiral which reverse the equation. *Nyim:korpa* by contrast, while in a sense free-floating and contextually attributable to either men or women; is not contradicted by anything, since it contains a more stable evaluation (*nyim* things are worthwhile things, *korpa* things are not). As far as strength and weakness are concerned, it is the concepts as it were, as well as the people, which are crossing lines.

A woman recognised as *nyim* is seen as behaving in a man-like way and is accorded some prestige accordingly. When women's activities (e.g. child rearing) are characterised as strong, a favourable evaluation may also be made of them as well, in comparison with men's prestigious activities which are also strong, though they are not ranked as equal. But there are situations in which a woman can be strong and no man-like at all. The strong-willed, obstinate female, who goes her own way, who pays no heed to others (i.e. men, i.e. is anti-social), is *not* showing proper male-like qualities. 'It is the epitome of all that is worst in females' (Strathern A.N. 1972:162). She is remaining female, and being strong in these ways makes her more female, more capricious, more out-of-control, more all the things men fear women can turn into. The woman has remained on the female side of the equation; when the concept of strength crosses the line to become openly attached to her it calls forth male condemnation. Similarly, should weakness afflict a man, for example if a prominent leader falls ill, the man remains on the male side of the equation even though powerless-ness has seized him. His male attributes are reinforced by anxious clansmen — they may look after him in the men's house and forbid women to come near. They try to keep the man himself from irrevocably crossing the line (and becoming permanently weak like a woman). When the concept of weakness attaches itself to males, then, other men show anxiety.[29]

There is an imbalance here. A strong woman is dismissed as exemplify-ing all the worst traits of females. A weak man is buttressed, his weakness denied as an inessential attribute, males rallying to his support. In both situations the incipient equation male: female: :weakness:strength is contradicted. In the first what is emphasised is not the actual helplessness of men in the face of the recalcitrant woman, but the destructive nature of her self-will. The equation is male:female: :good (socially productive) strength: bad (anti-social) strength. In the second case the weakness is interpreted as an affliction (from the outside — whether from angry ghosts or poisoners) and not as an inherent characteristic. The presence of women would reinforce the man's state of weakness, so that we have the formulation male:female: :resistance to weakness:spreading weakness.

The difference between the *nyim:korpa* opposition and the strength: weakness one is very clear here. When a man of little worth is dismissed as *korpa* in the way women are dismissed, there do not have to be any qualifications of the order 'Well he is after all a man ...'. In his behaviour he has crossed the line. For the fact that certain men are *korpa* is no threat to others regarding themselves as *nyim*; on the contrary, it enhances their status. Some men make of themselves the open admission that they are rubbish. The admission that males can be weak is another matter altogether: situations which put males into a state of weakness have to be explained away. The strength of victorious enemies, while recognised, is invariably referred to temporary. Moreover, the extent to which the defeated group can survive as refugees is put forth as proof of a 'fundamental strength' which enemies cannot touch (shown, for example, through ancestral support). When men are threatened by women or big-men by rubbish men, through menstrual pollution or poison, they are unlikely to admit that they are on the weak side of the equation and that women and rubbish men are on the strong side. They will either assert that they are strong enough to resist attempts made on their life; or bring that other contrast in to bear and side-step the issue altogether. They will say that the women and rubbish men in trying to poison them are behaving in a typically *korpa* way. The import is clear. Power is separated from prestige in this context. Thus even if the women are seen as threatening and thus powerful they cannot compete with and claim the legitimate prestige that is due to men. There is a notion of levels, that theirs is an essential strength which in the long run cannot be touched by the temporary attacks of women. Proof lies in the fact that ultimately men are *nyim*.

Perhaps strength and its absence are ideas too attractive for men not to apply to male-female relations. But they are slippery too. For although in some contexts they bulwark the contrast between *nyim* and *korpa* (to be *nyim* is to be strong), they also draw attention to the respective power positions of men and women, which is an area of ambiguity. We may conclude that men will do all they can to resist the downward spiral, to avoid the contrary equation men:women: :weakness:strength. And they will bring in that more stable contrast to do it. The safer ascriptions of *nyim:korpa* refer not to strength and its vulnerability but to prestige which becomes in this context an independent quality. People talking about poison veer from one position to another. Poison in one's own hand is a *strong* thing (but not particularly prestigious) to be used against enemies; poison in the hands of others is *korpa*, a rubbish thing (but no-one would call it weak). Notions of strength and weakness tend to be brought in, then, when the strength can be demonstrated on one's own (i.e. male) side, whether one is a clan faced by enemies or men confronted by women. Strength can be attributed to the other side if the attribution contains no threats to one's own: e.g. in those moments when men agree that women are 'strong' because of their domestic importance. But if the strength of the other camp is identified as dangerous, it becomes coupled not with prestige, for that would be acknowledging the reality of the threat, but with its opposite. The headstrong woman who openly admits to be influenced by nothing but her own strength of will (she is 'strong') is also *korpa*, rubbish, in terms of things society (men) value. The contrast between maleness (*nyim*) and femaleness (*korpa*) is preserved in spite of the dubiousness of power relations between men and women.

Power, Danger and Colour Signals

In claiming dominance, men put themselves into the position of admitting the possibility that they too could be the dominated. Their contrivances are explicable if we say that they are fighting at one level what their culture drives them to admit at another, that there are contexts in which the equation male:female: :weakness:strength does hold. There is another area in which a parallel admission is made with more ease, in the contrast between danger/safety (or solidarity).

In some situations there is an association between males and safety, females and danger. But not only is this not upheld consistently, contemplation of the reverse equation does not seem to lead to the same degree of anxiety as the strength:weakness case. We have argued elsewhere (Strathern, A.J. and A.M. 1971) that ambiguity in colour ascriptions reflects this. One cannot posit simple equations of the kind:

$$\begin{array}{cc} \text{in-group} & \text{out-group} \\ :: \text{male} : & \text{female} \\ :: \text{black colour} : & \text{red colour} \\ :: \text{friendship} : & \text{hostility} \end{array}$$

'We might argue that black signifies outward-looking aggressiveness with its corollary of inward-looking support and protection.... Friendship between men of different clans, on the other hand, is friendship towards outsiders, and carries a latent corollary of hostility within the clan itself, since outward links may weaken internal ones. It is appropriate, then, that both black and red can stand for danger and friendship.... If red means friendship towards outsiders, its opposite black means hostility; if red means danger to internal protection and solidarity, black carries an affirmation of these' (Strathern, A.J. and A.M., 1971:164). Friendship and hostility can appear on both sides of the equation, here the equation of male concerns with the colour black and female concerns with the colour red. For example, an individual derives strength and prestige from being a member of a particular clan and supporting its interests; he *also* derives strength and prestige from his extra-clan exchange partners, typically persons with whom he has contact through women.

In fact, an analysis of colour symbolism furthers the argument in another direction. Like the attributes *nyim:korpa*, the colours black and red seem to be attached to notions of maleness and femaleness. Thus black is associated with clan solidarity and aggression against (male) outsiders; red with the potential of extra-clan links, with wealth, with fertility (all benefits which flow from contacts with women), as well as with danger (from women) and supernatural threat (threats from spirits other than clan ghosts). But in certain contexts, especially on ceremonial occasions where fertility and sexuality are emphasised, men specifically put on red adornments. They do not actually go so far as to say they are making themselves 'like women', but they do say they thereby wish to make themselves attractive to women. It is reasonable to interpret these occasions on which they are appropriating female qualities (Strathern, A.J. and A.M., 1971: 106, 172), in the same way as fully decorated women appropriate certain male qualities. The contrasts are not blurred. It is individuals who display now maleness, now femaleness. They are, emphatically, *not* displaying sexual (genital) characteristics. These in Hagen eyes are demarcated by treatment of the hair and genitals, and head coverings and pubic aprons almost always continue to identify the physiological sex of the wearer.

Some evidence of the fact that it is men (those who are claiming that maleness is associated with prestige) who are the most vulnerable to belittlement of their status lies in the fact that the interplay between black (maleness) and red (femaleness) is not as simple as I have represented it here. Women's fertility is regarded as, on occasion, subject to male control (through cult performance). Males also have a further colour domain through which they can express access to this source of power without having to refer to femininity at all: white is a symbol of male fertility.[30] This protects them from equation of femaleness = fertility, which would be tantamount to femaleness = strength. As we have seen, the way in which they admit power as resting with females is hedged with anxiety. Females can be associated with power (symbolised in the colour red) it would seem only under the conditions: 1. it is an ambiguous power anyway, since red also signifies danger; 2. men have an equal and different, if not superior, source of power (symbolised by the colour white); 3. and finally, it is an attribute which men can appropriate for themselves on occasions (when they put on red decorations).

As in the case of *nyim:korpa*: :male:female, the equation

$$\text{black:red: :male:female}$$

is not touched by these manoeuvres. What the manoeuvres protect men from is any implication that in the association of red with females, females are being put into a power situation which makes a categorical equation between men and powerlessness.

CONCLUSIONS

Gender

Oakley (1972:e.g. 150) notes that the more sharply gender is defined, the more problems there may be for the individual whose person identity is connected to gender identity. Identity in terms of sexual (physiological) characteristics does not seem problematical for Hageners. What gives rise to anxiety, more acute in men than in women, is the prospect of success or failure. Moreover, given their structuring of *nyim:korpa* in terms of maleness:femaleness, we should not be surprised that much male anxiety turns on what females are going to do to their enterprises.

Throughout the Highlands exists the notion that women can 'pollute' men. In Hagen it becomes one of the pieces of evidence men have that they are working against odds to achieve their goals. Like the capacity for becoming *nyim*, the capacity of pollute is innate, but also modifiable. As well as their bodies, men's ventures (success in war, in exchanges, in encounters with the spirits) can be harmed too. Health, vigour, wealth, renown, personal well being and clan prestige are things which are achieved, and which women attack. Thus women and rubbish men alike threaten big-men with poison. It is basically success which the unsuccessful confront.

But at the same time women, and low status male supporters, attached to a big-man's household, are depended upon to produce the basic essentials of life and wealth. This dependency gives rise to fears that men will be betrayed, their plans wrecked and schemes thwarted. The only reliable women are those who have proved themselves to be *nyim*, for they are intent on raising their own and their husband's name at the same time.

It should be clear that this dependency of the big on the small, of a big-man on his supporters, of husbands on wives, is a quasi-domestic one, restricted to the sphere of production.[31] Hagen culture does not stress to any great degree the role of inferiors (women etc.) as an admiring audience for men's exploits, to the extent for example that is required among some Sepik cultures (e.g. Bateson 1958). Men seek admiration from their peers and rivals; big-men want the prestige other big-men will accord them. Their displays are not particularly for the benefit of the not-big, and dependence is not a public explicit affair. In any case, although big-men are dependent on their followers and partners, as they are also on women, ideology places emphasis on the man's skill in building up support and cultivating partners, in the same way as it is also part of his achievement to manage his wives or sisters so that they do act in his interests. (It is not the case that a man can *only* be important if he has so many sisters to provide him with potential avenues for exchange or so many wives to work for him.) If it were a matter of men demonstrating, rather than achievement, simple strength (e.g. evidence of physical growth or whatever), then this could be vaunted unambiguously in the face of the weak (those who could not participate in this kind of growth); vaunted in the face of other strong persons it would involve a challenge. A component of the displays Hageners put on at exchanges contain this element of aggressiveness against rivals. But prestige can be claimed without the necessity of a non-prestigious category of persons. In so far as assertions of prestige can be directed against equals, they are more autonomous, less relative, perhaps, than are claims of strength. At dancing displays the audience is made up of people of all sorts — rivals, big-men from other groups, one's own supporters, and women, all decked out in varying degrees of finery. The real struggle against *korpa* persons who may block one's advancement comes at home, privately, when a wife wants to send her pigs off against the husband's wishes, when a rubbish man steals valuables, when poison is slipped into the evening meal.

We may put it that Hagen men are not so concerned about their physical masculinity as about preserving and using to the full those social advantages maleness has endowed them with. They are not afraid of becoming women; they are afraid of becoming 'like women', *korpa*.

Gender: Physiology and Behaviour

From the absence of puberty and initiation rites it would clearly be fallacious to conclude that Hageners pay little attention to gender discrimination. Quite the reverse: contrasts between maleness and femaleness are used to symbolise potentialities in social life. Concepts of gender are tied not to physiological characteristics alone, but also to mental capacity and behavioural traits. There is a subtle interplay in the extent to which these are regarded as ascribed or achieved.

In one sense being *nyim* or *korpa* is a 'natural' produce of sex. But a man who becomes a big-man (*nyim*) has had to develop his innate capacities — they alone do not make him what he is; and the rubbish man (*korpa*) has failed to utilise his endowment. Showing maleness or femaleness in one's life-style, then, is not an automatic consequence of one's sex category. There is no reason why other aspects of gender should not have been ritualised in Hagen; but this aspect would not be amenable to such treatment.

At puberty a child begins to display the secondary physical characteristics which demarcate adults of his sex. But his mental characteristics can be demonstrated only through behaviour as shown over time. Physical traits cannot be used to symbolise the mental ones because there is only a partial identification between the two. A distinction of capacities is extremely useful for the models Hagen men make of their social arrangements, and operates to bulwark equally the domination of men over women and big-men over little men. Ritualisation of physiological changes at puberty would weaken the central equation, prestigious (*nyim*): rubbish (*korpa*): :male:female. Let us return to the two contradictory assertions, that male: female: :men:women and that male:female/men:women. The first assertion can become a rationale for men's domination over women. Women suffer from being female, inherently incapable, and such. The second can be used as a rationale for the domination of big-men over little men. Little men have become like women, for they too suffer from being female; while some women can enjoy the advantages which male qualities bring. If these interpretations of Hagen constructs are valid, they suggest that the model we are dealing with is not just a male one, but a big-man's as well. But this takes the matter only half way.

That such models should be widely accepted (by rubbish men and women too, as they seem to be) is to be understood in the relationship between the perceived interests of big-men and their clan groups. I have argued that when women are called man-like and men women-like these are more than trivial compliments or denigrating insults. The behavioural contrasts in fact point up certain significant processes from the viewpoint of big-men, and those who agree with big-men's aims. They identify the behaviour which leads to success. Although this paper stresses the big-man's position, there is also a congruence between his aspirations and the aspirations as a whole clan is likely to have. In some respects an analogy exists between the relationship of husband and wife and the relationship between individual clan members and the clan as a whole. It is the wife's contributions to the household which help bolster the husband's eminence, as it is only through the achievements of its individual members that a clan has a name. Or again, the anti-social clan member who does not heed the long-term interests of his group, is similar to a recalcitrant wife who cannot be forced to take her husband's values seriously. Clans, like big-men, are concerned with their corporate prestige and this is a salient value which gives meaning to group membership. But loyalty to clan interests cannot be a matter of coercion. The individual's aims must be seen to synchronise with those of his group. The ideas of *nyim/korpa*, which can make group prestige appear to be the summation of the prestige of its individual members, has a powerful force in this context.

The same young man who was referred to earlier, in pointing out that what really makes a woman *nyim* is her working towards her husband's reputation (acknowledging common ends), commented that a woman cannot really be *nyim* by herself. A woman, moreover, who goes her own way and does not concentrate on helping her partner is not *nyim* at all: she is *korpa*, he said, just like those clansmen who keep to themselves and do not participate in joint enterprises. The *korpa* woman is above all one who does not heed her husband's words; the *korpa* man one who does not or cannot help his brothers, who has no contribution to make to clan prestige. It is not enough to stop at a description of the ideology of Hagen gender; the next step should be to consider the application of this ideology, and thus its meaning for morality.

NOTES

Acknowledgements

Brenda Gray's unpublished thesis, *The logic of Yandapu Enga puberty rites and the separation of the sexes*, made me reconsider the significant absence of puberty rites in Hagen. To the following people I owe very specific help in discussion, and some of their points and criticisms have been incorporated in the paper though no separate acknowledgement is made in the text: Ann Chowning, Barbara Lloyd, Louise Morauta, Marie Reay, Inge Riebe, Erik Schwimmer and Andrew Strathern.

1 e.g. 'mannish' — behaviour, physique; 'woman' — sexual (genital) ascription.
2 See below the question of whose gender.
3 However, there are several assumptions here, e.g. that a model is bound to be manipulable, and is in the interests of one sex rather than the other (see below).
4 i.e. Where men's and women's natures are seen to contrast in the degree to which they are under cultural control. For a Highlands example (South Fore) see Lindenbaum 1973.
5 And those Kyaka Enga who border Hagen. It is possibly not fortuitous that there are indications of historical links between Hagen Mendi exchange institutions (*cf.* Strathern A.J. 1971b:263 for a hint); and that of all Highlands societies the roles Hagen women play in the exchange system are most closely paralleled in Mendi (*cf.* Strathern A.M. 1972:304-5).
6 It is of less significance for a woman of ambition to be the daughter of a big-man than to be the wife of one.

7 However this is not the place to discuss the question in full. There are many types of stratification systems and one might wish to consider Hagen in relation to the range. Clearly Hageners have *ideas* about stratification. It also seems clear that class stratification, as a special case, is not present.

8 In addition to the references cited here see also Vicedom and Tischner 1943-8; Strauss 1962.

9 It was restricted in distribution, and may possibly have been borrowed from eastern neighbours (e.g. the Kuma), as some say it occurred only in the Wahgi Valley region. Some status implications about adulthood seem to be involved in actual Kuma initiation ceremonies (Reay 1959).

10 The only reference to her new sexual status is in the name of the pig given to signify that among the rights established by the transaction the groom acquires sexual rights to the bride. This is more a matter of who holds the rights than a signal of a new physiological status for the bride.

11 Though maturity itself may develop to its full over a longer period and involve physiological changes (e.g. the number of children a person has which are not ritualised. I am not saying that physiology is only of significance when it is ritualised, but that in rituals which occur about puberty physiology is a common source of symbolism and this indicates something about gender-constructs.

12 Although I write in rather positive terms here, these ideas have not been tested directly through fieldwork. They were formulated in response to queries raised by considering the problem of gender, something not properly faced in *Women in between*, though much of the evidence for the present argument is to be found there. Most ethnographers in the Highlands have noted a value placed on individual independence of will or action (possibly associated with the big-man syndrome).

13 Unmarried girls sometimes dance with male clansmen wearing male decorations but distinguished by the treatment of genital covering (apron) and perhaps also hair and face decoration. They are being both 'daughters' (women) and 'clan members' (like men). Very rarely a man with no sons may dress a daughter up as a surrogate 'son', in full male attire, including a men's apron. (This was seen for the first time, out of a period of ten years, by Andrew Strathern in July 1974.) It should be added that there was probably no idea of 'passing' the dancer as male — her breasts were quite visible — but she was dancing as a surrogate man. As Hageners say, their daughters would have been sons were they not born female.

14 Both in the sense of mental and physical potential, and the range of appropriate, expected activity. I am not referring to the possibility of individuals doing things which would generally be regarded as abnormal or aberrant, even though within their capacities (e.g. women felling trees or men making net-bags).

15 I give several examples of the way in which women's opinions about events, distributions, the sharing of household tasks, may differ from (and conflict with) men's; but do not really treat the question of a female world view — e.g. the images in terms of which they perceive clan or other loyalties, or do not perceive them, as the case may be. However, one comment on Ardener's charge: while women as a category may indeed have a different perspective from men, this perspective may look nothing like a (male-type) 'world view'. Where the men's model, moreover, incorporates within itself the notion of competition or conflict between the sexes in an attempt to validate male domination, it may itself provide so many loopholes that women's divergent interests can be given ample scope within its terms. (*Cf.* the power situation of

Lele women (Douglas 1966).) Van Baal (1970:299*ff*) would posit that the 'tug-of-war between the sexes' comes first, and models incorporating notions of conflict in fact are made by men and women equally.

16   I am taking up an extremist point for the sake of argument. For an examination of recent thinking on male and female models see Strathern A.M. n.d.

17   How far they are 'persons' in the same way as men are in respect of descent group or political status is treated elsewhere (Strathern, A.M. 1972:ch.12).

18   Women's regards are ambiguous; yet they do conceptualise their claims as competing with men's. Competition can exist only within the framework of a commonly acceptable idiom, and this is what women utilise: 'You are not to send that pig to X — what about my brother whom you have never paid back?'

19   There must be a differentiation in their domains of reference, moreover, for the equations to have metaphorical power and not be tautologies (*cf*. Wagner 1972:4). Tokelau do something of the same in the realm of kinship and the category contrasts brother:sister (Huntsmen and Hooper 1976).

20   Although men know that women employ magic to regulate their menstruation and have fears they do the same to their ability to conceive children.

21   Women follow men's usage here, though in referring to another woman as like a man they may be denigrating her in the sense of pulling down someone who has got above herself.

22   They may be trivial in some societies. *Cf*. the example given by Huntsman and Hooper 1976.

23   Women largely concur in these styles and overt reasons for the designations, though judgements about whom should be considered *nyim* and *korpa* differ a little from person to person.

24   There is a combination of ideas here. A *korpa* man does not involve himself in clan affairs/associates too much with his wife/becomes a like a woman/leads a hand to mouth existence/does not plan for the future/ does not appreciate his clan's long term's interests ... The associations here open up a further area for commentary; they are referred to briefly in the conclusion. (There are similar moral overtones to the ascription of being rubbish in Fore (Lindenbaum 1973).)

25   Rubbish men themselves may be referred to as 'work people' (*kongon wamb*), and as persons who do things not for themselves but for others (for the *nyim*). Supporters are also 'men who come behind' (Strathern A.J. 1971a:188).

26   This is not to say that such an idea is applied to all men who actually aspire the leadership; claims are often disputed. But it is among the battery of concepts which can be applied to notions of leadership, and is perhaps particularly cherished by men of eminence. They may draw attention to their own prominence with a faint note of surprise, almost to suggest that their personal prestige is so obvious (so natural) that none can stand in their way.

27   Men's houses are built with a single central pole, the object of ritual (Strathern A.J. 1971a:90). Women's houses have no such focus. Tall forest trees also enter the imagery of strength.

28   Elements of this power include their perceived control over their ability to pollute men, and their capacity to oppose men's interests and disrupt their affairs. Van Baal discussed the general position of women in marriage exchanges in terms of this contrast: 'By consenting to being married off, the sister, physically the weaker, secures for herself a strong position' (Van Baal 1970:293).

29   I think there is evidence to suggest that men, as males and in some cases also as individuals, are emotionally anxious about the various powers women have at their disposal. It is not central to my argument, however, to prove the point.

If one were looking for some kind of drive behind the model-building described here, it might lie in such areas.

30 Although in some contexts men claim to be 'transactors' while women are just 'producers' they can also imply that men are *both* transactors and producers, while women are *only* producers. Men are associated with two colours (black, white); women with one (red).

31 In a general way a big-man is also 'dependent' on all others to accord to him prestige and political support — within and outside his clan — but I do not mean that here.

BIBLIOGRAPHY

Allen, M.R. 1967: *Male cults and secret initiations in Melanesia*. Melbourne University Press.

Ardener, E. 1972: 'Belief and the Problem of Women' in *The Interpretation of Ritual*, ed. J. La Fontaine. London, Tavistock.

Bateson, G. 1958: *Naven* (2nd ed.). Stanford University Press.

Douglas, M. 1966: *Natural Symbols, Explorations in Cosmology*. London, Cresset Press.

Glasse, R.M. and Meggitt, M.J. 1969: *Pigs, pearlshells and women: Marriage in the New Guinea Highlands*. Englewood Cliffs, Prentice-Hall.

Huntsman, Judith and Antony Hooper, 1976: 'The "Desecration" of Tokelau Kinship', *Journ. Polyn. Soc.*, 85:257-73.

La Fontaine, J. 1972: 'Ritualisation of Women's Life-crises in Bugisu' *in The Interpretation of ritual*, op. cit.

Lindenbaum, S. 1973: 'A Wife is the Hand of Man', in contribution to A.A.A. symposium 'Sex roles in the New Guinea Highlands'. Nimeo.

Oakley, A. 1972: *Sex, Gender and Society*. London, Temple Smith.

Reay, M.O. 1959: *The Kuma, Freedom and conformity in the New Guinea Highlands*. Melbourne University Press.

Strathern, A.J. 1968: Review of *Male cults and Secret Initiations in Melanesia, Journ. Polyn. Soc.*, 77,1,102-3.

———— 1969: 'Descent and alliance in the New Guinea Highlands: some problems of comparison', *Proceedings of the Royal Anthropological Institute*, 1968, 37-52.

———— 1970a: 'Male Initiation in New Guinea Highlands Societies', *Ethnology*, IX, 4,373-9.

———— 1970b: 'The Female and Male Spirit cults in Mount Hagen', *Man* (n.s.), 5,4,571-85.

———— 1971a: *The Rope of Moka*, Cambridge University Press.

———— 1971b: 'Cargo and inflation in Mount Hagen', *Oceania*, XLI, 4,255-65.

———— 1972: *Women in Between*, Seminar Press.

———— n.d.: 'An Anthropological Perspective', paper prepared for *Exploring Sex Differences*, ed. B. B. Lloyd and J. Archer, n.y.p.

Strathern, A.J. and A.M. 1968: 'Marsupials and Magic' *in Dialectic in Practical Religion* ed. E.R. Leach, Cambridge University Press.

———— 1971: *Self-decoration in Mount Hagen*. London, Duckworth.

Strauss, M. 1962: *Die Mi-kultur der Hagenberg-Stämme*. Cram, de Gruyter, Hamburg.

Van Baal, J. 1970: 'The Part of Women in the Marriage Trade: objects or behaving as objects', *Bijdragen tot de taal-, land- en Volken kunde*. 126,290-308.

Vicedom, G.F. and Tischner, H. 1943-8: *Die Mbowamb* (3 vols.) Cram, de Gruyter, Hamburg.

Wagner, R. 1972: *Habu: Innovation and Meaning in Daribi Religion*. Chicago University Press.

Ideology and Theory:
The Problem of Reification in Anthropology

ROY WAGNER

Culture, in its more serious forms, is committed to an idiom and indeed an epistemology of absolute knowledge and absolute meaning. This is particularly true of such arrogantly idealized manifestations as medieval religious doctrine and modern scientism, however clearly occasional theologians, like the medieval Berengar of Tours, or scientists, like the contemporary Gregory Bateson, may realize their relativistic and mediational underpinnings. Indeed, the very assertion that cultural meaning is relative must necessarily be phrased in absolute terms, recreating in succinct form the paradox which haunts all attempts to comprehend man's culture scientifically. It is perhaps because of this paradox that anthropology, with its relative and mediative praxis, has often fought shy of a complete ideological identification with scientism. Nevertheless, just as the idiom of learned discourse contrains the expression of our relative understanding through its absolute forms, so the rationalist and secular ideology of modern society demands the definition of anthropology as a science, and the enshrinement of its insights and perspectives as scientific 'fact'.

The ideological component of every cultural proposition amounts to the tendency to conceal or deny its relative basis, to replace the tenatative 'as if' of mediation with the assertive 'is' of cultural legitimation. Thus we may say that ideology transforms the relative into the absolute, and that the goal of mediation is to deny its status as such and achieve a relation of one-ness or identity with its object. The tendency is exemplified in Lévi-Strauss' interpretation of the significance of sacrifice,[1] wherein the sacrificial victim, representing a medial form between man and deity, is destroyed to bring about a union between the two. Likewise, in its attempts to speak the language of cultural absolutes, of laws, verification, and validity, science has often sacrificed any knowledge or consideration of its own cultural bases.

The ideological self-effacement of mediation is most apparent in the transformations and methodologies through which religious and scientific 'certainty' are constituted. In each case the 'means' of the operation, its temporal and historical beginnings and circumstances, the wafer and the wine of the sacrament, or the hunch or hypothesis of the scientist, is 'sacrificed' to the attainment of its absolute ends. Thus while both science and religion are cultural enterprises, each is obliged to deny culture in the interests of its own particular 'truth', and to mask the essentially mediative and extensive character of its procedure in references to the idealized goals, to 'verification' or 'communion'.

In formal terms, the operation could not be simpler; a metaphor is constructed, drawing familiar elements into an analogous representation, or impersonation, of the object of the mediation. Hence the priest celebrating Mass is likened to Christ, and the wine and wafer to Christ's substance, and in the same way the 'model' constructed by the scientist is said to 'represent', in an abstract way, the subject of his study. These metaphors, as mediative constructs, are transitional; they are bridges to enlightenment or understanding, and therefore they build a meaningful relation between the culture of the mediator and the object of the mediation. As such, they constitute extensions of that culture, and, insofar as analogy is the only means by which the supernal or the unknown may be grasped, amount to legitimate cultural relations. But the effect of ideological operations, such as communion or verification, is that of transforming the metaphor into an identity, and making the resemblance or impersonation absolute. This is accomplished by formally recognizing the points of resemblance between the metaphor and the element it represents, and simultaneously dismissing or denying the discrepancies. In a religious context, this ideological 'collapsing' of the metaphor is accomplished on the authority of Church tradition; in science the hypothetical analogy becomes 'verified' when the points at which it resembles the subject matter can be shown to accord with some generally accepted definition.

However promising this procedure may appear as a means of culturally having one's cake and eating it too, it can only succeed in eventually gobbling itself up. The metaphor by which culture is extended, and communion is facilitated, is abolished by its own success, for at the very moment of realization it is declared to be no metaphor at all, but an expression of absolute truth. Thus although the ambiguity of metaphor is overcome, its mediative qualities are also lost; the priest who becomes Christ is no longer human, the hypothesis which becomes truth is no longer challenging. From the absolute standpoint of ideology, mediation is only a stage in the attainment of truth, and fulfilment is reached in the transition from mediation to verification. If we choose to view verification skeptically, however, as a kind of semantic sleight of hand, it becomes apparent that culture itself is nothing more than a series of extensions, or metaphors, and that it is only by denying the ambiguity of the latter that the illusion of absolute meaning can be sustained.

A science which cleaves too closely to the ideologies of its culture can only teach a disregard for the mediative relations which ideology masks and denies. The reductionist who sees cultural differences as communicational 'static', and the dogmatist who cannot abide the implications of meaning as metaphor, ought to confine their interests to disciplines wherein mediation, as well as the understanding of mediation, is not heavily involved. Otherwise they will only achieve that species of reification, of reducing relationships to things, which mocks the dogmatism of one's ideological commitment by projecting it upon others.

Reification is the consequence of the quest for absolute knowledge in a science which deals with relative quantities, a by-product of the ideological antipathy toward metaphor. In anthropology, as elsewhere, it comes about when the scientist begins to treat the *means* of his investigation, the didactic constructs in whose terms his interpretation of the subject is constituted, as the *object* of investigation. Rather than acknowledge the heuristic nature of metaphors such as descent, society, social group, culture-complex, or lexical domain, the tendency has been to demarcate them as objects of study, and thus phenomenalize them. What begins as a figurative concept, an analogy created by the mediator's effort to 'translate' an experience through his own system of meanings, becomes an attribute of the thing to be understood, and a literal fact, in the process of verification. In its enthusiasm to 'factualize' an essentially relative and hypothetical understanding, anthropology has 'validated' a bizarre world of imaginary forms, a wax museum of putative social orders, heuristic dictionaries and grammers, unlikely species, and religious 'isms' which never have existed.

The fault of these 'fairy tales of science' is not that they are imaginary and hypothetical, but that, ambiguous and insubstantial as they may be, they are presented to us in the guise of literal fact. It is the special accomplishment of a good myth or fairy tale that it transmits meaning clearly and powerfully through the imaginative transformation of verifiable reality, and this is also the quality of good mediation. The mediative tasks of anthropology are likewise alien to the interests of verification, for the relational meanings which they would create must necessarily span a series of respective cultural 'absolutes'. Thus anthropology is committed by its professed interests and praxis to the standards of precise and conscientious mediation, to an ideal of excellence in the theory and practice of cultural extension, rather than the disciplines imposed by cultural legitimation.

If anthropology has consistently misunderstood its own dependence upon mediation, it is scarcely surprising that it should have failed to recognize the significance of mediative extension within its subject cultures. Characteristically, the ideological habit of our own science has been projected outward upon other cultures, so that we reify not only our own concepts for dealing with the latter, but also the analogies and other mediative techniques by which meaning is created there. Thus it comes about that when social and linguistic anthropology address themselves to the phenomenon of meaning, they apprehend it in terms of definition, dogma, and belief, that is its absolute and ideological, rather than its figurative and extensive aspect. Classification, definition, taboo and doctrine are concepts which mirror the pretensions of our own scientism and which, when 'discovered' to be operative in other cultures, provide a justification for those pretensions.

We might ask ourselves at this juncture what possible qualifications an anthropology which is primarily concerned with legitimation might have for the comprehension of creativity within its subject cultures. The verification of our own analogies produces a model of culture as a haphazard congeries of didactic constructs represented as 'fact' of grammars, descent systems, kinship domains, and the like. The emphasis on legitimation within the native culture results in a model of thought and action which is skewed along the dimension of obedience and deviation, and riddled with literalness, taboos, rules, and rituals. In both instances it is the emphasis upon 'absolute' meaning which excludes any potentiality for extensive change, for a culture whose form is 'fact' cannot change without denying that fact, and creativity within a culture whose essence is dogma and ritual must necessarily take the form of heresy. This is so because the effect of creative extension is the antithesis of ideological legitimation; it compromises the absolute meanings of ideology by metaphorizing them, drawing them into figurative constructs which have a mediating intent, and which parody the content of the original dogma. It is for precisely this reason that religious and secular regimes with strong ideological commitments have generally subjected the artistic, literary, and experimental activities to severe censorship and restriction.

The antithetical relationship between ideological sanction and creative extension makes the recognition of creativity a convenient touchstone in gauging the legitimizing and reifying tendencies of a given approach. The classical schools of diffusionism are a case in point, for their theory and methodologies are developed from an assumption of the essential non-inventiveness of human cultures. This initial assumption was all important, for it facilitated the explanation of differing cultural contents via the differential distribution of reified cultural traits, and thus fostered the reification of cultures into museum-like trait-complexes. The most ambitious of these schools, the German *Kulturkreislehre*, expectably evolved a set of verification procedures, the *Kritik der Echtheit*, for determining which complexes were to be recognized as 'cultures'.

The structural-functional approach, which largely replaced diffusionism in the early decades of the century, owed its initial inspiration to Durkheim's objectification of society in works like *Suicide* and *The Division of Labor in Society*. The latter work introduced the concept of society as a discrete, internally differentiated system, containing as it were the dynamic of its own explanation, in sharp contrast to the universal, intercultural dynamic of diffusionism. This shift in the scope of explanation accompanied a corresponding change in the focus of fieldwork, usually identified with Malinowski, and an abandonment of the historical incidentalism of the diffusionists in favor of a thoroughgoing rationalism. Programs for the study of culture as a rational system range from the utilitarianism of the British functional school and the French emphasis on the logic of the 'social fact,' to the more modern utilitarianism of ecological anthropology and the encyclopedism of linguistic anthropology.

The notion of adaptation, and with it much of the functional approach, is an attempt to explain the *effects* of creativity through random action. The status gained by the term 'adaptation' in the natural sciences has surrounded it with almost magical associations, but its glitter should not blind us to the virtual identity of this idea with the anthropological concept of 'function'. A usage which 'functions' thereby 'adapts', it attains the sanction of natural necessity, and hence a place within the synchronic balance of forces which forms the hypothetical basis for functionalism.

Since cultural 'order', via the pressures which 'select' for it, is resident within the system of natural necessity for the functionalists, they must regard the creation and extension of cultural forms as an essentially random process. Thus it is that the writings of Malinowski and Radcliffe-Brown are filled with scorn for the historicism of the diffusionists, for the approach which purported to explain, in incidental terms, the random mazeways of cultural usage. The 'culture' of the functionalists is an artifact of the adaptational legitimation of man's random errors and inclinations; its ideological content is sustained by the machinery of nature, its creativity is hypothetical, dubious, and inexplicable.

The logical approaches can be understood as attempts to reaffirm the non-natural, that is categorical or cognitive, basis of culture within the confines of the systemic approach. This is accomplished by a reversal of emphasis summed up in Radcliffe-Brown's 'turnabout argument'; instead of natural necessity, the order of culture is seen to emerge from the logical necessities of the mind. The selective and legitimating device here is cultural rather than natural, and randomness appears as the impingement of fortuitous natural events upon complex social or totemic structures. Paradoxically, however, this attempt to reinstate culture itself as a mode of explanation did little to render cultural creativity and extensibility explicable. Its effect was rather the opposite, for the decision to make logical order the absolute basis of culture also rendered it impervious to creative change. If culture is reified as logical order, and identified with a particular logic and a particular order, then a change in that order is bound to fall outside the 'system'. Thus although the naturalist models admit of a kind of change *via* serendipity, the logico-structural approaches have neatly eluded even that alternative, and are forced to look upon any ripple of extraneous motion as a potential threat to the delicate equilibrium of systemic meaning.

The scientistic study of culture as a closed, rational system involves a kind of 'double jeopardy' of absolute meaning, for it makes use of the verificational and deductive operations of academic rationalism as the communicative medium through which the meaning systems of other cultures are represented and understood. Thus the 'systems' analogies portray the natives as metaphoric academics, by rounding off and 'closing' their cultures into self-contained didactic paradigms. The purpose of such systems is twofold, for they are intended both to describe the subject culture and to render it meaningful. When, however, the systemic 'model' is verified and shown to be 'truly' descriptive of the culture it represents, its 'closed', paradigmatic nature also becomes a property of that culture. The attempt to analyze culture *via* methodology and verification thus leads to the comprehension of culture *as* methodology and verification, producing the well-known stereotypes of the 'commonsense' native, the native as scientist, or of culture as a set of tools or adaptations.

The more serious drawback, of course, is that a culture which is represented as a closed, 'synchronic' system has neither the necessity of extending its ideas and meanings nor the capacity of doing so. This is true of any consistent, ideologically absolute system, and would be true of our own culture if we chose to apprehend it in terms of its various taboos, doctrines, and dogmas. Creativity is unnecessary and impossible under these circumstances precisely because the relative and metaphorical means through which it operates is denied by the emphasis on the absolute. Cultural 'systems' are finished, sophisticated products of the anthropologist's creativity, but as such they are sterile, and have no innate creativity. One might say that their creativity has been pre-empted by the anthropologist.

'System' is uncreative because, as the object of an external creativity, it cannot by itself generate or initiate creative acts on the same level. Regardless of how extensively a set of 'rules', or a generative grammar, is capable of replicating cultural situations or sentences, it cannot bring about changes in its essential masterplan. A system 'works', but only within the limitations and parameters set down in its formulation. Those who are committed to reified 'system' models of culture must perforce insist that culture itself is similarly limited; that it does not 'extend' itself, but merely 'operates', like a washing machine or an automatic transmission. Concepts like 'deviation' and 'social control' have been created and pressed into service to explain or describe the 'defence mechanisms' of the cultural system, its resistance, *qua* system, to change.

The current interest in the construction of ethnographic models and simulations is of course a consequence of the analysis of culture as a 'system', and all too often the interest centers around our own logics, idioms, and representational techniques. Such considerations, of course, have a legitimate part to play in the study of culture, but when they are emphasized as ends in themselves, at the expense of the order they are representing, and when the latter is relegated to the status of mere 'data', then one might fairly complain of a 'manipulative' social science. It is only when we are able to develop a concept of culture which is relative, and which applies in the same terms to the analyst as well as his subject, that we will be able to comprehend the creativity of the subject culture through that of our own. This requires at least a viewpoint which can consider the means of cultural extension and legitimation in impartial terms, and recognize these operations in its own case as well as that of its subject, rather than impose its own standards willy-nilly upon the latter.

The point can be made even more explicitly than this, however. An anthropology which is conscious of the hypothetical and heuristic nature of its models, and convinced of the necessity of such models, represents a formidable advance upon the simplistic seeking for 'god's truth'. But the danger of such a creative self-consciousness is that, like other sorts of self-consciousness, it often comes to be an end in itself. If model-building, as an act of cultural extension, is a necessary facet of the anthropologist's task, then there is no reason why such extension should be denied to the cultures which the anthropologist studies. The challenge offered to anthropology is that of understanding culture through its means of extension rather than in terms of what it 'is', of creating a model, not merely of the native's 'culture', but of his own model-building.

If this proposition sounds somewhat involute and strained in contrast to the more usual plaints and projects of anthropology, this is perhaps because we have traditionally elected to make our pitch in the broadest terms possible. There are distinct advantages in this, but I have also tried to show that the overzealous simplification of the social scientist's tasks runs a great risk of transforming the means of understanding into its ends.

NOTE

1 Lévi-Strauss, Claude 1962: *The Savage Mind*. London, Weidenfeld and Nicolson, 225.

Deep Structures of the Dance

DRID WILLIAMS

It is true that we have really in Flatland a Third unrecognized Dimension called 'height', just as it is also true that you have really in Spaceland a Fourth unrecognized Dimension, called by no name at present, but which I will call 'extra-height'. But we can no more take cognizance of our 'height' than you can of your 'extra-height'. Even I — who have been in Spaceland, and have had the privilege of understanding for twenty-four hours the meaning of 'height' — even I cannot now comprehend it, nor realize it by the sense of sight or by any process of reason; I can but apprehend it by faith.

Edwin A. Abbott, 1884

Introduction

This paper is about a theory of human action derived from a sustained study of four idioms of dance. Specifically, an attempt is made here to elucidate some of the relations which exist between human danced movement and spoken or written language. The general theoretical orientation is that of structural/linguistic anthropology.

The paper is in two sections. The first provides an analytical framework for movements called 'constituent syntagmatic analysis' which states the rules for transformational, generative grammars for dance idioms. Thus, the first section represents a linguistic exploitation of the material. The second section deals with the conceptual space of the dance, i.e. the larger context of the transformational, syntagmatic rules. This context contains certain invariants which hold the syntagmatic structures together. While it is obvious that one invariant pertaining to this theory is the human body itself, a complete theoretical framework must include not only the person performing the actions but certain set features of the environment as well. There are, then, four structures involved in this paper. The structure of paradigmatic:syntagmatic relationships found in the first section and 1. the structure of interacting dualisms, 2. the canonical co-ordinate space and 3. the spatial system of the body-instrument, found in the second section. Finally, some notice is taken of the 'semasiological unit of movement', a unit of movement which is linguistically tied, mathematically structured and empirically based.

Obviously, such a theory of human action as this turns around preoccupations with units of movement and identity of behaviour. Of central importance to it, therefore, is the concept of the human semasiological body. Roughly, this is the human 'expressive' or 'meaningful' body (the word derives from 'semantic'). The semasiological body is also referred to as the 'body-instrument' in the exposition to follow. It is fully defined and specified in the second section of the paper, so only one other comment need be made about it here: the concept of the semasiological body draws

211

attention to an important distinction which must be made between the biological identity of the dancer and the social identity and/or the symbolic identities of the dancer, who, being human, is capable of consciously assuming multiple identities with reference to movement activities.

In this paper we seek, first of all, the constituent syntagmatic rules of the dance and throughout we are taking a semasiological point of view. The first section of the paper is purely instrumental in that it deals with some aspects of form and use of syntactical and grammatical devices in two dance idioms. While the larger, contextual section of the enquiry aims to study in broad, general terms the abstract principles involved in one domain of human activity and knowledge, i.e. the dance, rites, ceremonials and ritual, the paper begins at the level of *s*-structures, where events are generated (Ardener 1973). It shows how constituent syntagmatic analysis can be conceived in movement terms and uses analytical devices and notation styles which are Chomskyan.

Although some of the inspiration for this kind of analysis was implemented by Chomskyan linguistics, there are other, prior sources of inspiration which must be recognized. Interest in Chomskyan linguistics seems to imply an interest in what follows and it is true that social anthropology has lagged behind linguistics with regard to descriptive techniques: we could only point to Chomsky's work as a 'marker'; a partial realization of modern method. However, when a notation system for human action was examined, our way became clear. *Ex post facto* it became evident that the rules for speech and the rules for movement — related though they may be — are in different worlds. We assume a fundamental conception of human semasiological action, a concept derived from twenty years experience as a dancer and teacher of dancing. We assume ascending levels of semasiological competence; a Chomskyan concept, linked in this paper with Saussure's 'série associative' and Ardener's paradigmatic:syntagmatic scale. Such concepts, together with all the implications suggested in Harré's anthropomorphic model of human beings — 'architectonic' man and woman-kind — are basic, as is his exegesis of two paradigms of (spatial) action; Cartesian and von Helmontian (Harré 1970:266-7). In the main, these concepts and their implications are treated as negligible, and the aspects of human action on which they focus are treated as epiphenomena in traditional functional-behavioural approaches to movement.

The traditional functional-behavioural approach to movement is based on stimulus-response theory. S-R theory postulates, ultimately, that the same mechanisms which produce the so-called 'mating dances' of stilt birds and chimpanzees also produce human dance phenomena such as 'Swan Lake', the Ghanaian 'Sokodae', the north Indian Kathak dance or any example of any stable dance tradition in the world. 'Behaviour' in the traditional functional-behavioural paradigm is defined as a system of dispositions to respond or react in a certain way under specified stimulus conditions. I would assert, on a basis of research so far done, that no human dance, ritual or ceremonial movements can be adequately described as 'behaviour' of this kind. I assert that human danced action is not fundamentally of such a mindless, brainless, purely affective, basically meaningless kind.

The theory outlined in this paper depends on the *agentive* character of human beings: on the unique natures, powers and capacities which human beings possess. In this connection, we may recall Hampshire's study of thought and action (1965) which leads us to be able to postulate that human spatial points of reference are points of application for linguistic predicates. The theory I propose is not based on a mechanistic model of human beings, treating them, as both Winch (1958) and Leach (1961) have pointed out in criticism of other authors as 'clockwork mechanisms' or 'organisms'.

In common with all scientists, I seek rational explanations of continuity and change. In social anthropology, we seek such explanations for human custom, tradition and institutions. Although these undoubtedly exist in a biological field, there are legitimate doubts, most of them expressed by anthropologists, linguistics and philosophers, that humans can be wholly explained by the biological field in our relation to it. I see human custom and social institutions existing in spatio-linguistic fields and I would define human beings first as *'homo structuralis'*. With reference to continuity and change, I have been interested, as this paper aims to show, not only in what synchronic actions or units of movement *are*, but in the diachronic mappings of series of units of actions which make up the passing forms executed by one or more dancers. In addition, I am interested in the diachronic changes of the structural forms themselves through and 'in' time. These interests all require prior analytical structures: invariants which 'hang it all together', as it were, for it is these which prevent such domains of human actions from becoming a chaos. We may well ask, 'why isn't an epileptic fit or an hysterical fit a dance?' The answer is that while such fits happen to the body and movement is involved, they do not obey, nor do the movements obey, such rules as are set out in the following pages. To confuse this class of movements with danced actions or with ordinary, social, basically signal actions is to confuse the nature of movement which is symptomatic with that which is signal or symbolic, a subject dealt with at length in another paper (Williams, 1972).

Elsewhere, too, I have asserted that dancing is essentially the termination, through action, of a certain kind of symbolic transformation of experience. I submit that 'a dance' is a visually apprehended, kinesthetically felt, rhythmically ordered, spatially organized phenomenon which exists in three dimensions of space and at least one of time. It is articulated in terms of *dancing* on the level of the articulation of the dancers' bodies; in the body-instrument space which as I later show is ninety-dimensional. It is articulated in terms of 'a dance' on the level of a pattern of interacting forces; the form space of a dance, not dealt with in this paper but definable, briefly, as the empirically perceivable structure which modulates in time. Clearly, these distinctions between 'dancing' and 'a dance' and 'the dance' recall the Saussurian distinction between 'langue' and 'parole'. The semiotic of dance forms depend on space, time, light, actions, orientation, direction and force. Whatever its surface characteristics, a dance has limitations, 'rules' within which it exists and which govern any of its idiomatic or stylistic expressions. These rules are explained at the end of this paper in their general, basically spatial sense. First we focus on the principles by which movement is ordered in a much more specific sense.

Substantial and Sequential Realization Rules for Dance

Chomsky has asked the question: Are there other areas of human competence where one might hope to develop a fruitful theory, analogous to generative grammar? He answered his question by saying that, 'Very little could be said about that today' (Chomsky, 1968:64). His speculations in the form of a lightly sketched programme of research correspond in some ways to the enterprise undertaken by the author in 1971. He says:

> such a study would begin with the attempt to characterize the implicit theory that underlies actual performance and would then turn to the question of how this theory develops under the given conditions of time and access to data — that is, in what way the resulting system of beliefs is determined by the innate schematization that restricts and conditions the form of the acquired system (Chomsky, 1968:64).

This paper immediately turns to the question of how the theory develops under the given conditions of time and access to data. It examines the substantial realization rules for dances, rituals and ceremonial idioms and some, and only some, of the sequential realization rules for movement in specific degrees of freedom of selected members of the human semasiological body. The latter, in particular, are thought to represent some important aspects of transformational rules for movement utterances, of which semasiological units of movement are comprised. The rules will be explained with specific reference to the dance idioms of classical ballet and north Indian Kathak.

The Law of Hierarchical Motility

We shall conceive of X as a class whose members are a,b,c,d. That is in this case, X = leg and a = toes, b = foot, c = knee and d = thigh. The statement can then be made that X = (a,b,c,d). X' = the other leg. (NB: common language terms are used with reference to the parts of the semasiological body for ease in communication. Obviously, analytically, the small italic letters refer to points of articulation and the degrees of freedom thereof.)

There is a paradigmatic : syntagmatic relation of the above members a,b,c,d to X. There is a law of hierarchical motility involved: a, for example, may be moved without movement occurring at b, c or d, but b cannot be moved without moving a. Movement of b can occur without moving c and d, but, c cannot move without moving a, b and c; however a, b, and c can move without moving d. When d moves, displacement in space occurs at all the other points.

For our further exposition of rules, we will omit mention of any movements of body members other than X and X'. The omission is justified for the sake of clarity and simplicity. Obviously, each set of body members would at some point have to be handled separately and their relations and correspondences noted for rigorous analytical method and purpose, but it can be easily imagined, I think, that a 'concatenation' of moves of several body members — a 'polyphonic' conceptualization of movement — is too complex to begin with. The important point is that when considering X and X', there are only a limited number of possibilities available for any substantial realization of movement utterances in space. This is equally true for any other body members. Thus, we may say that for X and X':

$[X + X']$	=	body weight evenly distributed on both feet.
$[X - X']$	=	weight on one foot.
$[X' - X]$	=	weight on 'the other' foot.
$[X \leftrightarrow X']$	=	weight alternately on one foot or the other.

The Seven Basic Transformation Rules
(*for sequential realization in space*)

Given the constraints of the semasiological body's members X and X', it is easy to see that there are only a few possible ways in which the weight may be transferred with reference to the displacement (or not) of the whole semasiological body through space. It can further be seen that any and all 'steps' in whatever idiom of dance (rite or ceremonial) that is under examination, only the following deep structural transformations are possible with reference to X and X' (the 'moves' given below are from classical ballet):

Rule 1: $[X + X'] \longrightarrow [X + X']$ — *soubresaut* or *entrechat* class of jump.

Rule 2: $[X + X'] \longrightarrow X$ — *sissone* or *coupé* class of jump. An alternative way of stating this rule would be:
$[X + X'] \longrightarrow [X - X']$

Rule 3: $[X - X'] \longrightarrow X'$ — *pose* or *piqué* class of moves. An alternative statement is:
$[X - X'] \longrightarrow [X' - X]$

Rule 4: $X \longrightarrow X' \longrightarrow X$ and etc. — *pas de bourrée* class of moves.

Rule 5: $[X - X'] \longrightarrow [X + X']$ — *assemblé* class of jumps, or inverted, the *jeté* class of jump.

Rule 6: Either X or X' to another body member for support, such as a *kneel* or an *arabesque à terre*.

Rule 7: $[X - X'] \longrightarrow [X - X']$ — *Sauté* class of moves, such as *sauté en arabesque* or *attitude*, etc.

Rule 1 is the rule of equal weight stress.
Rules 2, 3 and 5 are rules of unequal stress.
Rule 4 is a rule of alternating stress.
Rule 6 is a rule of changing stress.
Rule 7 is a rule of repetitive, or 'iterated' stress on one member.

The three main motility characteristics of X and X' are, in common language terms, 'flexion', 'extension', and 'rotation'. X comprises, among its four articulatory members, seven degrees of freedom: a = one, b = two, c = one and d = three. X and X' therefore consist of fourteen degrees of freedom of articulation. Any moves of X and X' may be time (i.e., rhythmically) ordered or not. With regard to X and X', the linguistic concept of 'functional load' *might* be of importance, although at present, the author finds this very doubtful indeed, but a notion of articulatory emphasis would be very important. Either concept is not, however, necessary to the further development of this discussion. Below, I have included examples of direct realizations of these rules from the idiom of ballet:

I. For a type of *sur place* jump called *soubresaut*, the following notation would be correct:

1a. $[X + X'] \longrightarrow [X + X']$
1b. $[X + X' \longrightarrow (c_{fl} + a, b_{ex} + a, b_{fl}) \longrightarrow X + X']$

(the 'key' to abbreviations if fl = flex; ex = extend; b = beat; moves in around brackets comprise internal composition of move)

II. For another type of jump of the same class, i.e. Rule 1;

2a. $[X + X'] \longrightarrow [X + X']$
2b. $[X + X' \longrightarrow (c_{fl} + a, b_{ex}) + \left\{ X_b \ X'_b \right\} + (a, b_{fl}) \longrightarrow X + X']$

('curly' brackets indicate the vertical dimension; what the dancer does in the air at the peak of the jump)

Speculative Considerations of the Above Material

This type of notation could be used for any of the moves in ballet which have been listed, or, for that matter, any movements involving X and X' whatever, but notice that the above examples are 'separate steps'. This makes this conception analogous to a 'phonemic' or 'morphemic' level of linguistic analysis. Such rule analysis as the two examples given above, together with the previously stated seven transformation rules draw attention to a significant difference between 'rules' with reference to movement phenomena and linguistic phenomena such as 'a sentence'. That is to say, for instance, that there is no 'noun predicate, verb predicate structure' in the movement utterance, and it is also to say that while a linguistic morpheme such as 'book' or 'tree' presumably has a 'thing' referent, i.e. an actual (or tangible) book or tree, a *soubresaut* or an *entrechat* do not have such actual referents, although such steps as *pas de cheval* (step of the horse) and *pas de chat* (step of the cat) would. It is a little difficult at this present moment to see where such 'morphemic' or 'phonemic' analysis has great value in terms of the meanings of 'a dance' (seen to be at another level of the paradigmatic : syntagmatic scale of moves in the following pages) but such speculations may simply reflect a personal bias of the author. Certainly, such analysis *can be done* and perhaps that is the important fact.

The seven general transformational rules given above are of great value to an analyst because they are universal transformational rules which underlie any dance or ritual idiom anywhere in the world. Introduction of the notion of universality, however, poses other considerations to which we draw the reader's attention below.

Different Levels of Rules

At the outset, we noted the paradigmatic : syntagmatic relation of a,b,c,d to X in the context of the law of hierarchical motility. To see such a law in its proper context, in turn, it must be related to the larger notion of different levels of rules, for structures assume different roles and different values on a generalized scale of relationships. It is useful at this point to reiterate a statement of Ardener's (1971b:1xxxviii) with reference to the structure:

> The terms *paradigm-syntagm* — from later restatements of Saussure's opposition of *serie associative* to *syntagme* ... represent, however, a more basic relation, not restricted to language. Dr. Milner uses the opposition in a closely linguistic context ... The linguistic uses apply to 'linear chains'. In the anthropological language of structure, *syntagmatic structures* are apperceptions of relations between events as they are generated; *paradigmatic structures* specify the *kinds* of events generated. It may not at first be clear that the relationship *paradigmatic : syntagmatic* does not yield its significance through a model that is (*a*) static, (*b*) of two dimensions. If we take a model of the continuous generation of events, the syntagmatic axis must correspond in reality to a four-dimensional continuum (the three dimensions of space and one of time). The paradigmatic axis then becomes a fifth logical dimension of interesting properties. It is homologous with the expression in physics of the mode of specification of the moving 'present' (a 'time-like' displacement) in a four-dimensional continuum — for which a further conceptual dimension is required....

This structure can be diagrammed as in Fig. 1.

One has constantly to keep in mind that a 'phonemic' or 'morphemic' or 'lexemic' level with reference to movement restricts discussion to the first level of the scale (marked 1 ⟶ 2 above), or to a level *below* the scale, if one analyzes 'one gesture' as previously demonstrated in the case of the *soubresaut*. Clearly, level 4 ⟶ 5 is going to affect the 'meanings' assigned to all the levels below it. Theoretically, this means that the rule of contextual compliance (elsewhere discussed in the context of the credibility of a notation system for dance) must assume, at some point, the role of a guiding principle.

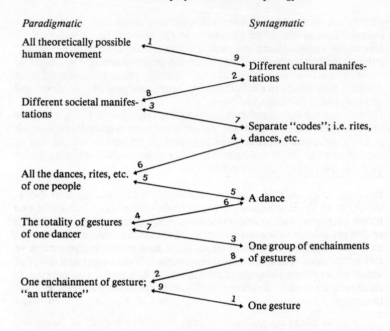

Fig. 1

N.B. The numbers represent levels; they can be read either way.

Thus, we can see that, while every movement sequence in the idiom of ballet which involves X and X' is generated out of the seven rules stated on p.215 (having a correspondence to level 9 ⟶ 10 above) which, in the case of ballet include such notions as the following: all movements, excepting those which occur in the classes of movements designated as 'character, demi-character, or mimetic' must occur within the framework of the Rule of Turn-Out; i.e. a rotation outwards (away from the centre line of the body) of X and X' at all times. The rationale for this idiomatic rule is 1. the outward rotation increases the possibility of geometric design possible to the semasiological body, 2. it provides a broader base for movements of the body, i.e. mainly visually, from the point of view of apperceptions of the spectator and 3. it increases the maximal possibilities of flexion and extension of X and X' in positions *en l'air* (specifically, leg gestures) in the spatial envelope surrounding the body instrument.

Out of all possible movements in the idiom of ballet, the Royal Ballet version of *Swan Lake* (after the Petipa-Ivanov version) for example, the 'step' or movement elements may be roughly classed as follows:

Poses: arabesques, attitudes (Rule 4)
Beats: *cabrioles* (Rules 5), *entrechats* (Rule 1) *petits battements* (Rule 7)
Cuts: *coupés* (Rule 2) *piqués* (Rule 4-1)

Glides:	*chassés, glissades, pas de basque, pas de bourrée* (Rule 4)
Raises:	*relevés* (Rule 7 or 1) *élevés* (same)
Hops:	*ballonné, temps levé* (Rule 7)
Jumps:	*eschappés* (Rule 1), *grand* and *petit jetés* (Rule 5) *sissonne* (Rule 2)
Turns:	*petits tours en chaîne* (Rule 4), *pirouettes* (Rule 7 or 1), *renversé* (Rules 4-7), *fouetté* (Rule 7)
Others:	(all *en l'air* figures or leg gestures) *développé, retiré, rond de jambe, pas de gavotte, pas de cheval, pas de mazurka, pas de valse* and *temps de flèche* (Rules 4-7)

Kinds of Movement Data

Basically, there are two kinds of data available to the analyst of movements, or to the investigator of movement phenomena. I call these two broad classifications 'track' data and 'gestural' data. The substantial realization rules mainly refer to the former broad distinction of classes of data, for the legs carry the dancer or ritual performer from one place to another in space (or, support him in one place) and the movements of X and X' either propel the agent in and through the displacement context; i.e. the stage, the church, the dance place under the big mango tree, etc. or, they support him/her in one 'spot', while the dance is done, which might consist of gestural material alone. The 'tracks' or 'patterns' in space are conceived in terms of semasiological units of movements based on the following linguistic propositions: *A is here; A was there,* and *A will be there.* Clearly, these units can be seen to apply either to the agent, substituting the A with the personal pronoun *I*, or from the point of view of the apperceptions of an observer, who empirically perceives that, for example, dancer A *was* off-stage, *is* now at centre stage and (*a posteriori* for the observer) sees that A takes a position downstage left. Track data from the point of view of dancer A is, of course all *a priori*; that is to say he/she *knows* where he was, is, will be, otherwise the choreography would become a chaos.

Both kinds of data involve selections; if A is in centre stage, for example, then A *is not* in any of the other places there are available in the displacement context. If A (in *Swan Lake*) arrived there by virtue of doing a *glissade, assemblé voyagé, coupé devant* and *posé en arabesque*, then A has *not* got there by virtue of any of the other means available in the idiom. Now *Swan Lake* is a pre-arranged choreographic structure of movements, but the dancer might be improvising so, because of the presence of a composer we do not rule out the Chomskyan notion of *creative* choice of moves within an idiom of dance; similarly, an actor might speak pre-arranged lines in *Hamlet*, but he might 'ad lib' in the idiom of the English language in the context of another type of play.

So far, we have dealt with substantial realization rules, which tell us something about how 'track utterances' are generated in ballet, but this material tells us little about how gestural data might be generated. We will therefore turn our attention to sequential realization rules for another selected member of the body instrument. We will choose the head which has five degrees of freedom of movement, but we will concern ourselves *only* with the field of possible utterances *in one degree of freedom* for the head: namely, that of up/down. These rules form another aspect of the 'implicit theory' behind performances of dance, rites, ceremonials, etc.

This degree of freedom of the head is chosen primarily because it is thoroughly explained and specified mathematically in the last half of this paper in the context of the structure of interacting dualisms and of how movements of the semasiological body can be defined and described — even computed and quantized. The following rules are based on 'positions' of the head as pictured in Fig. 2.

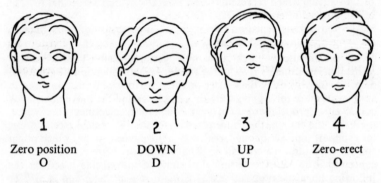

1	2	3	4
Zero position	DOWN	UP	Zero-erect
O	D	U	O

Fig.2

The notation used in the following rules has two expressions, also shown above; numerically, as 1,2,3,4 and alphabetically as O,D,U,O. The illustrations represent the 'original utterance'; i.e. 1,2,3,4. The question is, how and in what ways can we derive all the possible combinations of that utterance in movement? What are the transformational rules for the utterance? We will approach the problem systematically in the way that a dancer or teacher of dance might do: first by permutations of pairs of elements in the following way

1. 1 2 3 4 (= 4 2 3 1) = O D U O
2. 2 1 3 4 (= 2 4 3 1) = D O U O
3. 1 3 2 4 (= 4 3 2 1) = O U D O
4. 1 2 4 3 (= 4 2 1 3) = O D O U

The operation performed here is that of successive or cyclic inversions of the first, the second and the third pairs of positions. This ordering produces one pair of opposites; ODUO/OUDO. It produces one 'first and third element' transformation; DOUO, and one 'second and fourth element' transformation; ODOU.

In the above formulation (also to be seen in the illustration) the 1 and 4 positions are the *Identity* positions, or, in dancerly terms, the 'zero' position of the head. It is obvious that the two positions designated 1 and 4 are interchangeable; that they are *the same* positions. Notice also that the quantitative aspects of these number sequences are irrelevant. While one thousand two hundred thirty-four (sequence one, read arithmetically) is quantitatively very different from four thousand two hundred thirty-one, such considerations are immaterial in a non-metric mathematical model. Only the serial or sequential aspects of the numeration are important. Notice also that the third permutation has a distinctive feature; that of serial reversal in the bracketed set, thus, the paired set of opposites generated by successive inversion of pairs of elements yields a combination of movements which represents serial reversibility and sequential reversal of the original utterance; ODUO/OUDO.

The above transformation rule is *successive inversion of pairs*. Exactly the same operation could be performed on the R/L degree of freedom for the head; that is, taking $4 = (I = 0)$, $5 = $ (head turned right), $6 = $ (head turned left), and $7 = (I = 0$; head erect). Similar sequences would be derived to those shown above:

4. 4 5 6 7 (= 7 5 6 4) = O R L O

5. 5 4 6 7 (= 5 7 6 4) = R O L O

6. 4 6 5 7 (= 7 6 5 4) = O L R O

7. 4 5 7 6 (= 7 5 4 6) = O R O L

This exercise merely changes the paired movements, using the same rule, but that one rule by no means exhausts the possibilities for other similar rules.

Working with the same sequence we started with; 1 2 3 4, or O D U O one can derive a different set of sequential realizations by starting with a bi-lateral transformation of the original utterance thus:

1. 1 2 3 4 (= 4 2 3 1) = O D U O
1A. 3 4 1 2 (= 3 1 4 2) = U O O D

If the operation performed is that of double bi-laterial inversion of both 'sides' of the sequence, the permutation is the opposite of the above:

2A. 2 1 4 3 (= 2 4 3 1) = D O O U

These two operations yield the opposites UOOD/DOOU. If the original utterance is again treated bi-laterally, as two halves, but the operation performed is that of 'splitting' the first half, i.e. 1 and 2, and 'shoving in' the second half, i.e. 3,4 the sequence becomes

3A. 1 3 4 2 (= 4 3 1 2) = O U O D

A further operation of inversion on that sequence bi-laterally gives

4A. 3 1 2 4 (= 3 4 2 1) = U O D O

Having thus far derived two sets of four related permutations of this degree of freedom for the head, we now arrive at the final set of possible operations, which is as follows:

1. 1 2 3 4 (= 4 2 3 1) = O D U O

1B. 2 3 4 1 (= 2 3 4 1) = D U O O

In the second group of permutational rules (the 1A, 2A, 3A, 4A set) the first pair of the sequence was split and the last pair shoved in. In the B set permutations, the middle pair (2,3) are 'lifted' and moved to the left and the remaining pair are shoved together (1,4).

By performing a further operation on 1B, that of inverting the first pair as well as lifting it, yielding 3,2 — we derive the opposite of DUOO:

2B. 3 2 1 4 (= 3 2 4 1) = U D O O

If we lift, invert, and shove the middle pair to the right (instead of to the left as in the above) we derive:

3B. 1 4 3 2 (= 4 1 3 2) = O O U D

Finally, the last of this set of permutations is derived by inverting the last two elements of the above sequence:

4B. 1 4 2 3 (= 4 1 2 3) = O O D U

A Full Set of Permutations of One Degree of Freedom for the Head

The full set of permutations, numbering twelve, of the utterance 1,2,3,4 are these:

1. O U D O ⎫
2. D O U O ⎬ Successive or cyclic inversion of pairs
3. O U D O ⎪
4. O D O U ⎭

1A. U O O D ⎫ 1. bilateral inversion of sequence
2A. D O O U ⎬ 2. bilateral inversion of pairs in sequence
3A. O U O D ⎪ 3. split and shove bilaterally
4A. U O D O ⎭ 4. same, plus one inversion

1B. D U O O ⎫
2B. U D O O ⎬ Lift and shove operation with inversions
3B. O O U D ⎪
4B. O O D U ⎭

Stated in pairs, the twelve utterances are as follows:

UDUO/OUDO (1/3) ⎫
DOUO/UODO (2/4A) ⎬ will be perceived as discontinuity
ODOU/OUOD (4/3A) ⎭

UOOD/DOOU (1A/2A) ⎫
DUOO/UDOO (1B/2B) ⎬ will be perceived as continuity
OOUD/OODU (3B/4B) ⎭

There are two more possible operations which might be used in head movement sequences, e.g. *deletion*, which will generate utterances like OOOD, OOOU, DOOO, OUOO. Alternatively, *substitution* will give OODD, OOUU, etc. These rules would create further apperceptions of discontinuity.

The full set of permutations for the R/L degree of freedom for the head is (in pairs) as listed below:

ORLO/OLRO	
LORO/ROLO	These permutations hold for head moves in the
OLOR/OROL	third degree of freedom as well, i.e. for head
	movements TURNING right and left or for those
ROOL/LOOR	INCLINING right and left
LROO/RLOO	
OORL/OOLR	

Mappings which produce Longer Sequences

If the sequence ODUO is mapped onto the sequence ORLO by virtue of 'locking in' of the zero position, the sequence O D U O R L O is obtained. The same operation repeated with the third degree of freedom, i.e. inclinations of the head right and left, generates a complete sequence using three degrees of freedom for the head: O D U O R_t L_t O R_i L_i O, thus producing the full 'scale' of three degrees of freedom of movements. In numerical terms:

1 2 3 4 5 6 7 8 9 10

O D U O R_t L_t O R_i L_i O

Sequences which delete the Identity, or zero position, such as RDLU, ULRD, LURD or DLRU generate circular motions on different planes.

Serial Reversibility

An important feature of these sequences, either in shorter or longer forms is that they are capable of serial reversibility; the head exercise shown above can be done 10,9,8,7,6,5,4,3,2,1. Not only is the sequence of positions reversed, but the movements themselves are reversed as well. There is no loss of structural intelligibility either way, just as there is no loss of intelligibility in such a sequential reversal of musical notes. If we suppose, for example, that the I or O position is the note 'do' (middle C at 250 vps), the sequence would read do-re-mi-do-fa-sol-do-la-si-do — or the reverse.

When dancers speak of 'scales' of movements for various body members it is this sort of thing to which they refer. They refer, in linguistic terminology, to 'grammars' for the semasiological body; i.e. 'a device of some sort for generating all and only the sentences of a language' (Chomsky, 1972:85 and Lyons, 1968:156). In our case, a 'grammar' is a device for generating the utterances in a dance idiom and/or for generating 'scales' of moves, out of which only a few will be used in any given dance.

Obviously, exercises such as the above would correspond to plainsong or a musical form akin to Gregorian chant — a single linear sequence of movement (or notes). Movement would become 'polyphonal' as movements of other members of the body instrument are brought into action simultaneously with these. This particular utterance therefore (the 1-10 sequence above) represents one 'octave' — better termed 'decime' of actions through three degrees of freedom of the head. Other 'grammatical scales' could be constructed, of course. Grammars for Indian dance would include lateral displacements of the head and West African and Caribbean ones would include a similar *F/B* displacement.

Finite State Grammars?

It would be possible to show how such 'grammars', based on finite numbers of movements can be generated for other separate members of the semasiological body; the arms, the torso, etc. In fact, such things are done all the time in studios in the West and in India and among master drummers in Africa. What is interesting is that it would seem that with reference to the human body, we are confronted with a complex of finite state grammars, in connection with each separate body member, which, in virtue of the nature, powers and capacities of 'architectonic man' or 'homo structuralis' can then generate infinite sets of utterances (with reference to the body instrument as a whole) which we call 'dances' or 'dance idioms'. So far as we have gone in the present discussion, what these sorts of exercises 'mean' is that they are the syntactical and grammatical formal structures of any given idiom.

Semantics and the Dance

If we address ourselves to the notion of semantic 'meaning' in the sense that we may take the utterance ODUO/OUDO to mean 'yes' or as a gesture of affirmation in Anglo-American society, then we are led towards the question of syntactic vs. semantic 'meanings' in general with regard to structures in movement. Syntactic structures of movements such as the substantial and sequential realization rules we have just examined (and the societal values ascribed to the deep structures of the conceptual space of the dance, discussed later), are not constructed in aid of a 'grammar' in quite the same sense as a spoken language is. Spoken language seems to be used by humans in aid of a *propositional* type of grammar — one which constructs classificatory and categorical systems into grammatical 'sentences' having noun predicates and verb predicates, etc. They contain a certain type of propositional logical $p,\ \backsim p$ structure, which I show at the end of the paper to be strictly one-dimensional. An English sentence containing such a proposition is *'All men are mammals'*.

If we performed the same operation on that set of four-linguistic signs as we could on the movement utterance ODUO, i.e. sequential reversal, we would derive the sentence *'Mammals are men all'*, which is ungrammatical and, even if the last two elements are inverted to *'all men'*, which renders the sentence grammatical, e.g. *'Mammals are all men'*, it contains a proposition which is false. Whales are mammals, but they are not men and 'men' (assumed to include women as well) are mammals but not whales.

The sequence ODUO/OUDO can have the semantic meaning of 'yes' and the sequence ORLO/OLRO can have the meaning 'no'. It would be scientifically irresponsible at this time to say that we know that such head gestures have the same semantic connotations in every society[1] in the world, but these gestures do have these connotations in Anglo-American and European society. Whether this is a prescribed fact, or whether it simply has a negative value, that is, ODUO/OUDO in these societies will *not* mean anything *but* an affirmation, or 'yes', is not known by the author at this stage of the enquiry. However, the essential point is that such sequences have meaning on at least *two* levels. Such meanings as they may have at the level of socio-cultural *signs* indicating a state of affairs, i.e. signs indicating a state of affirmation or negation, is the least important level. May we hasten to say that, from a human point of view, such signs were (and are) extremely important, for example in the context of a Roman circus, where 'thumbs up' meant 'yes' and life, and 'thumbs down' meant 'no' and death. We are not trying to minimize the importance of such things, but our aims, on a syntactical level and in this paper, are to show that, in terms of human communication systems, the gesture ODUO/OUDO has infinitely more meaning, not as a 'nod' of affirmation but as *a conscious differential* between 'up' and 'down', or in the case of ORLO/OLRO, as a differential between right and left. Elsewhere this differential has been described as the important distinction which must be made between movement which is symbolic and that which is either signal or symptomatic.

Syntactical Context

The reason why we say 'more meaning' is because such facts point to an extremely important theoretical, methodological and practical realization: the syntactical context *itself* provides the resources in the dance or ritual semiotic for both the creation of and the understanding of meanings in any given idiom. Dances, rites, etc., are *not* simple enactments of myths, or any other verbal material. Dancing provides a resource by means of which things are done and ideas are understood. Dances and rites are used, created, performed and watched precisely because they provide differential syntactic and semantic structure. If dancing had only been a poor substitute for spoken, propositional types of grammars, then obviously, especially in England and America, dancing would have died out long ago, just as E.B. Tylor, among other Victorian anthropologists , thought it would do.

Dancing is one of the things humanity does. 'The dance' is something we both create and have. Here, in dances (and in liturgies, etc.) we see 'structural' or 'architectonic' man- and women-kind at work. The dances, and most of the rites which are created and transmitted from generation to generation are *felt* structures represented in four dimensions; in a space-time continuum. These felt structures are analogous to force fields. A force field is itself a structure, and, so is 'a dance'. Moreover, unless an observer can *see through* the dance structure to the potential structure beyond, he or she is not only *not* seeing that particular dance, but is simply *not getting the point*. That is, not seeing that 'this' or 'that' or 'something' *is the case*.

Semantic Fields

By way of further explanation, since at the outset we specified two classes of movement data — track and gestural — let us suppose that the dancer's gestural unit is ODUO/OUDO, and that the track unit of movement *simultaneously* performed (cf. Ardener, in this volume) is that of a straight line of moves from UCS to DCS (up centre stage to down centre stage). The track data in this case will convey or 'express' the opposition 'near/far' or proximity/distance. 'Up' in this case means upstage and that the dancer is far from the audience. 'Down' is downstage and near to them within the contextual confines of the stage area. 'Up' and 'down' can thus be seen to have two distinct dimensions of meaning in movement; 'affirmation' (or differential between up and down) on a vertical axis and distance/proximity on the horizontal axis of the floor plane. If the track unit is U⟶D, bringing the dancer nearer the observers, the total move will have a different shade of meaning from a case where the track is D⟶U. In either case the meaning is syntactic, and, perhaps, semantic only in relation to a general notion of 'values', in relation to the semantic fields connected with the particular piece.

Such 'semantic fields' for ritual movement phenomena, liturgies and dances might be said to begin with just such examples as that given above. As a bare indication of what is meant, for much more research needs to be done here, may we draw attention to the contrast which exists in the situation above and a dance situation in West Africa? For a start, the near/far axis in many Chanaian dances is a relational axis between dancer and master drummer not dancer and 'audience'. The pivotal point of the dance space is the centre, usually of a circle, so this axis lies on a horizontal plane of centre/circumference. The near/far relation is totally oriented on the drummers and not the observers. The vertical axis could, in cases I have seen, be said to be the same as the western example, that is to say ODUO/OUDO would have affirmative semantic content, but the whole focus or the direction of the move would be different. One extremely significant factor in West African dance is whether the horizontal track of the dancer is moving clockwise around the dance area from the master drummer, or counter-clockwise. If the former, in the Krachi state, then it is a secular dance. If the latter, it is a sacred dance, regardless of what individual gestures the dancer may be making.

These are all very fundamental syntactical and semantic features of structure in dances. I have risked being boring because the examples are so very simple, but, it has been suggested, in connection with this aspect of our subject, that maybe movement is not basically a semantic device at all in any sense akin to spoken language. Maybe, it has been said, it is *purely* syntactic. The suggestion poses a very difficult problem and one which will by no means be answered in this paper, indeed, maybe not for many years, but it is worthwhile, and necessary, to state the problem — for it is crucial. There are those who cannot help thinking that, for example, in any case where dancers are symbolizing birds or animals that they are reproducing some of the 'syntax' of the swan's world, or the bull's or the emu's — or whatever. Those, including the author, who would argue against this position would ask: in how far does that mean that we are assigning the same nature, power and capacities to animals and birds as we are to human beings? And, if they, too, have syntactic structures and semantic fields in which their 'dances' take place; if they, too, use spatial points of reference as points of application for linguistic predicates, then why could not a chimp dance in the Royal Ballet?

Further Example

It is important to note that this paper has not aimed at showing how the idiom of ballet, or any other idiom, was 'developed' in any mechanical or mechanistic sense (cf. P. Winch 1958). My sole concern is, I believe, similar to that of Chomsky; to demonstrate how the complexity of human movement phenomena is decreased in the light of such generative rules for human movement as I have defined: the law of hierarchical motility, the substantial and sequential realization rules. I started from a criterion of showing how syntagmatic structures of actions 'apperceived as events as they are generated' (Ardener 1971b) follow certain classes of rules. In conclusion, I draw attention to similar principles as they operate in a dance form which has a much more highly structured metric: the North Indian (Lucknow) form of the Kathak dance. Again, this exposition is only of elementary, beginning stages of the idiom.

The rhythmic base of Kathak is called 'Tatkar' (the bell-work) and this part of the total dance involves the feet and legs only. An accomplished dancer must be able to perform Tatkar in Japtal (seven), Ektal (ten) and Trital (sixteen) beat measures. The dancer learns the syllables for the measure while learning and while performing Kathak. There are sets of 'nonsense syllables' which only 'mean' movements which are designated for each part of the dance form, which include Tatkar, Tukras, Amads, Ghats and Parans. Tatkar is performed mainly on one 'spot' on the stage or performing area. On each of the dancer's legs are tied approximately three to four pounds of pitched bells; those on the right leg are the male bells, those on the left are higher pitched and are the female bells. The basic movements of X and X' consist of a 'slap' (s) of the whole foot and a 'beat) (b) of the heel only.

Elementary permutations of the Trital measure are as follows:

TA	TAI	TAI	TAT	A	TAI	TAI	TAT	TA	TAI	TAI	TAT	A	TAI	TAI	TAT
R_s	L_s	R_s	L_b	L_s	R_s	L_s	R_b	R_s	L_s	R_s	L_b	L_s	R_s	L_s	R_b

rule 4   rule 7 rule 4   rule 7   rule 4   rule 7 rule 4

This simple sequence, the basis of the permutations to follow, is based on the rules of alternating and iterated stress, as marked above. The next set of permutations is obtained either by accenting the italicised beats or by deleting them:

TA TAI TAI TAT   *A* TAI TAI TAT   *TA* TAI TAI TAT   *A* TAI TAI TAT

TA *TAI* TAI TAT   A *TAI* TAI TAT   TA *TAI* TAI TAT   A *TAI* TAI TAT

TA TAI *TAI* TAT   A TAI *TAI* TAT   TA TAI *TAI* TAT   A TAI *TAI* TAT

TA TAI TAI *TAT*   A TAI TAI *TAT*   TA TAI TAI *TAT*   A TAI TAI *TAT*

The above combinations follow a rule of cyclic or successive patterns of accent or deletion. The next series uses deletion only:

TA TAI TAI TAT TAT ＿＿＿＿＿   TA TAI TAI TAT TAT ＿＿＿＿＿

TA TAI TAI TAT TAT ＿ TAT ＿   TA TAI TAI TAT TAT ＿ TAT ＿

TA TAI TAI TAT TAT ＿＿＿＿＿   TA TAI TAI TAT TAT ＿ TAT ＿

TA TAI TAI TAT ＿＿＿＿＿＿   TA TAI TAI TAT *TA* ＿＿＿＿＿

TA TAI TAI TAT ＿＿＿＿ TAT   TA TAI TAI TAT ＿＿＿＿ TAT

As can be easily seen, the next combination works on a principle of 'crossing' the lines of the underlying 4/4 time measure:

TA TAI TAI TAT TAT ＿ TA TAI TAI TAT TAT ＿ TA TAI TAI TAT

DHA GI NA TA   GI NA DHA GI NA TA GI NA DHA GE NA GE

DHA GI NA TA   GI NA NA GE TA   TAI TAI TAT A TAI TAI TAT

DHA GI NA TA   GI NA ＿＿＿＿ TA   GI NA DHA GE NA GE

There are many more complicated measures, but we will complete this exposition of permutational rules in Kathak with a whole dance 'phrase'; the opening 'salaam' or 'bow' of the dancer at the beginning of the Tukra section. Notice the underlying structure of the Trital beat measure:

tat	＄	tat	dhigida	dhigidi	dhigida	dhigidi	tat	tat

tai		ya	tai	ya tram	tat	tat	dhigida dhigidi	dhigida dhigidi ⫴ tat	tat

The gestural pattern which is simultaneous with this is nearly impossible to describe verbally but it starts with a strong R/L movement of the arms followed by one counter-clockwise turn ending in a vertical axis gesture of 'blessing', followed by three open, high arm gestures, a fast repetition of the R/L arm movement and the turn, ending in a 'Kathak pose'. The spatial sequence is in this pattern: R/L; turn; U/D; R/L; turn; ending pose.

The phrases chosen are of the simplest, most elementary kind, but they are thought to demonstrate some of the ordering principles underlying the idiom. Such 'constituent syntagmatic analysis' demonstrates deep structural similarities of movement utterances. We do not mean to say that ballet dancing and Kathak dancing *look alike* on a level of surface structure, or that they look alike as empirical phenomena to an observer. We have not advanced any naive theory of universalism such as one which might try to say that every time the utterance UDUO/OUDO is seen it 'means' yes or affirmation. The aim has been to leave no doubt in anyone's mind that such ordering principles are cognitive, they are inherently logical and they form some, although only some, aspects of the implicit theory behind dance performances.

Most of what has been said so far in this paper does not follow traditional approaches to the study of movement, which up to now have been dominated by functionalist, behaviouristic and positivistic ideas. Even now, ethologists, for example, are consistent in their definitions of the word 'ritual' where anthropologists are not. That is to say, in ethology, ritualization refers to the evolutionary change which the signalling movements of lower vertebrates have undergone in adaptation to their function of communication. From an ethologist's point of view, ritual movement is adaptive, repetitive behaviour which is characteristic of a whole species. But such definitions have little relevance for social anthropology. As Leach pointed out (1966:403), ritual is looked on, if anything in anthropology, more as occasional behaviour by particular members of a single culture.

From some ethologist's point of view the capacity for speech is itself merely one example of ritualized adaptation in the species *homo sapiens*. In the context of this view, the findings of contemporary structural/linguistic anthropology can have little relevance, and practically, no bearing on the matter. Fortunately, it does not preclude the possibility of anthropologists studying the relations between the dance and spoken language or between a liturgy such as the Catholic Mass and spoken language. We may well ask where is a better place to study this relationship if not in the stable dance traditions and liturgical traditions of the world? Here, we see human semasiological bodily competence in its highest and most complex forms. Except in 'studio' situations in the west, east and Africa, where are the practitioners of these 'arts'; where else have many of the body-mind, body-movement relations been studied, practised and utilized except by dancers — and their societies — one might almost say 'since the year dot'? Obviously this paper has not answered any of the classical or 'perennial' questions to which we all address ourselves. It does not pretend to. But it does focus attention on some of the highly abstract, extremely elaborate computations which form some of the deep structures of dance movement. However, even constituent syntagmatic analysis is not enough, though it does provide us with the rules of constructing transformational, grammatical structures. Following these rules produces such structures, but we must next turn attention to the larger spatial contexts of the syntagmata.

NOTE

1 In Bulgaria, the ORLO/OLRO utterance means 'yes' not 'no', for example.

REFERENCES

Abbott, Edwin A. 1962: *Flatland — a Romance of Many Dimensions*. Oxford, Blackwell.
Ardener, Edwin W. 1971a: 'The New Anthropology and its Critics. *Man*. vol. 6, no. 3, September.
_____ 1971b: 'Introductory Essay' in *Social Anthropology and Language*, op. cit.
_____ 1973: 'Some Outstanding Problems in the Analysis of Events', papers read at A.S.A. Decennial Conference. Oxford,. In this volume.
Chomsky, Noam 1968: *Language and Mind*. Harcourt Brace, New York.
_____ 1972: *Syntactic Structures*. The Hage, Mouton.
Hampshire, Stuart 1965: *Thought and Action*. London, Chatto and Windus.
Harré, Rom 1970: *The Principles of Scientific Thinking*. London, Macmillan.
_____ 1971: 'The Shift to an Anthropomorphic Model of Man', *JASO*; 2,1, 33-7.
Leach, Edmund 1961: *Rethinking Anthropology*. London, Athlone Press.
_____ 1966: 'Ritualization in Man in Relation to Conceptual and Social Development', in J.S. Hurley (ed.), *Ritualization of Behaviour in Animals and Man*, *Philosophical Transactions of the Royal Society of London*, 251, 772.
Lyons, John 1968: *Theoretical Linguistics*. Cambridge University Press.
Williams, Drid 1972: 'Signs, Symptoms and Symbols', *JASO*, 3,1.
Winch, Peter 1958: *The Idea of a Social Science and its Relation to Philosophy*. London, Routledge and Kegan Paul.